Liberty, Equality, Fraternity
a Refutation of Liberalism

Liberty, Equality, Fraternity
a Refutation of Liberalism

Groen van Prinsterer

Translated by: Jan Adriaan Schlebusch

RefCon Press

Liberty, Equality, Fraternity: a Refutation of Liberalism

Originally published in Dutch by Guillaume Groen van Prinsterer as *Vrijheid, gelijkheid, broederschap: toelichting van de spreuk der revolutie*, first edition by Roering (The Hague) in 1848; second edition by Van Nifterik (Leiden) in 1871. This is a translation of the second edition, which is in the public domain.

Library of Congress Control Number: 2022933786

ISBN: 978–1-954504–00–4

Translator: Jan Adriaan Schlebusch
Editors: James Robinson-Prior, James Ryan, Joseph Crampton

To the Reformed Conservatives
Defend. Strengthen. Build.

Contents

Translator's Preface

Guillaume Groen van Prinsterer (1801–1876) was a Dutch Christian statesman and historian whose Anti-Revolutionary political theory was characterized by its opposition to the anti-Christian liberalism and socialism inspired by the Enlightenment. Groen was convinced that society stands before an inevitable choice: either submit to the authority of God and His Revelation, or reject it and decline into the revolutionary abyss. Groen's core message was that forsaking the supremacy of God's transcendent moral order for the supremacy of mankind and mankind's ability to determine the standards for societal and political norms leads to the kind of anarchy from which government tyranny alone offers liberation. For Groen, the French Revolution and the nineteenth-century European revolutions of his own time were merely political manifestations of an epistemological revolution—a rebellion against the authority of the Triune God of the Bible.

It was at the age of 19, while I was a freshman at the University of the Free State in South Africa back in 2008, that I first became familiar with the name Guillaume Groen van Prinsterer. Perhaps surprisingly, it wasn't by means of my studies, though. Despite being one of the greatest and most renowned nineteenth-century opponents of the anti-Christian philosophies of the Enlightenment, Groen—as he is commonly referred to—is sadly not well known outside the Netherlands, not even among the Dutch Reformed folk in South Africa—and this despite the renown his successor, Abraham Kuyper, enjoys in the circles in which I grew up. During a semester break I visited my parents, and my father was reading a book—neither of us can recall which book it was—in which a passage from Groen's magnum opus, *Unbelief and Revolution,* was quoted. My father was so intrigued by the quote that he came to me and read it to me out loud. This incited me to read up on this astonishing figure, and it started my journey with Groen.

And what an edifying and productive journey it has been so far: one that has taken me to the Netherlands where I completed a PhD on Groen in 2018 and, since then, I have also published four scholarly papers on this astonishing Conservative and Anti-Revolutionary figure. One of my passions has always been to make Groen's original contributions more widely available to a broader audience. Translating this book, one of his works that impacted me most during my PhD studies, from the original Dutch into English, was a natural next step in this journey—and one I thoroughly enjoyed.

Only a few of Groen's works have hitherto been translated into English. The Dutch-Canadian Scholar Harry van Dyke translated Groen's magnum opus *Ongeloof en Revolutie: Eene Reeks van Historische Lezingen*, originally published in 1847, into English back in 1989 as *Unbelief and Revolution: A Series of Historical Lectures*. He again published a revised translation in 2018. Another book by Groen is one of his major works written in French, *Le parti anti-révolutionnaire et confessionnel dans l'église réformée des Pays-Bas* (1860), which has been translated by Colin Wright as *Christian Political Action in an Age of Revolution* and published in 2016. The only other book by Groen that has, until now, been translated into English is his memoir of Friedrich Julius Stahl, translated and edited by Ruben Alvarado entitled, *In Memory of*

Stahl, and published in 2022 by Pantocrator Press.

This book, originally published by Groen in Dutch as *Vrijheid, Gelijkheid, Broederschap* in 1848, refers to the famous triad that originated from the French Revolution, namely "liberté, égalité, fraternité" which is translated as "Liberty, Equality, Fraternity" (or Brotherhood). There is a very good reason why Groen wrote this in 1848. Although his lectures on *Unbelief and Revolution,* published the year before, had been well-received, he desired to reach a broader audience who were, in 1848, enchanted by the motto which was commonly employed as propaganda for liberal and socialist political revolutions, not only in France but throughout Europe. So, in order to reach a broader audience at such a crucial stage in his battle against the revolutionary ideas of the Enlightenment, he wrote this book as a concise overview of the nature of the conservative Christian's battle against Revolutionary Enlightenment liberalism. The work addresses the very heart of the Enlightenment's epistemology and political philosophy and shows how the Christian epistemology and political theory and practice offer not only a better alternative but the only truly viable one. Groen himself often recommended this book to friends who sought to gain better insight into his political thought.[1]

It will, from the very first chapter, be noted that the work is decisively contextual. Despite addressing principles and theories throughout the book, Groen often references historical figures, events, movements, and even stories that may not be familiar to the readers of this translation. Therefore, I decided to also provide a light annotation along with the translation. Most of my annotations are aimed at explaining historical events, figures, works, or movements that Groen refers to, but I also provide a few very brief comments on his own political theory. Groen references the Bible more often in this work than in any other. He often lumps various passages from Scripture together, and annotations with the relevant Scripture references are therefore provided throughout the book. Whenever Groen quotes

---

[1] For example, in a letter written to Abraham Kuyper in 1872, more than two decades after originally publishing *Liberty, Equality, Fraternity*, Groen writes that he hopes that Kuyper had received the copy of this book that Groen had sent him (Groen van Prinsterer, 1964 (1872). *Schriftelijke nalatenschap: Briefwisseling* 1808–1876. Edited by C. Gerretson, A. Goslinga, H.J. Smit, and J.L. van Essen. The Hague: Marthinus Nijhoff, 301). Groen had republished this work, which originally appeared as a series of pamphlets, the year before, but without making any significant changes to the original text, however.

directly from Scripture, I have used the New King James Version, as opposed to simply translating the original Dutch from the *Statenvertaling*—from which Groen quoted throughout the book (with one exception). In the few instances where Groen used French phrases, I have kept the original in the main text and provided the translation by means of annotations.

One of Groen's most characteristic tropes, irony, is just as prominently—if not more prominently—employed in this work as in any of his other writings. By employing verbal irony, he often writes the opposite of what he means in order to mock the revolutionary liberalism and socialism of his time. But this shouldn't scare the reader, as you will soon realize that Groen quite brilliantly writes in a sarcastic tone that is easily picked up even if translated from the original Dutch into English. In fact, it makes for a delightful read and the way he uses this trope to mock his opposition is guaranteed to bring a few smiles to readers' faces.

I owe a special word of thanks to the donors of this project as well as the publisher, without which this work would never have been possible—a translation which I am convinced will benefit and edify the reader just as much as I was by reading the original Dutch. After all, the principles, ideas, and truths expressed therein remain as relevant as ever. The battle for our faith and for Christendom against the forces of evil is one that Groen rightly noted to span all of history—a battle and a history of which the reader is just as much a part as Groen himself was. May this work encourage you to continue fighting the good fight, for the glory of Christ and his Kingdom.

Jan Adriaan Schlebusch, March 2022

Foreword

The French author Albert Camus once wrote that the French Revolution of 1789 marked the "disincarnation of the Christian God." No human event, of course, could disincarnate Christ, but Camus' point is well taken: this Revolution—a monumental event of history—set Western Europe on a course of secularization, a rejection of its Christian heritage, and toward a metaphysics of negation. The envisioned "progress" seemed positive—liberty, equality, and fraternity was the stated goal. But, as Groen van Prinsterer demonstrates in this work, the fruit of progress was anything but positive. The promises were never met and the goods never delivered; but how could they be? Reality itself was negated by unbelief, and delusion concealed in man's mind his fallen state. War was declared not against sin and oppression but against God's order itself and his remedy for sin; and hence, ironically, the politics of man came to be directed, perhaps unwittingly, against man himself.

We are a long way from 1848, the year that Groen published this work. The liberalism of our day is shaped by the aftermath of World War II. Whereas the revolutionary spirit of Groen's day was majoritarian—a concern for the condition of man *in general*—today this spirit is minoritarian, concerning itself with liberty, equality, and fraternity of "oppressed" minority groups. Indeed, today the activists for progress are not the ones making the promises but demanding that the *majority* keep its promises—to the old guarantees of liberty and equality found in, say, the Declaration of Independence or the Civil Rights Act of 1964. Thus, we are in the peculiar situation where liberalism relentlessly attacks and critiques the majority on behalf of an ever-increasing set of minority groups. A liberal nationalism for the majority is now a liberal nationalism for the minority.

But fundamentally liberalism has not changed since Groen's time. Revolutionary liberalism must proceed. The abuse of language must continue unabated. The politics of negation cannot stop. Having made Western man fit for maximal production and consumption—having formed mass-man—the revolution shifts to sexual libertinism, women's liberation, racial equity, and the undoing of gender. From its beginning, revolutionary liberalism affirmed a robust universality, including the idea of universal human rights as the foundation for human relations. Thus, for the revolutionaries, "the organic development of society" needs to be destroyed, writes Groen. That is, the *particularity* of a people, developed from time immemorial, is not a reliable body of law and custom for social organization, says the liberal, but is a product of systems of oppression. The liberals claimed that the discoveries of the "Enlightenment" would correct these abuses, by replacing rather than reforming the system. Of course, now the universality of the Enlightenment, having destroyed the organic ties that bind people to place, is rejected as oppressive, and the liberal politics of negation proceeds on its predictable course to a valueless void. The liberals who once championed the abstract Man, now celebrate the abstract Other. Yet the struggle has the same end: freedom from oppression, equality, and universal fraternity. One wonders how it will all end.

Despite all the liberal bluster about "systemic" oppression, the advancement of the latest sacred minority group through the institutions indicates that the "system" is working. For, after all, leftwing liberals control the institutions. Liberalism won long ago, and the "system" is directing its efforts not against the old aristocracy on behalf of the sacred masses but on behalf of a few sacred identities at the expense of the majority. This is how I understand my own country's situation. The people of the United States, being subjected to an unprecedented level of moral insanity, are an occupied people. We are controlled by a hostile and transformative liberal imperial power based in Washington DC, which seeks to overthrow every authority independent of the state (especially parental authority).

But the people of the Unites States and the West generally are not powerless; they are not defeated. Groen's work here is a call for Christian action. He writes, "Patience is a Christian virtue, but where the opportunity for action exists, passivity would be most inappropriate" (pg. 141). Crucial for our time is Groen's emphasis on authority. He refers not to the sort of pseudo-credentialing that we see in our day, as people use their "PhD" or security clearances to legitimize a regime narrative (that often proves to be false). We live in the *age of credentials* in which regime institutions confer vacuous titles on regime representatives. Groen, however, refers to more venerable authorities: natural authority (e.g., parents), the authority of long memory (such as the historic norms and institutions of the organic nation), the authority of the old hierarchy, and the authority of the Word of God. Ever the Burkean—the Dutch Burke!—Groen is no reactionary. He recognizes the need for changes and reform. But he opposes the liberal revolutionary spirit, the overturning of natural order and traditional authority in the name of abstractions.

Each in our own way, the peoples of the West must recover our authorities, chiefly the authority of God. We are past the time of "conservatism". In another work, Groen critiqued the conservatism of his day for "refus[ing] to change its erroneous principles." He criticized a "timid conservatism that, acting under the motivation of fear and calculation of interest, has at times remained passive and indifferent."[2] Anti-revolution in our time needs

---

[2] See: Groen's *Christian Political Action in an Age of Revolution*, translated by Colin Wright (Aalten, The Netherlands: Wordbridge publishing, 2015 [1860]), 98, 101.

to be pro-renewal—for what people once called *instauration.*

I welcome this lucid translation of Groen's work by Jan Schlebusch. As civilization faces an onslaught from domestic enemies, Groen's work should be a vital part of the conversation among Christians about the future of the West. Groen was a man of action, as each of us must be today. Though some of his concerns seem distant from our own, we should ponder the deep principles and instincts that animate those concerns—the concerns for one's people and place and for the glory of God in national life.

Stephen Wolfe, April 2022

1

THE FRUITS

"For every tree is known by its own fruit."

–Luke 6:44

*L*iberty, *Equality, Fraternity!* It is not the first time we have heard this cry in the Netherlands. In 1781, in 1795, in 1830, and in 1848 it was also heard.

In 1781: Where did it come from? From that country which always gave us so much love in words, yet so much hatred in deeds: from France. From French books, we learned these words. But it did not remain limited to books— we had to gain pleasure from it. The French liberty could no longer be missed in the Netherlands. There was, in our country, peace, rest, prosperity; poverty was virtually unknown; trade flourished; from the colonies, we gained abundance; we were satisfied with the money. Liberty was there also, as in virtually no other country on earth.

But all of this, they said, was not enough—it was nothing—if we didn't have the new French liberty. And with that liberty, our wealth and abundance would also be doubled. And there was, they claimed, so little needed to acquire all these blessings. Merely the humiliation of the Prince of Orange along with war with England was all that was required.

War: The dear French loved it and were friends of liberty. The hated English, however, were proponents of slavery. For England, the war was inconvenient. They wanted to remain friends with Holland. But no, we had to, and we would have war. We would teach England a lesson. There was no crisis because the French were with us. Now Holland would acquire wealth and power and fame, like in the golden years, along with unprecedented progress.

So they spoke for years. So they continued to speak at the stock exchange in Amsterdam after England, tired of the mockery, declared war on December 27, 1780.[3] Five days

---

[3] This would mark the beginning of the Fourth Anglo-Dutch War (1780–1784). The war was the result of disagreements between Great Britain and the Netherlands regarding the legality of Dutch trade with

later, on January 2, they did not speak like this anymore. England had already destroyed 60 ships and, after one month, this would be 200.

In 1780, Textel and 't Vlie received 2,641 ships; in 1781, only 1,322.[4] In 1780, 2,058 Dutch ships sailed through the Sound; in 1781, only 11.[5] The French help never came. Most of the Dutch colonies were lost. Peace was desired in vain. Finally, when peace was acquired in 1784, it was both painful and shameful.

Later it would become evident that the people did not learn from this pain and shame. It would have been better to side with the Prince than take on England.[6] He was very kindhearted and did not want to harm even his enemies. Therefore, these brave men spread the rumor that he was a tyrant. They were so dedicated to humiliating the ruler that he became completely powerless.

Britain's enemies in light of existing Anglo-Dutch trade agreements.

[4] Textel and 't Vlie are Frisian islands north of the Dutch mainland and were vital for maritime commerce at the time.

[5] The Sound is the strait that separates Denmark and Sweden.

[6] Prince William of Orange was a grandson of King George II of Great Britain (1683–1760) and had close ties with the British monarchy.

And thus was the beginnings of *liberty, equality, fraternity* in Holland, in the manner desired by the French.

And do you wish to know the nature of this threefold gift? Allow me to explain.

Liberty

Liberty namely to do and say all that they who are in power approve of; liberty to slander and insult the Prince; liberty to slanderously reduce all those who had previously been in power to oppressors; liberty to form militias to keep dissidents in check; liberty to enact capital punishment upon those who sing the anthem of Orange or wave the flag of Orange;[7] liberty to deny liberty to all others. And so, the whole Fatherland was set free—free to do all that the French commanded.

Equality

Yes, there was equality especially. There was not only one, but even two equalities: one for the party at the top and one for those at the bottom. Equal rule or equal submission. Equality in privilege and equality of injustice. To this was added another common equality for both parties, for the Orangists and the Patriots:

---

[7] A reference to the banners representing the Dutch people and the royal House of Orange.

equality in impoverishment and decline of the Fatherland.[8]

Fraternity

A familial bond in which the majority of the Dutch nation, who were Orangists, were excluded. A brotherhood of the enemies of Orange. Nonetheless, this brotherly love did not last long. It was a brotherhood in which men hated and scolded each other, in which they threw each other out of bed, in which they grabbed each other by the throat and would have slaughtered each other had the Prussians

---

[8] In the period between 1781 and 1787, an internal conflict marked the Dutch political landscape. An Enlightenment and Revolutionary minded party, known as the "Patriots" opposed the rule of the Prince of Orange and desired an overthrow of the existing order. The movement was kickstarted by a pamphlet written by Van der Capellen tot den Pol and distributed all over the country in 1781 entitled, *To the People of the Netherlands: A Democratic Manifesto*. In the spirit of the ideals of the French *Philosophes*, the pamphlet stated that "those who are governing you, the Prince, or whoever has any authority in this country, only do so on your behalf. All of their authority derives from you ... All men are born free. By nature, no one has any authority over anyone else." The Patriot Party was opposed by the "Orangists," supporters of the Prince of Orange and the traditional Christian Social Order.

not intervened and brought an end to the internal conflict.

It happened really fast. Everyone, except the liberty-loving tyrants and their followers, after all, desired the intervention. Oh, how brave were these sons of liberty when the enemy was not expected. Utrecht was reinforced and at one stage had 200 artillery and 7,000 men ... but the city was abandoned. When? Even before the breach—even before the enemy appeared. "In seven days," they moaned, "all was destroyed that was built up in seven years. The nation was defeated."[9]

No, not the nation. In the Netherlands, we do not allow 20,000 foreign troops to establish the law. We learned that in 1572 and 1672 from the Spanish and French.[10] But the nation was not blessed by this new liberty. The disappointed ringleaders eventually acknowledged that it was a sad time. The nation had not yet reached the desired new heights; a

---

[9] The Prussian invasion of Holland was a military campaign of the Prussian army during September and October 1787, in which the rule of the Prince of Orange was restored and the Enlightenment-minded Patriots were defeated.

[10] The year 1572 marked the start of an important rebellion against Spanish rule during the Eighty Years' War between the Netherlands and Spain (1568–1648). In 1672, the Franco-Dutch War began and lasted until 1678.

small portion rebelled—individual persons, a faction, that were killed due to lack of support among the people. The nation was ultimately relieved to be liberated from this liberty and relieved to see inequality brought back and to be redeemed from fraternal governance.

So it was between 1781 and 1787.

Let us now see what happened in 1793.

Liberty, Equality, Fraternity!
The House of Orange was out, and the French were in. For the friends of this anti-Dutch liberty, this was a reason to rejoice. At Scheveningen, the Pink sailed on January 18, 1795.[11] A Batavian, not a Dutch republic, was proclaimed, and the French were welcomed as saviors and brothers. People planted liberty trees and hung tricolored flags; they gave each other the hand; they sang and danced. Men held titles and parades and feasts. They passed

---

[11] Scheveningen is a beach at The Hague. A "Pink" is an eighteenth-century fisherman's boat. The expression seems to be akin to "the ship has sailed." Groen seems to indicate that the opportunity to restore the traditional political model of a Christian social order under the leadership of the Prince of Orange, had passed. On January 19, 1795, the Batavian Republic was declared in the Netherlands following a French invasion, becoming, essentially, a vassal state of the French Revolutionary Republic.

around the wine glass to seal the holy covenant of liberty and wished to crush dissidents with the thunder of their wrath. This joy was, to the friends of the old Holland and the friends of Orange, a bitter sorrow. But how long did this joy of the drunk Batavians last? Maybe eight days. In January, the French immigrants had come. By February, there was a housing shortage in many Dutch cities and towns. Many families had to resort to beggary. For every worker, widow, and orphan, there were two, four, even six French soldiers. And the French requests did not stop. Whatever they requested was to be granted without delay or complaint. Food, fuel, vehicles, horses—they had to have it all. Trade soon collapsed. Many of those who had invited these foreign friends into the country now wished that they would just leave. But they had no intention to. They were here to stay.

Still, the French made numerous improvements. Sure, they consumed all that the Dutch had worked for and saved. But surely they paid? Yes, with *Assignat*—with paper, the worth of which was equal to wastepaper.[12] A good deal

---

[12] *Assignat* was paper money—a fiat currency without any intrinsic value and not backed by any physical commodity—issued by the French National Constituent Assembly between 1789 and 1796.

indeed, to buy for a guilder and pay with a penny.

They came as friends; therefore, they had the right to a friendly reception. As brothers, therefore, they could share whatever we inherited from our fathers. It endured for longer than six years. The tragedy would continue until 1813. But what did we gain? Power, money, peace, or perhaps liberty?

Power? We were a wealthy commonwealth. We were reduced to an insignificant dependency of the French empire. We had outposts of our people to the east and west. We lost it or (because England was now master of the seas) we couldn't reach it. Before, we had impressive fleets. The ships we now had could not leave our harbors because they were controlled by the English. And if we still had any power left, it had to be used in service of the overpowering French.

Money? There was much profit—for the French. They were taken in, but for the effort of coming in, they demanded 100 million guilders. They wanted to relieve us of our surplus silver and gold. For example, we had to maintain and clothe 25,000 of their troops. Twenty-five thousand homeless then entered the country from France and, once they were taken care of, another 25,000, just as needy, would enter. So perhaps 100,000 entered the country and we simply had to be pleased and thankful that there were not more coming. This situation was managed by various schemes, which proved quite profitable. We had to pay what was due, even if it meant a little tax. Between 1795 and 1804, this meant giving 615 million guilders, of which 276 million was normal tax and 339 million were taken by extraordinary taxes; furthermore, the interest on loans amounted to 34 million. Initially, the figures could be negotiated, but negotiations later ceased. By 1797, the damage to our fleet amounted to 120 million.[13] Finally, a time came when no negotiations were allowed anymore. No ship came in, and none went out. Making money became impossible. And had it carried on any longer, the loss of money would have made survival impossible.

Rest? There was unrest, bustle, division, threats, perpetual deliberations on what to do, continual destruction of what had already been accomplished. We had a new government in 1795, another in 1796, another in January 1798, another six months later, and then again in 1801, 1805, 1806, and 1810. But was it always as

---

[13] Accounting for inflation, this total figure of 769 million guilders amounts to about $797 billion at the time of this publication.

tumultuous as it was at the beginning? Oh no. Eventually the rest came, until there was much internal stability in Holland. We had Napoleon coming over and he was a friend—a very powerful friend of unity and rest. He realized that the time of deliberation was over and that it was now time to keep quiet. He demanded quiet obedience, quiet payments, quietly sending children off to the battlefields to die. This rest and order was not often interrupted.

Liberty? Free from the House of Orange, that is true, but in its place came submission to the rule of Paris. Free to do all that was approved by the French, by the 100 or so members of their national assembly, by the 12 who ruled over the provinces, by the one who was known as the Grand Pensionary.[14] Free to be slaves of a foreign occupier. The sound of chains was the echo of the liberty cries. There are still now, in 1848, countrymen who remember the words "conscription," "classification," "police," "censure," "tax department," and "customs officer." Amsterdam lost one-seventh of its population within just a few years. In Haarlem alone, 500

---

[14] Historically, the Grand Pensionary was the highest non-royal political office in the Netherlands. In practice, he was the political leader of the Dutch Republic when there was no Prince of Orange exercising authority.

houses were demolished. Nonetheless, the saddest of it all was that which lies closest to the heart of a parent. What happened to the sons who were drafted for military service? They died in Germany, Spain, and Russia under snow and ice. What prospects were there for the Fatherland? The collapse seemed imminent, when, through the hand of the Almighty God, redemption came, and in 1813 the Prince of Orange returned from a 19-year exile to the beach of Scheveningen and The Royal Hague.

Liberty, Equality, Fraternity was also the cry in 1830. Not here in the Netherlands, but in France and especially in Belgium.[15] This happened in our lifetime. The commonwealth of the Netherlands was a prosperous one. Not everything was outstanding, but there was more than enough to be pleased with and thankful for. The friends of *Liberty, Equality, and Fraternity,* however, believed that we would not be happy as long as the King was not exiled, Belgium's close relationship with Holland ended, and the state was turned upside down. Holland did not cry for the loss of Belgium; even

---

[15] Groen experienced the Belgian Revolution of 1830 first-hand, as he was working in the royal cabinet at the time. This Revolution, in which the spirit of the Enlightenment and the French Revolution were once again manifested, had a tremendous impact in shaping Groen van Prinsterer's political thought.

if we had pain, we had no reason for shame. The Belgian Revolution was, after all, the reason that our troops would be away from their homes for four years and that the national debt increased to 300 million.[16] The annual budget of both Holland and Belgium respectively was about the equivalent of that of both countries combined before the Belgian Revolution.

Liberty, Equality, Fraternity is now, in 1848, particularly poignant, given the consequences of the February 24 Revolution in Paris.[17] In many countries where the people are new to this game, many are particularly pleased with this development. In France itself, with its series of similar episodes in recent history, the joy is less common. In fact, there is actually no joy to be found other than among hotheads, fortune-seekers, or those easily deceived, who place their confidence in empty promises. As for the rest, there is merely surprise, shock, terror, and sadness over what has come to pass—desperation and misery.

Everything was supposed to go well, but it all went wrong. There should have been a

---

[16] Accounting for inflation, 300 million guilders amounts to $313 billion at the time of this publication.

[17] Groen is referring to the famous February Revolution in France of 1848, which occurred shortly before he wrote this book.

reduction in taxes, but the taxes were increased. There should have been employment for everyone, but everywhere the economic activity ceased. There should have been liberty, but everywhere compulsion increased. Everyone should have become equally rich, but all became equally poor.

But soon it will be better, they say. In May, the representatives of the people came together, and just in case they couldn't find the right solutions, there would be 200,000 armed men at hand in Paris to take care of matters as they ought to be taken care of.

On top of that, the Parisians are particularly concerned about the well-being of others. They send Frenchmen or French-minded men everywhere to incite unrest, so that, if possible, the whole world would be as wise and happy as the people of Paris.

Let us calculate the benefits that our Fatherland has received merely in the past few weeks thanks to French boldness and nonchalance:

1. A decline in funds.
2. The complete disappearance of many fortunes.
3. A decline in possibilities for many potential employers to provide jobs like they used to.
4. A standstill at many factories and a decline in trade. No orders, no work.

5. Pretty protests, but not ones that provided bread or jobs.

6. And, lest we forget, the prospect of a government, as they say, better and more beautiful than any the Netherlands has ever seen.

I'm not getting ahead of myself. I am not judging the constitution, of which we only have a concept at this stage.[18] Nonetheless, I cannot regard a document that revives the spirit of the revolutionary maxim as a guarantee for the eminence of future polity. I am not an unconditional supporter of preserving the past; however, I do not see retired ministers as the true patrons of those rights that I hold to be dearest to the Dutch nation. Therefore, before making a final judgment, I will wait until not only those who are past but also the policies of those to come are known to me.

My opponents call me prejudiced and mistrusting. They say that man is becoming wiser and is now less temperamental than before. Now is the time for true *liberty, equality and fraternity.* Maybe, but I have honestly already had enough. I am already beyond satiated. "But," they say, "this is a delicious

---

[18] Groen wrote this during the prelude to the constitutional revision in the Netherlands in 1848, which most historians regard as officially initiating the era of constitutional democracy in the Netherlands.

meal, and it only tasted bad because it was not well prepared." This is the fruit of a good tree, the liberty tree, that we have planted.

I would have thought that it would have been enough to point to the bad fruit, but let us then investigate what this *liberty, equality, and fraternity* means. Let us examine the tree which gave us these bitter fruits.

2

THE MIRACLE TREE

"Woe to those who call evil good,
and good evil."

–Isaiah 5:20

*L*iberty, *Equality, Fraternity.* It most certainly will not be superfluous to investigate these three branches of the French miracle tree—these three words of the Revolutionary motto—separately.

What is *Liberty*? In days gone by, the people had been pleased with the existing liberty, when they were not subject to arbitrariness and injustice, when they had the opportunity to utilize their talents and abilities appropriately, when their legitimate rights were protected. The people realized that, for this protection, authority was also necessary, and that every government needed to have legitimate authority to have a positive impact in society. They also realized that government, although limited by the rights of others as well as by the principles of justice and equity, were to remain independent of the approval of those whom they governed. They wanted a government that governs, a government that reigns *over* its subjects. They were convinced that no people would be able to enjoy liberty had it not been subject to legitimate authority, either in a monarchy or a republic. Now it is completely different. To be free, the people now essentially want no authority in society whatsoever. This is a strange desire indeed. Because without authority there is no order, and without order there is confusion, and in the midst of confusion, I am, even with the most delicious fruits of the liberty tree on my plate, not guaranteed my right to life or property. I am as free as a bird, but it is well known what "freebird" means in our language.[19] For free movement, a foundation is necessary, and I certainly have no reason to delight when the ground beneath my feet is taken away.

But my opponents claim that there is no sense in comparing the present with the past. Our current liberty is in accordance with the

---

[19] In Dutch, to be *vogelvrij* or "freebird" means to be outlawed.

spirit of the age and the progress of enlightenment. We have the essence of true liberty—not merely the past shadows thereof.

But let us investigate what this liberty is that they call "true" and how it has impacted us.

They claim that only those people are free who are never subject to the will of another. But how would that work? The matter is simple. Only those who are their own lord and master are free. However, everyone together chooses for an executive government, one elected by the will of the people—a government that is governed: one elevated like a weathervane, going back and forth in accordance with the alternating bouts of the general will. The government is subject to the people, that is, the elected representatives of the people. And because I belong to the people, because I have the right to vote and to overthrow the government, therefore I am free. Therefore, I am subject to laws, they claim, that I have effectively made myself. Therefore, Lamartine[20] could recently tell the people of Paris: "You are all sovereign!"

Nobody would deny that this proclamation sounds pleasant. Who wouldn't

---

[20] Alphose de Lamartine (1790–1869) was a liberal French poet, historian, and statesman, who played an important role during the February Revolution of 1848.

want to have the power? But if we analyze our so-called sovereignty and liberty and count the privileges and rights that are truly thereby granted to us, then the claim that we have made a good trade becomes highly questionable.

Because I belong to the electorate, they claim that I am free. Therefore, those without the right to vote are not free. Because I am on the electoral roll, I am free. But to what degree? What if:

1. The majority elects a representative and the choice of the majority is for one that I did not vote for? Then I become a threat to those in power.

2. The person I voted for gets a seat in the assembly, but the majority of the assembly votes against him, and then their decision is directly opposed to my wishes and principles?

3. The person I voted for disappoints me by doing the opposite of what I desired?

4. The representatives in power conspire against the people, to the detriment of the people?

You see, fellow electorate, in such cases, there are for the realization of your will, simply no chance. You are free in the same sense that someone who bought a lottery ticket is rich.

They claim, however, that all have an equal chance to make their will heard. An equal chance? If you are a quiet and order-loving citizen, I doubt it. The chances are not equal. I may be called equally free to another, but I may not truly be if he is stronger or has a pistol to my chest. By means of the changing of the guard, I may by apparent coincidence also get my chance at political power, but not if my party is deceiving me. Furthermore, the voting process isn't always without irregularities. All are free, but the majority decides. To get the majority, therefore, becomes the goal and, for that, people often use guile and violence. Eventually, they start to make exceptions: all have a right to vote, except those with differing political sentiments.

In 1795 and later, many in the Patriot Party said that all patriots have a right to vote, except those who aren't good patriots or patriots with different principles or different opinions. One also has a free vote: you are free to vote for that which is proposed. You are free, but only free to use your liberty according to their guidelines. It was peculiar that, when Napoleon became emperor, one colonel told his soldiers that every soldier had the right to vote for him, but those who voted against him were to be executed. It is the same currently in France. All are free to vote for the form of government they prefer, but one would be robbed of life and property if one voted against a liberal republican form of government. One has a free choice of representatives, but there would be only barricades and civil punishment were one to opt for anything but the most extreme form of republicanism.

There is one more thing we should take note of in order to grasp the value of this new liberty. In the past, one often heard complaints about arbitrariness in government and absolutism. These complaints are no longer possible. Why not? Because there is no more absolutism or arbitrariness? No, because we as citizens are considered to be the embodiment of the all-powerful government itself. Your dear liberty lies in your right to vote, in your participation in the influence exercised by the free people upon the governance of the state. But after you have voted, you may not object to what the majority decides. There used to be a legitimate authority able to deliver one from the tyranny of the majority—one that could maintain one's property and rights, even if all conspired together against you. Now, one has to be content with what the majority decides. In exchange, you get the opportunity to see your political will executed if you can manage to get the majority to agree with you. Because what the majority wants is final. They have the rights over your money and your life. Because you are a fellow member of the sovereign government, you have to tag along in whatever direction the most powerful faction of this government steers you.

But you claim that you are not unconditionally bound to the majority of the representatives or the government. In fact, when they act at odds with the rights and interests of the people, then revolt is a sacred duty. Undoubtedly, but in the application of this principle, also remember the proverb: "So many heads, so many minds." In other words, consider that your sentiment does not necessarily reflect the sentiment of the majority. Many may regard the government you despise as ideal or be sworn enemies of a government you support. And consider that, in practice, there is usually an audacious minority which, often by illegal means, dictates to the majority. Consider that, with this system, there is also always an ever-present pretense for rebellion and strife. Consider that the government is neither compelled nor inclined to recognize in your criticism and enmity the voice of the people and that over and against the principle of revolt, each government sets the principle of self-preservation and actively takes steps against what it sees as a threat. Because it is always threatened, it is always occupied with self-preservation and takes necessary measures in this regard. The preoccupation with the necessity of self-preservation always entails tyranny. Strict laws characterize internal affairs; wars characterize international relations. The people consequently suffer great restrictions and are brought under control by bloody laurels. This transformation from liberty to tyranny is now by no means odd anymore.

Imagine, for example, a ship with one hundred men on board. All are free, and all have an equal right to vote for a captain or coxswain. Imagine that after the vote they decide that every decision of the captain and coxswain must be subject to public approval, in order to check the men they elected, to advise them and to ensure that they act in the best interest of their voters. Imagine that they refuse complete obedience and are thrown overboard. Imagine that this had already been done to yesterday's captain and coxswain. How would this impact the newly elected officials' behavior?

It is pleasant to be able to do whatever I want. But if I live in the midst of many people who each do whatever they want, then there is conflict, force, and then the general will becomes worse than slavery. It is pleasant to rule over your opposition because you belong to the triumphant majority, but I surely cannot regard it as a characteristic of an excellent liberty to be free to do only whatever the majority allows me to do.

If we have direct elections, wherein will your liberty consist of? That you, if you pay enough taxes, would have one vote among thousands to vote for one representative that would have one vote among many in a convention along with perhaps a king and other conventions that have almost unconditional authority over your rights and interests.[21]

Unconditional? They say it isn't so because we have a constitution—one that dictates each person's responsibilities and limits powers. Sure, but hereunto I also have an objection. The constitution, which existed from 1815 to 1848, dictated that budgets and finances be made public, and yet, for a long time, it was not made public. The constitution dictated freedom of religion, and the *Afgescheidenen*[22]

---

[21] The Constitution of 1818 introduced the franchise (the right to vote) to adult males who paid a certain amount of taxes. Universal adult franchises for all adults—both male and female—would only be introduced in the Netherlands in 1922.

[22] The *Afgescheidenen* or "Secessionists" were a group of conservatives who split from the Dutch Reformed Church in 1834 due to theological liberalism. Although Groen remained within the Dutch Reformed Church, he had

were persecuted. The constitution dictated that only public schools be regulated by the government, and yet everywhere the erection of private schools was prohibited. The constitution dictated that there be no coercion of conscience, and yet everywhere parents were forced to send their children to schools teaching ideas that they objected to because the government judged that these schools were "Christian enough." The constitution dictated the protection of general and particular rights and liberties, and these were not always protected.

We can hope that things will improve, but we must not hope to find in a constitution, however liberally formulated it may be, a guarantee against the arbitrary interpretation of the highest government convention in the land. One must not forget that, to them, although bound by the constitution, this very constitution is also a very stretchable band. One cannot think that, because you have the liberty that is written on a piece of paper, you also have the certitude of its actual enjoyment.

And now on to the second word: *Equality*.

----

much sympathy with the theological objections of the *Afgescheidenen*. The Secession of 1834 would play a decisive role in the 1857 split between the Reformed Church in America and the Christian Reformed Church in North America.

All people are equal. This is not true. A common equality is, much like the common liberty, unachievable. The people are not free. In fact, by virtue of the nature and development of society, they are placed in various relations which entail either authority or submission. A proposed liberty which destroys these relations would lead to a licentiousness which in itself would make true liberty impossible and arbitrariness and coercion inevitable. The people are not equal. In fact, in terms of the abilities of body and spirit, in the tendencies of character, in eagerness, in courage, and in perseverance, deviations exist whereby providence has established the differences in class, position, rank, and financial abilities. In this, the organic growth and health of society is manifested. If you attempt to erase the outcomes of these inequalities, there will only arise new inequalities. Do you know what was meant by earlier generations when they mentioned "equality"? That everyone was equal before the law and that there was no respecter of persons when it came to applying the law—all while remaining in harmony with the variety of ranks that made up a given society and provided the foundations of each state. Men even regarded these inequalities as things that cannot be missed and which are in everyone's interest.

People thought that there ought to be differences in terms of property and pleasure on earth, and that the abundance of the rich was necessary for the wealth of the middle class, whereas the wealth of the middle class, in turn, was a guarantee against the impoverishment of the laborers' class. They were also convinced that the rights with regard to and influence on the organization of the state were to stand in relation to these inequalities of rank and financial abilities and that through these means alone the stability and durability of those institutions desirable for both the strong and the weak could be guaranteed.

They were especially aware of the fact that for the difficult art of governance, special knowledge and talents were required and that not everyone was equipped thereunto. Moreover, that it was in the interest of all to be governed by the most able. Especially with regard to this aspect, the general opinion has now changed. Everyone must now be equal in terms of the governing of the state. This is embodied in the ideal of universal franchise. What do you think: If a thousand people, completely ignorant of the science of medicine, were to vote on who was to become a doctor, would there not be a great chance of falling into the hands of a fraudulent physician? And when all vote to elect the physicians of the state, would we be immune to political fraudulence?

Now on to the final beloved word: *Fraternity* or *Brotherhood*.

Allow me to, in simple terms, define to you what this word means in the revolutionary dictionary. This *brotherhood* entails that, either by heart or by force, one confesses these pitiful principles of *liberty* and *equality*; that you embrace the triumph of those who adhere to these principles, even when it means surrendering your own rights, trampling the rights of others and destroying, if need be by force, all opposition to these revolutionary principles. Therefore, another threatening word is necessary to complete the motto: *Liberty, Equality, Fraternity, or Death*. This addition is indispensable in practice. It could be read on all public buildings in Paris during 1792 and 1793, but it was seen most clearly through the series of unmistakably gruesome deeds committed in validation of this closing word. But, they say, these kinds of acts are not possible in our country. Already in France they have now abolished the death penalty and, with the current revolutions, almost all citizens were spared. In this, however, I find no assurance. In fact, in 1789, most people in France would have regarded the bloodshed they would see and even take part in within four years to be an impossibility. Circumstances and the inevitable outcomes of principles often lead to unintended consequences. While I appreciate the current hesitancy against the shedding of blood, it must also be remembered that, for a long time, even Robespierre was an opponent of the death penalty.[23] I appreciate the composure characteristic of the Dutch people, but remember that also in 1787 it was sung in the Netherlands that: "Liberty is worth it, even if it costs the blood of citizens!" The Prussians and also the French in 1795, with the aid of capable advisors, were, however, able to stop the bloodshed. Yet, one of the most capable revolutionaries claimed in 1801 that, in retrospect, it would have been better to hang the anti-revolutionaries or, at least, beat them senseless. According to at least one reliable eyewitness account, it was common in 1795 in Amsterdam for songs to be sung glorifying the bloodshed in France as well as the guillotine, called the "national razor."

---

[23] Maximilien Robespierre was a liberal French politician and lawyer famous for overseeing the Reign of Terror between June 1793 and July 1794 as Chairman of the so-called "Committee for Public Safety." During his tenure, Robespierre murdered an estimated 27,000 dissidents, mostly Christians.

The nature of this Revolutionary brotherhood, maintained with determination and zeal, which threatens death to each who refuses to adhere to its vile doctrine, can be indicated by one passage from Holy Scripture. Cain was evil and murdered his brother. And why? Because his works were evil and those of his brother were good.[24] The creed of *Liberty* and *Equality* is, in its *Fraternity*, just like that brotherhood of Cain.

Therefore, we now see everywhere:

Liberty: the overthrowing of all authority.

Equality: the destruction of everything good that has come about through the organic development of society.

Fraternity: the oppression and, if necessary, the murder of everyone who refuses to be a collaborator of injustice.

But no, they say, if only the nations accepting these doctrines achieve a sufficient level of civilization and enlightenment, then there will be good choices made, and one will see governors who love the people as well as peaceful and considerate citizens. But to them, I would ask: By what standard? What do you mean by "enlightenment?" When is the level of enlightenment sufficient? When does your guarantee have any value? I would go further

---

[24] See: Genesis 4.

and note that no enlightenment of the mind will offer any guarantee against passions and desire. Sure, maybe we could have rest assured if enlightenment of the mind was the end of it all, if the mind always conquered the heart, if the storm of passions were always tempered by right arguments, if there was no distinction between will and knowledge, and if, in order to obey God's commandments and to take the path of righteousness and equity, we only needed light and were not in need of strength.

Know yourself. Know that you are a sinner before God. Only then the ideas underlying the doctrine of the natural goodness of man would be set aside. But for now, there is no setting aside of these falsehoods but merely a renewed application thereof. Understanding this tendency is the key to understanding the extent of the dangers of our time.[25]

---

[25] In the first edition of this work (1848), Groen concluded this second chapter with a few references to the Dutch law regarding private, religious schools at the time as well as its implications. This short addendum was removed in the revised edition he published in 1871.

3

THE PRACTICAL REALITY

"The fool says in his heart: 'There is no God.'
They are corrupt, and have done abominable
iniquity..."

–Psalm 53:1[26]

*L*iberty, *Equality, Fraternity.* I advocate the setting aside of these Revolutionary doctrines. What foolishness they are! What heresy! They say we must continue on this good path—not retreat backward but move forward. If the tree bore no good fruit, it was only because it was not granted the liberty to grow freely. The

---

[26] In most English translations of the Bible, the text quoted here by Groen is Psalm 53:1. In the Dutch *Statenvertaling* used by Groen, however, this is indicated as the second verse of the Psalm.

failures were due to a lack of full commitment to the Revolutionary ideals. They argue that either through fear, through personal interests, or through the desire to please certain individuals, slackness in the adherence and application of these doctrines were justified. The failures were the result of not applying the theory in practice since there was never a political order purely based on the ideas of the Revolution.

Now, if this were the sole reason for the embarrassment and adversity, then the solution would be easy, as we would at least know how to rectify the situation. Let us then call upon those with the right intentions and let us draw up a petition entitled: "Full application, no half measures anymore."

Allow me, however, to inquire in light of our revolutionary duty, while we are still busy drawing up this document, whether it is in fact due to incomplete application of these doctrines that almost no good and so much bad came out of this endeavor. Furthermore, allow me to investigate the nature of the full and complete application that is spoken of here.

For about 60 years now, this Revolutionary doctrine has been put into practice, and it has been applied in a variety of ways. Here in the Netherlands as well an impressive number of experiments have been done.

The House of Orange was disbanded and banned in 1795, and the old Dutch Republic was demolished. They claimed it was a weak and impractical structure that could not be maintained. In its place came the little Batavian Republic, which was established, divided, and governed according to the demands of their art—as we were taught, in word and in deed, by the French philosophers in their model French Republic. It is undeniable that, since then, there have been numerous different forms of government in the Netherlands. We have had many different kinds of rulers. At one stage we were a French puppet kingdom, later a province under the dominion of the French emperor, since Napoleon regarded our country as no more than the sludge and mud of the rivers of his empire.[27]

In 1813, things were completely different. The Netherlands was free. The calls of *"Oranje*

---

[27] The Batavian Republic lasted for 11 years, from 1795 to 1806. The Kingdom of Holland was established in 1806, with Napoleon's younger brother, Louis, appointed as monarch. Napoleon, however, ousted his brother from the throne in 1810 and incorporated Holland as a province of the French empire. In 1813, the Netherlands became a constitutional monarchy as the son of the exiled Prince of Orange, William V, returned from England to reclaim the throne.

Boven!"[28] echoed in the streets and in our hearts. But now, they said, we must be careful not to take the precious new liberty for granted. We must have a king like the nations around us.[29] But we especially need a constitution—a piece of paper on which everything the king may or may not do is written. We must have a constitutional monarchy. And it happened. We got a constitution in 1814 and 1815, with a revision in 1840 and a host of new laws and decrees, just as numerous and disjointed[30] as the sand of the beaches. Since 1795, many constitutions, charters, and laws have been designed, accepted, and discarded. They say the laws reflected youthful ignorance, yet they are continually discarded as old and outdated. New constitutions now seem to come out annually, like calendars, and a bookstore owner recently appropriately remarked when asked for a copy of the constitution that he does not sell periodicals.

At times, there were conventions where everyone chose representatives, and at times the choice was left to only a few. At times, they

---

[28] This can be translated as "Hail Orange." It is a Dutch folk song honoring the relationship between the Dutch people and their royal family.

[29] Groen is rhetorically referencing I Samuel 8:20.

[30] The word *onsamenhangend,* here translated as "disjointed," literally conveys the idea of incoherence.

wanted nothing to do with that which is old, and at times they valued the old as something that could positively contribute to the new state. This was how it was in the Netherlands, and this was how it was elsewhere. Trial upon trial, and yet no one was ever happy with what, in accordance with the new doctrines, was achieved.

But, you would ask, why did they remain so loyal to these damnable doctrines? To me, this remains a mystery. If I were to attempt to build a house of poor-quality lime and bricks and it constantly collapses, yet I continue to imagine that if I only arrange the bricks differently, I would be successful, it would certainly not be strange if I were to make no progress despite continuing to work hard. Now, this is how it has gone with the building of our state. The architects were convinced that only their own crumbling bricks were any good. They never came to realize that the cause of the failure was the incongruity of the Revolutionary doctrines themselves. Whatever they did or did not do, whether they broke down or built up, to the Revolutionary doctrine, they always remained religiously attached—even if they were at times hesitant in the application thereof and remained speculating about it without proceeding to apply it. They even at times did the exact opposite of what was demanded by their doctrine but never dared to question its eminence. Its inherent goodness and its orthodoxy were never questioned. Circumstance may have necessitated that it could not be consistently applied in practice, but it was still regarded as the only source for the happiness and perfection of mankind. If I may speak freely, the doctrines of *liberty, equality, and fraternity* have become an idol. If anyone dared question their eminence, then all would cry out as with one voice, "Great is Diana of the Ephesians who does not know that her image fell down from heaven!"[31] While these teachings are therefore unquestionable, tremendous care will be taken not to see the glory of the goddess to which the whole of the Netherlands and all of the world has sworn allegiance is diminished.

In this manner, the people argued; in this manner, they spoke. So they restarted the same failing project time and again whenever the opportunity arose. But to serve an idol is a tough religion to adhere to. Countrymen, you who love the Fatherland just like I do: read and consider what has happened to the Fatherland since men have become so cocky. Remind yourselves of what you have seen and heard, and you will acknowledge that I am not exaggerating. After every series of disappointments, a new

---

[31] Groen is rhetorically referencing Acts 19:28 and 19:35.

disappointment is added yet again. The bitter experiences were always at odds with the sweet delusions. Every form of government based upon the Revolutionary ideals caused division, misery, dissatisfaction, and the eventual collapse of the government and the state. Revolutions and wars, cruelties and foolishness always followed the application of these doctrines.

And yet, the people still did not develop an aversion to it? Not in the least. In fact, they constantly looked for the heart of the problem in trivial matters. They complained about everything, except for the foolishness of the people in accepting these false doctrines. Have you ever seen an accountant who continues to look for the mistakes in his calculation without paying any attention to his flawed formula? How he suffers and goes crazy in continuing to search endlessly for the reasons why his balance on paper differs from the amount he has in the bank? We would remind him: "It's not your calculations, stupid! Look up and acknowledge that you started with an incorrect balance." Politicians who fail time and again, look up! See that the reason for your self-deceit does not lie in the error of your conclusions but in the falsehood of your principles!

I only wish that my readers who agree with the revolutionary confusion could understand the confusion and that my words will have an effect upon them. But I doubt it. We already have the lessons from ample experiences and catastrophes. But in order to learn, lessons aren't enough; one must also pay attention to that which is taught through these lessons. Chastisement only serves its purpose if it is followed by repentance. What do you think: is their desire to learn, and is repentance visible? And as this is by no means the case, shall we not fear the continual future fulfillment of the saying, "Those who refuse to hear, must feel"?[32] But let us not judge too harshly. It is natural for these men to remain attached to their convictions as a mother is attached to her child. And, of course, you wouldn't judge a mother too harshly who refuses to acknowledge the shortcomings and evil of her own child, even if it were evident to everyone else. Furthermore, we know that it certainly is not easy to publicly acknowledge mistakes, especially if you were preaching from the rooftops that you have uncovered the greatest wisdom there is. Therefore, their attachment to revolutionary

---

[32] This is a Dutch proverb meaning that if a man foolishly refuses to pay attention to warnings, he cannot escape facing the consequences.

principles is understandable, despite how often it has been revealed as foolishness in practice. They would rather renew their experimentation time and again. In this regard, however, they are just like a gambler who continues to throw the dice, oblivious to the fact that in the nature of the dice itself lies the inevitability of his failure.

If half-measures have generated such terrible consequences, imagine what the full application of these doctrines will entail. Yet, they argue that only through the full application thereof will all be well. Then we would know that the liberty tree is indeed a miracle tree. The root of our misfortune is not too much but too little revolutionary liberty. A double dose of this poison is, therefore, what they propose.

Poison? Is this denouncement not too harsh? I'll leave the judgment to the reader—on the condition that we first investigate the practical implications of the full application of the creed *Liberty, Equality, Fraternity.*

In order to describe this, I am forced to make use of four words with a foreign origin. The first is "radicalism," the second "socialism," third "communism," and finally "pantheism." These words are so often heard nowadays that it is vital to know what each of them means. Strange words they are, and they convey strange ideas. But now that these alien ideas have come to the Netherlands, we ought to become acquainted with them in order to heed against the dangers they pose. We ought to be as heedful against dangerous ideas as we are against dangerous people. If murderers and malicious people are exiled to far-off regions, people can continue living without fearing them. But if they walk freely in our own country, it would be good to be aware of the threat they pose so they cannot surprise us while our guard is down.

Radicalism: What is a radical? A radical (derived from the Latin word *radix,* which means "root") is someone who is not satisfied with pruning or chopping but desires complete uprooting. Now that is all fine and good, but the question remains what the man desires to uproot and what he plants in its place.

Let there be no doubt: the radical uproots all that he considers to be at odds with *liberty, equality, and fraternity.* And in its place, he plants those seeds he found from the so-called "liberty garden." If its teachings and doctrines were good, he would have earned praise and trust; but if it is damnable, it would be vital to see that he never gets appointed as the caretaker of the Dutch garden. Because then the result would be the same for the Dutch garden as was said of Israel's garden in the Psalm: namely that swine from the woods have come to destroy it.[33]

Again, so what is a radical? I will explain by comparing him to something more familiar, a liberal. For simplicity's sake, I will explain it in this way: a radical is a complete liberal in the same way that a liberal is a half-radical. A liberal is a radical stopped in his tracks. A radical is a liberal who, by virtue of suitable circumstances, was able to grow to maturity. Or, to put it even more briefly: liberalism is the seed of which radicalism is the fruit.

All of us pretty much know what a liberal is. Although there are many different kinds of liberals, in general, they are those who, to a certain degree, promote those Revolutionary ideas which exhibit great aversion to the authority of a legitimate government but show great contentment with the power of their own allies and friends. They are those who promote these ideas to others in order to achieve their agenda. But the golden age of liberalism is over. Now they are mocked and shunned. All those who do not desire constant and continuing revolution are counted as heretics and worshippers of idols. The liberal is also out of place in this society. To find your place in the new Europe, you need to be a radical. To bow

---

33 A reference to Psalm 80:13.

unconditionally to the logical consequences of the Revolutionary doctrines is the *shibboleth*[34] distinguishing the radical from the liberal. While the liberals were certainly not free of political recklessness, it is the nature of the radical to continue further along the path set out by the liberal.

Should I develop this distinction in more detail? Everything that is not agreeable with the new philosophy, but which had been previously tolerated, must now be completely eradicated. The liberal acknowledges that the king can have some authority, that the franchise should preferably not be completely universal, that not everyone is born a fellow-regent, that a nation is gradually educated to enjoy full liberty. But this capitulation to truth is, in the eyes of the radical, high treason against the cause of mankind. He desires no limitations and no postponement. All states must be republics; that is, they must be ruled by the people. Is a radical, therefore, always a republican? No, he has—at least temporarily—no objection to the monarchical principle so long as it is applied in a republican

---

[34] The book of Judges records the use also intended here. In an ancient Hebrew dialect, the term *shibboleth* meant "ear of grain" (or, according to some, "stream"). The Ephraimites, who did not have a "sh" sound in their language, pronounced the word with an "s," revealing themselves as the enemy.

sense. The radicals want a government that is under them and, therefore, would tolerate a kingdom where the king is under the rule of the people. A king? Why not? As long as he remains obedient. What the people want, the king must do. If they want another government, the king must give them another government. Driven by the will of the people, he is, if he carries the title of "king," merely a royal marionette.

When it comes to elections, the radical is particularly consistent and exhibits his confidence over and against every objection of others. In every state, not only the right to vote but also the right to get elected should be afforded to all without exception. In France, they also call manual laborers, shoemakers, and artisans to participate in the country's legislature. The expression, "Cobbler, stick to thy last," is apparently not applicable any longer. I believe this touches the very heart of the character of the new political system.

Nevertheless, I still have one other objection. I have respect for people from all the different classes of society—for the king on the throne as well as for the laborer in his hut. I want equality, but I fear equality applied to work and career. I would not want to see a politician occupying himself with making or mending my clothes. Likewise, I fear when artisans, however knowledgeable at their trade they may be, occupy themselves with governing the state. The state must also only be ruled by those knowledgeable in the art of politics. It can lead to—and allow me this expression in order to remain true to my parable—the state being most excellently clothed, but the clothes and shoes simply don't fit.

I would prefer a carpenter if I want something to be built, a skipper when I'm sailing, a soldier when the enemy is at the gates, a doctor when I'm ill, a farmer when I'm in need of food, and a carter when I'm riding out. I want an experienced boatman when the wind at sea starts to pick up, and an experienced politician, men who know the art of politics, in the assembly or cabinet, when I see the political hurricane, the disappearance of the throne and hear from the mouths of the children dancing on the ruins the words *liberty, equality, fraternity*.

But they tell me that this is an arbitrary distinction that is not applicable anymore. It is aristocratic concepts by which I promote the fatal distinction of classes. Men are ignorant of what, through the enlightenment of our age, one person is able to achieve in different spheres of work. The time will soon come when it will be announced that the doctrine of equality demands that all people, without distinction, are everything.

Allow me to proceed to the second word, which in the eyes of many isn't any less admirable: *Socialism*. I will have to write only briefly about it, lest my argument becomes too long. The socialist is a proponent of a form of socialization but in a heretofore unknown way. He argues that until now not nearly enough has been done for the sake of equality. Thrones have been overthrown, the nobility have been robbed of its privileges, the difference in the classes has been greatly diminished, the inequality of political rights has everywhere been eradicated—a good start, but what has been gained? One inequality has remained, and that is the worst one of all: the inequality of property. There are still wealth and poverty, abundance, and shortage. What do liberty and the right to vote mean when someone can live idly off an inheritance while another has to work hard to make a living? What does liberty mean to me when I have to do hard labor at the command of the wealthy? If I am hungry, is it really to my advantage to have my name on the electoral roll? Is that *liberty, equality, and fraternity*? They would have the Revolution renounce its motto if it is unable to bring an end to the gravest of inequalities.

But, my friends, how can that be? "It can be so," the socialist would answer, in a very simple manner and without long delay. It can only be made possible if the state ensures a better distribution of property. The root of the evil is that the state, from prejudice, has actually failed to take the unequal distribution of property into account.

But should there not be respect for property rights? I thought I was the owner of my property. No, the socialist opposes such prejudices. The free and equal people have united themselves in one state, and this state is just as much the owner as it is the lawgiver of that which it rules. The arrangement can therefore be simple. Through many kinds of taxes, through prohibiting inheritance, by transferring the property of the dead to the state, the equality they have in mind can very speedily be achieved.

And there is something else. All trade and industry will henceforth, in order to combat a future rise in inequality, be run by the state. Communal labor will be arranged at the command of the state, which will give to each his job and salary. This state's monopoly will be the start of a unified society in an earthly paradise. The people need not fear disorder or violence. Socialists loathe that. They would never require anything from you by any other means than the authority of the state and the rule of law. They will take into account all formalities and, when they take away your very last penny, you wouldn't have the slightest reason to complain about irregularities. You don't even have to resort to beggary as there will always be a job for you in one of the large factories.

Let us proceed to the third kind of contemporary wisdom: *Communism*. The communist wants rich and poor to own everything communally, not as a result of Christian charity, but through the force of the state. At times, it is difficult to distinguish between communism and socialism. The difference in many regards does not so much touch the essence but the form of the two systems. The socialist makes you pay; the communist takes it himself. The socialist veils that which you and I regard as an injustice with the concept of the rule of law, while the communist is less courteous. He regards the ceremonies and formalities as unnecessary since looting is a much easier means. He desires definite and immediate equality. All that the earth has to offer, they argue, must be the property of humanity as a whole, while they consider property rights as a form of greed and theft. What these people call theft, however, is in fact, the reasonable, noble attempts at true justice. These honest and brave men, in their care for the welfare of all, also have other ideas opposed to what we, in our ancient way of thinking, have called ethical. Communists are convinced that family life is at odds with universal brotherhood. Marriage they count, along with private property, as detrimental and harmful institutions.

Now let us proceed unto the last and, in a sense, the most godless system of doctrine: *pantheism*. It ties together all the related principles mentioned above. This doctrine has recently made a lot of inroads in Germany in particular. They say this doctrine's implications are very deep, and indeed men go down deep with it, deep into the abyss. The more well-known name of atheism is also an appropriate description of this form of divine denial. To know the distinction between godlessness and pantheism is to us who know God the Father of our Lord Jesus Christ, the Father of all mercy, and the God of all solace, rather redundant. But it is not redundant to know that the various ways of forsaking God are, in neighboring countries, praised shamelessly as the pinnacle of science.

Often, however, the revolutionary doctrines have been veiled by a show of religiosity and, even now, we find socialists and communists twisting various passages of Scripture, abusing the commands of the Lord to justify their evil ways. But many have moved beyond this form of artistry. Do you know what these knowledgeable men teach? Christianity is a failed human experiment attempting to satisfy the human desire for eternal salvation. Man is his own god. God is a figment of human imagination. Here on earth alone can paradise be restored. Immortality is a myth, and there is no end beyond gaining maximum pleasure from this earthly life. Virtue to them exists in name only. They make no distinction between good and evil, and in actuality to them, all means that lead to the realization of the revolutionary ideals are good. Every crime in service thereof is counted as a revolutionary duty. The current crisis, in which everything has been turned upside down, is apparently to our benefit. Society is too sick to be healed. The building is too heavily decayed to be restored. A totally different society is needed, a building with different foundations. The blessings of the Revolution will only be experienced after many years of theft, murder, war, and destruction. But who in their right mind would object to establishing heaven on earth?!

But no, some people say, these ideas are too radical to have any influence. It is evident to all that these doctrines are utterly destructive to all peace and safety. Religion and morality are not seriously threatened thereby. In the extravagance of these ideas lies the guarantee of their failure.

Guarantee? But have there never been extravagant ideas embraced by man that had a great impact and caused much damage? Besides, you call these ideas damnable. That is your opinion. The opinions of others may be different. And allow me to bring to your attention something else that is most often not considered. These ideas are most certainly damnable when judged by the ordinances of God, nature, and the essence of reality.[35] But in terms of the spirit of the age, they are in order. Society had long ago already almost unanimously declared that the service of God and Law of God are not suitable for civil

---

[35] When Groen refers to the ordinances of God, he has in mind those divinely-established laws which govern creation and whereby God maintains His covenantal relationship with mankind, i.e., in terms of the inescapable negative consequences of sin and positive consequences of obedience to divine laws established thereby. See: J.A. Schlebusch, "Strategic Narratives: Groen van Prinsterer as Nineteenth-Century Statesman-Historian." (PhD diss., University of Groningen, 2018), 122.

governance. An appeal to God's commands and laws is inadmissible. Do they consider this setting aside of divine law as without consequences for the state and society? Do they believe that the very cornerstone of the building can be ripped out without doing damage to the building? On what is the sacredness and legitimacy of property then based? On what are political rights and the distinction between classes based? On what is fidelity in marriage and the authority of the father based if not upon God's will? What is left is merely a multitude of individuals among whom no relationship or standard exists apart from reciprocal desire and approval.[36] If people find authority handy, it is maintained. If it becomes a nuisance, it is destroyed. If property rights serve the common good, it is maintained, but if it does not serve the interests of the state, it is destroyed. When all are free and equal, they have a duty to rid themselves of all hindrances to this liberty and equality. It must be cut off, as was the case in France in 1793, when thousands were slaughtered.

Let me emphasize the point: even the greatest extravagance, in alliance with the

---

[36] Hierarchy is supported upon family per the Westminster Larger Catechism and agreed upon by all theologians of merit since.

wishes and worldview of the sinner, is not regarded as extravagant anymore. It is approved by godless hearts. The calmness of reason is powerless against the excitement of the godless heart and the desires of self-interest. The deception becomes particularly irresistible when its evil tendencies are not only hidden but recast as principles. When you propose to a man working hard to put food on the table for his family that stealing is not only permissible but praiseworthy: as the taking of that which in fairness should be his; as making himself master of a small part of that which, if the earth's riches were equally divided, would be awarded to him. This is the essence of the catechism of communism. The theory is clear and simple, as well as in its practice.

When some journalists incite restlessness and division by ignoring all that has been done for the plight of the poor, presenting the rich as unwilling to provide jobs and as conspiring against the poor, then the temptation for socialism would understandably be great. It cannot, in fact, be resisted without the shield of faith, by which one can deflect the fiery arrows of our evil enemies.

Yet, even if the half-hearted application of the Revolutionary doctrines has evidently led to much destruction, and even if the full application is unachievable, would it not be our duty as Christians to take sides against these doctrines that are bringing tumult and destruction to the whole world? Must the Christian be content with all that the government commands?

Must all abuses and perversions simply be patiently tolerated? Is it not better to embrace *liberty, equality, and fraternity* for the good and improvements that can potentially come from it?

I would argue that, by their nature, these doctrines make improvements impossible. They don't mitigate abuses but worsen them. And the very cause of the gravest abuses is inherent to them.

4

THE RADICAL REMEDY

"Men longed for the time of healing,
but behold, trouble came!"

–Jeremiah 8:15

*L*iberty, *Equality, Fraternity*. Under this
motto is promised constitutional
restoration, full purification, and radical
healing. And as some have asked me, "Would it
not be possible to use the revolutionary doctrine
for good?"

Undoubtedly so, had the Revolutionary
doctrine been true, and had its proponents been
right. But, they say, if only the extravagance of
some would be stopped and the Fatherland
would be saved from abuses, then everything
that gives cause for complaint would disappear.
The state would be saved if we did away with

them who, backwardly and childishly, rise up as protectors of prejudice and injustice, who oppose all improvement and express an aversion to liberty. Those who deliberately turn away from the light: darklings, Roman Catholics, or Protestant Jesuits,[37] unpleasant or irritating people who would for the sake of their own interests oppose the realization of *liberty, equality, and fraternity.*

Honorable proponent of a position I reject, your sketch certainly has no lack of color, but your portrait in no way corresponds with reality. Of course, I oppose the Revolutionary motto in the sense which it is proposed by its supporters, but does that mean that I oppose liberty? Am I a proponent of injustice and force? Is my opposition to abuses based on self-interest?

I hear many such reproaches but without any proof. In response, I would say that I am certainly a proponent of liberty, order, and justice. I desire reformation, but reformation is only possible by means of the principles I propose—politics in opposition to revolutionary ideals. Allow me to be blunt: I acknowledge no

---

[37] I assume Groen meant to write "Protestants and Roman Catholic Jesuits." He includes the Jesuits here because, throughout the late eighteenth and the first half of the nineteenth centuries, they were well-known opponents of the Enlightenment and the French Revolution.

reformation that is revolutionary. Revolution means upheaval. Revolution is, according to the meaning of the word as well as its history, destruction of that which man upheaves. Reformation, in contradistinction, is improvement of that which man conserves, not upheaves, but improves to protect it against the threat of upheaval.

You would say that I have no idea of the extent of the disease. But I know that all of society is sick. I desire healing and restoration. But I have no confidence in the physicians to whom I ascribe the very origin and aggravation of the disease. And, if I don't drink the medicine offered to me, it is because I have ample evidence that your magic potions are deadly. I am hesitant when you speak of rooting out abuses. Why? Because I love these abuses? No, but because every time the Revolution promises improvement, things just go from bad to worse.

Hesitancy is therefore inescapable. Before we allow the Fatherland to be destroyed by means of the revolutionary medicines of the doctors, it is important to investigate what exactly these so-called reformers have achieved thus far in terms of rooting out the abuses. To what degree has the so-called purification of the state and society been achieved by them? By what exemplary exercise of the medical profession have they proven themselves trustworthy? To what degree can, judging by the results of their patients, their self-confidence, and the boasting about their remedy be justified?

I believe we can gain clarity regarding these inquiries by briefly answering the following questions:

1. What has been considered an abuse?
2. Has that which is often promoted as improvement outweighed the decline?
3. Are, by the rooting out of abuses, the institutions improved?
4. Has respect been shown to unchanging principles?
5. Has the new doctrine lived up to its promises?

People have defined abuses as everything that does not agree with the doctrines of the Revolutionary designers. Therefore, before I can agree with the success of their battle against abuses, I would have to agree with the Revolutionary definition thereof. Or is it not sufficient proof of the mistakenness of a cause, if it is in agreement with error? Am I to be convinced of my guilt when I am accused by a violent rioter? Or when the rioter calls me a coward? Men of the Revolution! You lay before me a long list of abuses that you have dealt with by means of your wisdom, though I surely could not be blamed for, in accordance with my convictions, using a different standard for judging the authenticity of your so-called improvements. Between you and me there is, in the calculation of your achievements, a marked difference.

Allow me to proceed to the second question without delay. Have the improvements based on the Revolutionary doctrines been greater than the negative consequences thereof? A cause can be good, and yet the price to be paid is too high. A cure can be worse than the disease. I cannot thank you when you, in taking away a light fever, leave me with a serious illness. Similarly, in politics also, the gratitude for the curing of a disease can only be conditional. For example, before 1795, there were legitimate complaints about the stubbornness of governors. Does it then follow that the Fatherland must overthrow them for suffering 19 fearful years under French tyranny?[38]

The list of examples can be expanded indefinitely. It is not necessary, especially since the truth will become even clearer through answering the third question. Have the

---

[38] The revolutionary Batavian Republic in the Netherlands lasted from 1795 to 1813.

institutions associated with the abuses been affirmed, secured, and improved? No, they have been overhauled. Men have destroyed all institutions—also those that could have been reformed. Here and elsewhere, every national institution has been sold to the Revolutionary demolishers for destruction. This was no benefaction to the nations. I would not be doing you a favor if I burned down your badly built house. You wouldn't destroy a dyke because it has a hole in it. You wouldn't uproot a fruit-bearing tree because it grows askew. You don't kill a suffering man because he is sick. And yet, man has done all of this. There were many cases of abuse, much had grown askew, there were holes in the system, the building of the state had problems, the state was sick. But in order to heal, they murdered; in order to improve, they destroyed. Oh, reckless physician, do you not know that one only amputates the ailing limb in order to save the healthy parts of the body? The friends of the people, in caring for the health of the people, followed the example of the all-too-smart and benevolent bear, who became the gardener's ally. The fable is well known. In order to save his sleeping friend from an irritating fly, the giant animal decided to kill the fly by means of hurling a giant stone at him, but in the process crushed his friend's head and, thereby, albeit in a rather inconvenient manner, relieved his friend from the irritation of the fly forever.[39]

That is not all. Also, regarding the fourth question, there is no agreeable answer. No, these people did not leave even the principles alone. In order to fight abuses, not only the institutions were destroyed, but the very principles which ensured their virtuousness and durability were rejected.

What a shameful *modus operandi*. Just because I dislike a house built on rock, I don't simply break it down only to build a new one in the sand. When I desire the good fruits of a tree, I don't start by cutting off its roots. Let, therefore, in politics, whenever a constitution is written, the unchanging nature of virtuous principles and the vitality of the political alphabet be acknowledged. In 1795, it was claimed that the Netherlands was not happy under the House of Orange and couldn't be happy under it. Was it, therefore, necessary for the state to regard as first principle the idea that, apart from the people themselves, there exists no Lawgiver? Their liberty entails freedom from the God of Revelation, their equality demands

---

[39] The fable of "The Bear and the Gardener" is a fable which originated in India. It warns against making foolish friendships. The author, Jean La Fontaine (1621–1695), introduced the fable to the Western world in the seventeenth-century by adapting it into French free verse.

no distinction between faith and idolatry, and their fraternity the unified rejection of the commands of the King of kings to the nations.

Improvement was in our country the goal and motto of men such as Slingeland, Fagel, and van der Spiegel—men whose names and achievements I hope will never be forgotten by our nation.[40] But if improvement was considered impossible, if people were convinced that our system was irreparable, one in which the Dutch nation experienced the joy of prosperity, power, fame, and civil liberty, if a whole new system was needed—in which better care was taken for the unity of the state and the citizenry was given more influence—was it then necessary to accept a false philosophy with which all justifiable demands are irreconcilable? Their philosophy tore apart the state in various parties, only to generate from this a unity by force. Multiplying the deliberations and conventions is equally useless as it was before—

---

[40] All three men served in the position of Grand Pensionary of Holland. Prior to the liberal Batavian Revolution of 1795, this was the most important political office in the country apart from the Prince of Orange himself. In practice, the position was similar to what is more commonly known as the position of prime minister. Simon van Slingeland served in the office from 1727 to 1736, Gaspar Fagel from 1672 to 1688, and Laurens Pieter van der Spiegel from 1787 to 1795, when he fled to Germany during the Revolution.

in fact, it has only made things worse. The individual citizen is now more vulnerable than ever and more separated from the actual governance of the state now that the standard has become the artificial will of the majority.

With the building of the state, have we not set aside and disregarded the true foundation based on the will and ordinances of God—the rules of politics that presuppose human depravity? And by destroying everything by common approval and creating by common approval, we have cut off the roots necessary for a new institution to grow, because only then would it be based on legitimate historical foundations and gain genuine national strength.

Let us proceed unto the fifth question and its answer. The people have exchanged the principles upon which peace, wealth, and liberty are dependent for a set of doctrines that is very brave in terms of what it promises but ever failing in terms of what it delivers.

It was not long ago, not in a distant past, that our fathers and we ourselves were both witnesses and victims of men who proclaimed the kind of liberty by which all true liberty is destroyed: a law that annuls all true rights and an order based upon the desires of those whom we happen to, at any given time, call the government.

Liberty, Equality, Fraternity. Under this motto, you have desired freedom, but you have received confusion. You have begged for order, but you have received arbitrariness.

What was the true nature of that liberty of 1789?[41] You know that the licentiousness was there right from the start and eventually revealed itself most clearly in those horrendous scenes of 1793, which should never be forgotten by any generation. But, just in case you may have forgotten, allow me to remind you of the impact of these doctrines in France a mere three months after the Revolution. All property became subject to theft, castles were burned, monasteries destroyed, farmhouses were looted, taxes remained unpaid; there was no law and order and not even a shadow of the existence of due process. So it was, even when the Revolution was still in the cradle.

The liberty of 1830: How long did it last?[42] I think perhaps from July twenty-ninth to August seventh, when Louis Philippe

---

[41] Groen is referring to the French Revolution.

[42] Groen is referring to the Second French Revolution, which led to the overthrow of King Charles X, the restored monarch from the House of Bourbon, who had governed France prior to the first French Revolution. He was replaced by a new monarch, his cousin Louis Philippe from the House of Orléans.

attempted some strict reforms[43] to tame the free flow of the Revolution and by which he managed to govern for 18 years. Speedily, the reborn sovereignty of the people would be dissolved into the power of a single despot, who, by virtue of the fear for an even worse government, had the support of even his enemies.

And the liberty of 1848: What is it, and for how long?[44] It already shows signs of disarray in the way that it flatters and concedes to the mob, with the result already being complete disorder. It also shows ample signs of the arbitrariness that is always demanded by the friends of the Revolution in terms of pushing through their agenda.

When this is achieved, the compulsion and violence will only increase further in order to stop the very development that these men originally had in mind. People always tell us how lovely this new liberty is, but it is only lovable

---

[43] The word used by Groen here is *conservatieve* which literally translates to "conservative." From the context of the passage, however, it is clear that he does not have the kind of conservatism in mind with which he himself associated and therefore the meaning he conveys here is best translated as "strict."

[44] Groen is referring to the February Revolution of 1848 in France. During this Revolution, the monarchy was again overthrown, and the Second French Republic was established. This republic would only last until 1851, when a self-coup was staged by Napoleon III, who then established the French Empire.

from a distance. When it comes to the fore, it shows us just how unacceptable it really is.

But do you desire another standard by which to measure the blessings bestowed by the Revolution? I find this standard in the terrible disasters that men desire simply to escape it. False liberty gives birth to the force and compulsion by which people are carried away in cuffs. After Robespierre, Napoleon came—and what did this experience teach us? What is it currently teaching us? In comparison to anarchy, despotism is desired as a beneficence. People are, simply for the sake of being protected against the mother, highly infatuated with her ugly daughter. And is this infatuation so strange? Would you not be thankful to those who take away your liberty in order to save you from the death claws of those whom you have seen murder others? Would you not gladly exchange a common liberty for a common submission by which you are at least protected against death? Would you not look for guarantees against those who have blood on their hands? And when a new call for liberty is heard, would you not say: "I know what kind of liberty you have in mind?" Would you not be glad to be disciplined by a tyrant? Would you not rather be chained up than fall again into the hands of this kind of liberty? Would you not prefer to remain locked up in prison than to be taken into the valley of death?

But then the calls for liberty become a vain cry and its realization a mockery. Certainly, this is the end result in spite of all the glittering promises of the revolutionary doctrines. These are the characteristics of the revolutionary ideas in practice: every promise not only ends in disappointment but ends up delivering the opposite of that which was promised in the political program. Liberty becomes slavery, abundance becomes shortage, and the series of so-called generosities all become regrets. Thereby their relationship to the father of lies is revealed, who promises his children bread but gives them a snake.[45]

The proofs for this are, in light of recent events, ample. I do not only mean the liberty whereby thousands of freed prisoners and beggars have made the streets of Paris unsafe for French citizens. I speak not of an equality which, under the pretense that there is no difference anymore in rank or class or calling, elevates the mob to the sole rulers of the land. I don't even mention the brotherhood, which reveals itself in every conceivable form of hatred. I would ask in what way the liberty of the February Revolution deserves the adoration of

---

45 A reference to Matthew 7:1–10 and Luke 11:11.

Europe? Is it because a small number of ambitious men came to power in the midst of an uproar? Is it because all of France was forced to submit to the will of a local Parisian mob? Or is it because the officers of the new government have placed themselves above the law and do not recognize the independence of the judiciary? Or is it because in these apparent blessings of the Revolution, the seeds of disorder and misery can be seen? Or are they convinced of the beneficence of the revolutionary projects because the government, in expectation of the time when communism can be fully implemented, has started to bring in socialist reforms by the most arbitrary means?

But I will not count all the consequences of this so-called liberty. I ask not how many and what their nature is. I ask not to what degree Lamartine, in his daily praise of these events which he had prepared himself, has added to his talent of poetry, the talent of embellishment.[46] I will put all of this aside. I want to accept all that is acceptable and believe all that is believable—namely that the shocking scenes which we have seen over the past few weeks in France are merely a passing and inescapable malfunction

---

[46] The figure of speech employed by Groen here is impossible to convey into English. The Dutch word translated as poetry is *dichter* and the word translated as embellishment is *verdichter*.

of society and that we are now at the end and not the beginning of a series of foolish, revolutionary misdeeds.

But even if I were to show such lenience, it would not be for the sake of sparing you, oh political reformers of the day! It is because I want to test the very heart of this system of doctrine. It is because it would be to the benefit of others to see how the foolishness of your ideas has been revealed alongside its apparent triumph.

This is not difficult to prove. We only have to look at what the chief advocates of the wisdom of the age have proposed as the greatest secrets of this wisdom. In the prescribed literature, philosophers and philanthropists reveal the shining lights of the revolutionary heaven. Saint-Simon,[47] Fourier,[48] and others advocate with the most excellent rhetoric that for the achievement of the true equality of humanity, only one modification is needed. Only one! How little is needed! And which one is that? The organic society must be replaced by

---

[47] Henri de Saint-Simon (1760–1825) was a liberal political theorist who laid much of the philosophical groundwork for the development of socialism in the thought of Karl Marx and Friedrich Engels.

[48] François Marie Charles Fourier (1772–1837) was an early French socialist thinker. He is credited with inventing the word "feminism" in 1837.

an artificial one. Envy and opposition would stop as soon as society has been reformed into one of brotherly cooperation.

But alas, it cannot be achieved. Why not? Because the people are unwilling; because they do not have brotherly love. Because envy and resentment live among them, because sin brings separation between them, and the tendency to selfishness and self-interest rules them.

We would not tolerate this. Once we come into power, we will not cater to these tendencies. We would make people, whom we love so dearly, happy, even by force if necessary. We would bring people together in spacious common workplaces, where they would receive work and wages and food and entertainment and all those worldly desires. By means of common labor and common enjoyment, the state will arrange and distribute it.

Your plan may be pretty, but I think you have left all liberty behind and out of sight.

No, there is liberty they claim and, if you don't see it, you have only your own ignorance to blame.

So it always goes when these men are granted an opportunity to speak. One would certainly be tempted to ask questions, but the dialogue is always suddenly brought to an abrupt end. Now I realize why this liberty is seen by my opposition and not by me. I desire liberty for all, but the opposition seeks liberty for them alone. Under the name of liberty, their free rule over the citizens and residents of this country is intended.

The proponents of this social order ordained by the state, of this society not of clans and families, but companies and corporations are, in terms of the implementation of their system, content with the peace and liberty of the government—the liberty and omnipotence of those who take care for the discipline of society and are the heads of the herd who provide us with this new grazing. They have convinced so many of the greatness and superiority of their ideas. But, as soon as the point is reached where these ideals become a reality, they change their minds and the enchanting portrait changes, and many who had been proponents thereof now stand with de Lamennais[49] who wrote concerning this Revolutionary religion: "I am convinced that this system would condemn the nations to the kind of slavery that the world has never before seen. Man would become a tool, and we would be more miserable than the negro over which the farmer rules according to his

---

[49] Jean-Marie-Robert de Lamennais (1780–1860) was a conservative Roman Catholic priest and philosopher who played a decisive role in the revival of Christendom in France after the French Revolution.

own pleasure, and we would be degraded to the level of an animal. I don't think a more nonsensical doctrine has ever arisen from the human mind."

Another example is Louis Blanc,[50] who was previously one of the most celebrated Revolutionary theorists and, in 1848, was a member of the provisional government, who expressed the greatest sympathy for the lower classes. For him, the impracticality of Saint-Simon's theories was evident, but he had discovered another recipe for success: managing the labor. For all there was work, by means of the loving care of the supreme state. For all there is an equal wage.

How then? For the hard-working man and the sluggard an equal wage? The same wage for the one who got the job done and the one who achieved nothing! Undoubtedly! Because, as Blanc claims, surely there will not be any more sluggards. But how can you provide assurance for such a claim if there is no monetary incentive to work?

What guarantee did Blanc provide? Look at his design, and while you are venerating its

---

[50] Louis Blanc (1811–1882) was a French socialist, political philosopher and statesman who, in addition to being a member of the provisional government after the 1848 Revolution, was also a member of the French National Assembly in the early 1870s.

simplicity, honor it for the immense knowledge of human nature of which it bears witness. In every workplace, a sign will be erected which says: "A sluggard is a thief." And looking at this sign will provide more incentive for work than despicable money. The conscience will provide sufficient motivation, and the honor of the laborers will have the magical power necessary by which miracles will be achieved in the service of the industry.

The state-run economy is based on the idea that this sign at the workplace provides an infallible guarantee. But the previous French government had no eye for these theories. Old Guizot,[51] they claimed, with his stubbornness and stupidity, who remained attached to the past and the idea of learning lessons from experience, with his conservative opposition to this new philosophy; he definitely needs to be shunned for denying the peoples of the world the revolutionary blessings, and if a king is in agreement with a prime minister like that, a revolution is inevitable.

And now, after the Revolution, everyone has been promised a job, but, if I may ask, have

---

[51] François Guizot (1787–1874) was a conservative French statesman who was Minister of Education (1832 - 1837), Foreign Minister (1840 - 1847), eventually Prime Minister from September 1847 to the February Revolution of 1848, and France's only Calvinist leader.

these jobs also been provided? Many people had, according to my sources, an abundance of work and pay before this Revolutionary promise, but not after. Blanc's speeches were very beautiful, in which he argued according to his own convictions, but the practical reality was at odds with what he proposed. And what do we read in the papers who espouse the correct viewpoints, for example, in the *Haarlemsche Courant*?[52] The most republican-minded papers and even the majority of the working class agree that, despite how beautiful the words of Blanc's speeches may sound, there is indeed a great discrepancy between saying and doing. The new newspaper, *La Republique*,[53] even goes so far as to claim that, if ever a system according to the ideals of Blanc were to be implemented, it would mean the end of all industrial progress, and there would be no creation of jobs, no more competition in the job market. They admit that the policies of Blanc, which aim at equalizing all wages, would be a grave injustice towards those working hard, as they would be forced to share

---

[52] The *Haarlemsche Courant* (currently called the *Haarlems Dagblad*) is the oldest newspaper in the Netherlands that still circulates. The first edition was printed in 1656.
[53] *La Republique* was a liberal French newspaper in the nineteenth century.

the fruits of their labor with those who are incompetent and lazy.

Gradually, some have come to realize and admit the shameful foolishness of these overhyped doctrines. Many have come to realize that true liberty is almost always sacrificed for the sake of equality. This leads to a common monopoly of the state, and the guardianship of society is transferred into the hands of the executive branch of government. In the absence of all competition, progress becomes impossible.

The laborer is doomed to a lifelong servitude of the state—one he can only leave at the risk of starvation. All personal responsibility is taken away, and, in short, we see the greatest mental and moral decline ever witnessed.

It is indeed a good reason to rejoice whenever people come to realize the error of these ways. It would have been great if they had realized this in France before February twenty-third.[54] This would have been beneficial to Louis Blanc, as well. A high position may be desirable, but not when you boast before France and all of Europe about your foolishness. Even an honorary chair must feel most uncomfortable when—if the reader would allow me to use this

---

[54] Meaning before the February Revolution of 1848 broke out.

expression—is no different from what we call a common footstool.[55]

I have one more comment for you, oh doctor of the revolutionary medicine, whose degree has been awarded by the High School of Revolution. You argue that *Liberty, Equality, Fraternity* would take away all abuses. But against this claim, I have one important concern: the very antidote you recommend brought about the illnesses against which you recommend it. The abuses we are currently suffering are the consequences of the application of the very principles for which you zealously advocate.

What is advertised as improvements by the revolutionaries?

1. No more persecution on the basis of religious convictions.
2. No more neglect of the most important matters of the state.
3. No more centralized control of the life of the common people.
4. No more extreme poverty and unemployment among the lower classes.

I do not doubt the excellence of the promises, but only their fulfillment. And do you know why? I don't have a drawn-out argument, simply

---

[55] The Dutch word used here for "footstool" is *schabelletje*.

this: I distrust the boldness of your prophecy of salvation because it would mean that your doctrine would have to have the opposite effect of what it has had up to now. With a few words, I hope to show this with regard to each of the four points.

With regard to the first claim: It is disgraceful how you have taken away many people's right to religious liberty and liberty to educate children according to their religious principles. Many people were displeased with the way in which the Dutch Reformed Church persecuted those Reformed folk who seceded from the church,[56] and the relentless opposition to the establishment of Christian schools. A number of different causes contributed to this, but the most notable is certainly the actions of the current government. A government founded in liberal principles is, from the very nature of its relationship to the people, shaky. It governs for the people and by the grace and will of the people, but if the people become displeased, if the sovereign people become discontented and knows its power, this government becomes threatened. It is therefore preferable that the people remain like a sleeping lion, which is not easily tamed once it is awake. And when the beast finally awakes and shows its teeth, a

---

[56] See: footnote 21.

double chain is sought. This is the essence of the lovely relationship between the people and the government in the new state. While claiming to be far from intervening with the so-called free development of ideas, the government is indeed cautious about every independent development when it comes to our national religion[57] or national education. When, after a long, dormant period, a revival of religion is witnessed, the government seeks for pretexts to quench or extinguish this.

You can be sure that no one who possesses political power searches for pretexts in vain. Those who have ample pretexts never suffer from a shortage of plans. But there is more. The excellence of the revolutionary doctrine is particularly evidenced in her usefulness and her flexibility in service of every government that is completely incompetent and incapable of *savoir faire*.[58] One would think that the doctrine of liberty would supposedly limit the government. But it is evident that this is not the case—not in the least.

---

[57] The word *volksgeloof* used by Groen here does not convey the idea of a state church. It rather signifies the collective and covenantal relationship of the Dutch nation to God.

[58] *Savoir faire* is a French expression meaning the capacity for appropriate action.

What is the purpose of the state? In days gone by, people used to say its purpose is to protect the rights and liberties of all. In practice, this was a problem for the government because no one could be forced to give up his property to the state. Now things are completely different. Government has been liberated from this difficulty. Government does not have to be shy anymore. Now it has an irresistible weapon by virtue of its political foundation. What is, after all, the purpose of a state formed by means of a convention of free and equal individuals? The common good. In practice, the common good means the interest of the masses and the state, and therefore individual rights and interests are always subordinate thereunto. Rights are only acknowledged as rights as long as they are not in conflict with the chief end of this political theory.

But surely the common good is a virtuous cause, as is the general will and the self-rule of the people. I will grant this if you answer me the following question: Who determines what the interest of the state is and what corresponds to the common good? Surely it is those who have gained the majority of the votes or have the strongest political power. Well then, an injustice is no injustice anymore as long as it serves the interest of the majority at the cost of the minority. And the majority is always with the government for as long as the government remains in power, whether it is by means of a national convention, a directorate, or a king— whether it is under the leadership of Robespierre, Napoleon, Louis-Philippe, Lamartine, or Ledru-Rollin.[59] Remember, here we have reached the point where someone can steal this precious liberty with one grab. The people say to the government: "You are responsible to work for the common good." That is the official command from the sovereign people. But what is granted? That the government itself may define what the "common good" or the "interests of the state" means to them. In turn, the government promises the people: "You can live according to your sovereign will." But what is the secret agenda, the *arrière-pensée*?[60] Oh, popular sovereign! Whose crown is worn and whose scepter is swung by your government! Most certainly, your will is the standard by which every government must rule, but every government would have to teach you what your will truly entails.

---

[59] Alexandre Auguste Ledru-Rollin was a liberal French politician who briefly served as France's Minister of the Interior after the Revolution of 1848.

[60] *Arrière-pensée* is a French expression meaning ulterior motive.

Advocating for liberty for the church and the school has brought us to this view. You realize that this means that we can only serve God and only educate our children in God's ways as long as you do not deem it damaging to the common good.

"But the parliament!" they counter. Oh yes, I have forgotten about them. Is it surprising that I have such difficulty remembering that they have any influence?[61]

"But the houses of representatives!" they say. For some time, we haven't only had one, but two houses.[62] These surely offer a guarantee of proportional representation! Supposedly, they represent the spirit of the Fatherland.

You will have to excuse me for not addressing the issue of parliamentary psychology here. I will limit myself to the observation that since 1795 we have had an elected representative council that has consistently, in accordance with the principles of *liberty, equality, and fraternity*, proceeded to implement, albeit in the name of the nation,

---

[61] Continuing his preceding argument, Groen here counters the idea that a parliament of elected representatives in itself serves as a guarantee against tyranny.

[62] In the Dutch political system, a "house of representatives" is literally known as a "room of representatives."

only those policies which they themselves have regarded as good. When a certain party, with the help of the French military, exiled the Prince of Orange and brought in the French, they claimed it was the will of the nation. When division became evident, and another government took their place, people again claimed that it was the nation that willed this. Likewise, the tyranny of Napoleon was, in the opinion of his comrades, a most outstanding example of a national government of the people.

We would surely, then, not be amazed if a Dutch government, made up of both parliament and the king, regards itself as representatives not only of the "constitutional people" but of the historical nation, especially when it claims that with regard to education only their policies are truly national. And that it, therefore, deserves preference and the almost exclusive right to be universally implemented. On top of that, the revolutionary desire is to let every resident on Dutch soil have the right to vote; then, the danger is the establishment of an essentially foreign and imaginary nationality to be forced upon the nation.

A free man does not choose to be tall or short, weak or strong, and he cannot by mere will liberate himself of his inherent tendencies or temperament. He is bound by his nature and the nurture that shaped him. He cannot exchange his own inherent characteristics for that which he finds more appealing. A nation, just like an individual, did not create itself and, as man is bound to his nature, so is a nation. But I have heard that these notions are currently considered to be the silliness of the Historical School based on falsehoods.[63] The will of the sovereign people, they claim, makes national that which it regards as good. But the will of the people, or those who present themselves as the people, acts on the basis of ever-changing opinions according to the fancy of the day. No national memories come into play then. Therefore, we could not regard it as strange that in a nation shaped by the gospel unto

---

[63] The nineteenth-century Historical School was characterized by a belief in the authority of a historically developed common law, a romantic reaction to the Enlightenment's disregard for history's pedagogic value. The Dutch scholar W.G.F. Van Vliet has pointed out a number of elements in Groen's thinking derived from this school: 1. a rejection of striving for a perfect society, 2. an emphasis on the particular and unique character of a people or nation, 3. the organic symphony of the character of the nation, its laws and its political forms, 4. the necessity of sensitivity and tentativeness when it comes to reforms, 5. the idea that new reforms must be rooted in the old, and 6. opposition to the codification of laws based on the rational insight of one generation of politicians. See: W.G.F. Van Vliet, *Groen van Prinsterers Historische Benadering van de politiek.* Hilversum: Verloren, 2008, 32.

sanctification, a love of liberty, and the duty of rightful submission is then subjected to an exclusive national education where children are not taught that the Bible is God's Word, that Christ is the only Way unto salvation, that their ancestors were martyrs of the faith, that William I[64] was not only a great, but God-fearing man, and that there is no power outside of God and that there is no power that is not under God.

With regard to the second claim: People find it worrisome that so little has been achieved in terms of those issues which affect the nation the most. People notice that, in the meetings of government, so much is said but so little is done, and that at these meetings the most important issues are ignored. With regard to education, welfare, and legislation, the mistakes aren't rectified and the status quo is maintained.

Shall we try to conceal that which is widely known? Thirty-three times, we have solemnly celebrated the third Monday of October.[65] We see the arrival of the train, the

---

[64] William I or William the Silent (1533–1584) was the leader of the Dutch Revolt against the Spanish Habsburgs that set off the Eighty Years' War (1568–1648) and resulted in the formal independence of the United Dutch Provinces in 1581. He was a renowned defender of Dutch Protestantism against Roman Catholic persecution.

[65] Groen is referring to the celebration of the defeat of the French at the Battle of Leipzig, and the consequent return of the Prince of Orange which took place in October 1813.

speeches, the responses, and the joyful hope of improvement is there. But what happens when the houses of representatives conclude their sessions at the end of every year?[66] I don't want to deny that there were also exceptional years, in which the harvest that followed planting season was spectacular. But what was the rule? The hope disappointed time and again and, apart from raising taxes and taking out loans, not much was achieved. The truth of this accusation is indubitable, but with whom does the fault lie? I certainly don't excuse the Second House of Representatives, but I would prefer to see, now that most of the terms of its members are coming to an end, that they take responsibility for their actions. But it would be too harsh to lay all the suicidal actions of the Revolutionaries at their door. I don't intend to praise them but, when it comes to the destructive nature of the Revolutionary ideas, these representatives are certainly not the chief culprits. If improvement under the banner of the dangerous Revolutionary doctrines is impossible, if every step brings us closer to damnation, from fulfilling their role, and if the king cannot propose any reforms apart from

---

During much of the nineteenth century, this was celebrated annually in the Netherlands on the third Monday of October.

[66] This is a rhetorical question with a negative answer.

those spoiled by Revolutionary distortions—
which are in themselves propelled forward by
Revolutionary violence—then the Houses can,
to a certain degree, be excused. If you can only
do damage, then perhaps it is better to do
nothing. You can't progress by means of
confusion and, if every modification only
further worsens the current situation, then
there is no better option than preserving and
maintaining the current system. Or would you
continue to walk if you are but one step away
from falling off a cliff? Would you allow work to
be done on your damaged house if it only led to
more cracks and walls falling over? Would you
put up a fence if the sparks from the steel fell on
the ground covered with gunpowder?

So much was promised with regard to
common deliberation, but that nothing has been
delivered can be clarified from another
perspective, as well. According to the new
political doctrine, people see the guarantees for
improvement and deliverance in the political
forms. They spend so much time designing a
political system for the state that they have no
time to address the actual issues facing the state.
Of course, if one is too obsessed with the form of
the container of the liquid, it wouldn't be a
surprise if one forgets to pour it in altogether. As
long as people remain preoccupied with

agreeing on the form of the cup, crying for water will be in vain. You may be shaking from the cold, but you won't be helped as long as there is no agreement with regard to the cut or materials of your clothing. Do not be surprised, therefore, if matters truly relating to the interests of the people are postponed as long as there is constant deliberation over the nature of the election and the extent of the franchise.

With regard to the third claim: The extravagant centralization! This is one of the main complaints and not without good reason. The oversight and control of everything, including that which does not need to be overseen, the arbitrary control over local town and provincial councils, the banning of free associations, and the obstruction of all free operations are all tendencies about which people rightly complain and protest. But it is one of the logical consequences of the current political philosophy that all the parts of life are to be controlled by the big government of the central state, all in the name of the sovereign people. Never forget that this central state would use this to its own advantage to cheat and restrain the very people in whose name they govern once the people become a threat.

With regard to the fourth claim: The worst evil, they claim, is poverty. Poverty and unemployment, a broken relationship between the higher and lower classes, no relation between work and wages, conflict between the proletariat and capitalists. What will be the end result of it all? This remains uncertain, but what is certainly not unsure is what gave rise to all of this: liberty and equality in the Revolutionary sense. Allow me to provide just one example. When the Revolutionary motto came, guilds and corporations had to be demolished. Free competition was desired along with no barriers to the development of artistic endeavors and industries. There were to be no more spiteful monopolies of persons or companies, and thereby the free development of industries would have provided the necessary guarantee for a better future. The future they desired is here, but can it be called "better?" In this regard, I am in agreement with the leading figures of the current Revolution. It is this so-called liberty, this unlimited competition, this removal of the natural relationship between employer and employee which has destroyed healthy societal relationships and has led to the tyranny of the banks and the rich, which often takes away the livelihood of workers and divides society into two opposing classes, leading to the creation of a massive poor population, and prepares the way for the war of the classes. They have brought to Europe an economic condition that is bad enough for many to call for the re-establishment of those guilds and associations which were so recklessly destroyed by the revolution.[67]

Therefore, let us proceed to the conclusion of my argument. I do not oppose the remediation of the system, but I am convinced that the radical remedies proposed to us today are equivalent to death itself. Therefore, I propose not this radical remedy but rather the remediation of the radicals. Therefore, I chose to start this chapter with the words from Jeremiah 8:15: "Men longed for the time of healing, but behold, trouble came!" or if you were to follow the translation of Van der Palm: "Men longed for restoration, but behold, devastation came!"[68] Therefore, I also think it is

---

[67] Groen is here lodging a critique against both the free market and socialism. He seems to be advocating for an alternative and traditional guild-based economic model akin to the Distributism that would later often be associated with G.K. Chesterton.

[68] The *Palmbijbel*, the translation of the Utrecht University professor of theology, Johannes van der Palm, was finalized in 1830. It was based on the same Greek and Hebrew texts of the *Statenvertaling*, but sought to use what was, at the time, more modern Dutch. As a rationalist, Van der Palm did, however, dissent from the Dordtian and Westminsterian view of Scripture in that he was an adherent of lower (textual) criticism and, therefore, in some places deviated from the Received Text, for example in I John 5:7.

necessary to point out what follows in the text: "Is there no balm in Gilead? Is there no physician there?"[69]

So, if you desire improvement, do not look for it in the principles that brought about this disaster, but respect true rights and history, and seek the Christian principle, which, by virtue of adhering to the highest truth, is the only principle immune to the deceptive theories.

From Scripture alone, the Christian can learn what duties are expected from him, how to judge the developments of the age, how great the blessings are that he receives in the midst of the disorder and suffering, and what the nature of the true liberty of the children of God entails, as opposed to the essentially evil liberty of the world.

---

[69] A reference to Jeremiah 8:16.

THE LIBERTY OF
THE CHILDREN OF GOD

"Therefore, if the Son makes you free,
you shall be free indeed."

–John 8:36

*L*iberty, Equality, Fraternity: Truly a lovely
motto, and the motto also of the Christian,
but only if it is understood in relation to the
liberty of the children of God.

But many revolutionaries also say: "But
we do that. We also desire the liberty of the
gospel. We also honor the Redeemer, and we
also proclaim a Christian doctrine." But here is
a misunderstanding, perhaps by mistake and
perhaps on purpose. Let us, in order to avoid a
fatal semantic confusion, give a brief overview of
what we understand to be the liberty of the

gospel, from which I have derived the title of this chapter.

The liberty of the children of God: "But as many as received Him (the Word who became Flesh), to them He gave the right to become children of God, to those who believe in His name. For as many as are led by the Spirit of God, these are the children of God."[70] This is liberty from the deception of the devil, by which people are held captive to his evil will. We are liberated from the condemnation of the law. We are liberated from sin to be able to serve God as His beloved children: "Being then made free from sin, you become servants of righteousness."[71] We are liberated from eternal death: "Jesus Christ destroyed him who had the power of death, that is, the devil, and liberated those who through fear of death were all their lifetime subject to bondage."[72]

Liberty from all that would impede our willing obedience to His commandments, by which we enjoy the true liberty: "Liberated from the hand of our enemies, to serve Him without fear, in holiness and righteousness all the days of our lives."[73]

---

[70] Here, Groen quotes John 1:12 and Romans 8:14 together.
[71] Romans 6:18.
[72] Hebrews 2:14–15.
[73] Luke 1:74–75.

Our liberty is founded on the merits of Christ and Him crucified.[74] It is the kind of liberty that makes the liberty of the world look like nothing in comparison since man, without this liberty, always remains a slave of sin and is, in reality, only as free as someone who is locked up in prison.

The liberty of the Christian is the kind that arises from faith and reveals itself in faithful obedience. Let us evaluate if this is the same liberty that the revolutionaries propose and is often promoted by them as a Christian liberty. Also, if their liberty arises from faith and whether the fruits thereof are of the kind that faith ought to produce.

Is it the same liberty? Surely not, because the Revolutionary liberty is a worldly kind as opposed to a heavenly kind of liberty. It is a kind of liberty that desires to become free of the authority of others, but not the sin in one's own heart. Of course, it is true that the desire for just liberty with regard to earthly relationships is in line with the Christian's faith and duty, but how Christian is the liberty of the revolutionaries, who accuse us of unfairly denying their agreement with the spirit of the gospel? I do not have to look hard to find the perfect examples for refuting their claim.

---

[74] A reference to I Corinthians 2:2.

De Lamartine was considered by many to be an excellent Christian when he published his *Meditations and Harmonies*.[75] Just as he is regarded, in praising the Duke of Bordeaux,[76] a true Legitimist.[77] He once made a journey to the holy city of Jerusalem and, in his prose, he praised Christianity. He also claimed to be a Christian. Do you realize, however, what kind of faith he regarded as sufficient? This can be learned from what he wrote in his very last publication regarding the revolutionary principles of the eighteenth century. We believe this was an era of unbelief.[78] Not according to de

---

[75] *The Poetical Meditations and Religious Harmonies* of Alphonse de Lamartine was a publication of his poetry and prose.

[76] Prince Henri, the Duke of Bordeaux and Count of Chambord, was the King of France for seven days in August 1830, although he was never officially proclaimed as such. He was the last legitimate descendant in the senior male line of Louis XV of France (1710–1774), whose grandson Louis XVI was executed by the guillotine during the French Revolution.

[77] The legitimists in nineteenth-century France were royalists adhering to the rights of dynastic succession of the dynasty of the House of Bourbon, which was overthrown in the 1830 July Revolution.

[78] See: Groen's *Unbelief and Revolution*, translated into English by the Dutch-Canadian scholar Harry van Dyke and published in 1989 by Wedge, with a revised edition published in 2018 by Lexham Press. In this, Groen's magnum opus, which he originally published in 1847, only a year prior to publishing *Liberty, Equality, Fraternity*, he explains his understanding of both history and politics as essentially the battlefield between faith in

Lamartine, who regarded this as an era of faith in which there was merely an appearance of unbelief. But how then?

Well, in the eighteenth century, there was much delight in the ethics and societal influence of the gospel. What Christianity called "revelation" philosophy called "reason." A difference in wording, but similar in meaning. The doubt of the Enlightenment merely did away with the external forms of Christianity's supernatural doctrines.[79]

Do you see how modest and faithful this unbelief was? This unbelief only applied to that which reason cannot comprehend, that is, only the essence of divine revelation. When reading such an apology, it comes as no surprise that this so-called Christian would be willing to replace the Ten Commandments with the *Declaration of the Rights of Man*.[80] For such a

---

God or the Kingdom of Christ on the one hand, and unbelief in or rebellion against Christ's Kingdom and Lordship on the other.

[79] This is the argument of de Lamartine. In a footnote, Groen quotes directly from the original French of the liberal statesman's final work, *Histoire des Girondins*, published in 1847.

[80] *The Declaration of the Rights of Man* was the constituting document of the French Revolutionary government. It was drafted by Emmanuel-Joseph Sieyès and the Marquis de Lafayette, in consultation with Thomas Jefferson. The document proposed an abstract theory of rights, one completely detached from reality.

so-called Christian, it is natural to regard the doctrines of Rousseau[81] and the theory for which Robespierre had murdered thousands as Christian.

Let me refer to another example of a so-called Christian revolutionary who, despite his talents and abilities, is really no better: Lamennais.[82] You inquire concerning his faith or his rational convictions at least. Do you really want to know what it entailed? In his writings, he exhibited himself as a defender of simultaneously Roman Catholic errors as well as Christian truths. If you want to know what his convictions were, tame your curiosity. Don't bother reading his latest writings. You will only discover what he is not. He would himself only be capable of a confession of doubt and ignorance. His most remarkable books were published under the title *Words of a Believer*.[83]

And what are these words? In this work, there is no mention whatsoever of depravity and

---

[81] Jean-Jacques Rousseau (1712–1778) was one of the leading philosophers of the French Enlightenment which led to the French Revolution. He is famous for his promotion of the ideas of egalitarianism and the social contract.

[82] Hugues-Félicité Robert de Lamennais (1782–1854) was a liberal Roman Catholic priest and is considered to be the main forerunner of liberal Roman Catholicism. He is not to be confused with his conservative brother, Jean-Marie-Robert de Lamennais (see: footnote 46).

[83] *Paroles d'un croyant.*

redemption, of sin and grace, of apostasy and sanctification, of the essence and power of godliness. This so-called believer has too much interest in worldly matters to have any time to occupy himself with the heavenly citizenship. He does, however, often use the name of the Lord. But in his case it is an idle and blasphemous use of the name. He uses the language of the prophets, of the parables of Biblical visions and symbols, and his works sometimes read a lot like biblical language. It could be because he borrowed many phrases directly from Scripture. But always remember that among the prophecies of Scripture are also prophecies regarding the actions and performances of false prophets. They are to be recognized by their words and deeds.

His theo-political system is simple: God willed Revolutionary liberty and equality. Therefore, there is no other legal framework or authority. Every authority that commands something to another bears the fruit of guile and violence. All governance is evil, and every government is a vessel in the hands of Satan. To overthrow all authority and restore the so-called original equality is the task of the brotherhood according to this gospel, and the task of Christian love and part of the holy war for a suppressed humanity.

Let me put it simply: This is the language of a false prophet. It is an admonition to the nations to destroy all divinely ordained ties, the preaching of rebellion against God, and a combatting of the gospel with words borrowed from that very gospel.

Wherever there is sin, authority is a blessing. Liberty without authority is a curse. True authority is a guarantee against the liberty of evil people to do everything they desire and a guarantee that provides liberty to benevolent people to do that which is in accordance with duty and right. Let us hold to what Article 36 of the Belgic Confession teaches:

> We believe that our gracious God, because of the depravity of mankind, hath appointed kings, princes, and magistrates, willing that the world should be governed by certain laws and policies; to the end that the dissoluteness of men might be restrained, and all things carried on among them with good order and decency.

The goodness of God is also revealed in His institution of government. Rather than the *Declaration of the Rights of Man,* we will, as of old, seek in the Ten Commandments the standard of our rights and duties. Following the command to "honor our father and mother," we would show love and respect to all those who have been appointed over us, while having sympathy with their shortcomings and weaknesses, since God wills to govern us by their hand.[84]

Why are people so often so easily deceived by unwholesome writings? Because they are not guided by Holy Scripture.

No creed of unbelief, no argument for the desires of the flesh would intoxicate those who are familiar with the contents of Revelation. They simply return to those first principles that they were taught in the Bible. Many seem to be clueless in the maze of political arguments but seek the line by which the Holy Scriptures guide us. Many remain in the dark in the midst of the political developments of our time. Open up your Bible, and you will experience that "the entrance of Your words gives light; it gives understanding to the simple."[85]

Many feel that they are weak in the battle against the giants, the prominent men of our time. But if you are familiar with this one necessity, namely Scripture, you will always have a weapon with which to resist injustice.

---

[84] A reference to the Heidelberg Catechism's explanation of the fifth commandment. See: question and answer 104.
[85] Psalm 119:130.

The Revolutionaries boast of their liberty which destroys all authority. One thing I know is that those who resist authority oppose the ordinances of God. An equality which makes you master of that which belongs to another. One thing I know is that "thou shalt not steal."[86] A fraternity that reveals itself in envy and hatred. One thing I know is that he who hates his brother is a murderer.[87] A brotherhood in which the presupposition is a natural love of everyone towards all. One thing I know is that it has revealed itself in evil, envy, and hatred towards each other.

Their doctrine of liberty desires no governance anymore: No king apart from a king who is the vice-regent of the people, no government that is not subject and neutered, no authority apart from that which acknowledges the sovereignty of the people.

To those who have been granted true wisdom I say: Remind yourselves of the teachings of the Bible, and discern whether there is agreement between these human pearls of wisdom and the Word of God. "Render therefore to Caesar the things that are Caesar's. Fear God. Honor the king. As free people, yet not using liberty as a cloak for vice, but as

---

[86] Exodus 20:15.
[87] I John 3:15.

bondservants of God. Fear the Lord and the king; Do not associate with those given to change. The Lord knows how to deliver the godly out of temptations and to reserve the unjust under punishment for the day of judgment, and especially those who walk according to the flesh in the lust of uncleanness and despise authority. They are presumptuous and self-willed. They are not afraid to speak evil of dignitaries."[88] Can we, in meditating upon these passages, take seriously the guarantee of the radicals that they are proponents of a Christian theory and would dare to claim that the apostolic accusation, namely that "they speak great swelling words of emptiness in that while they promise liberty, they themselves are slaves of corruption,"[89] is not applicable to them?

The doctrine of liberty of this age desires no inequalities. The distinctions of rank and class they want to see disappear. Submission is, to her, a stumbling block, regardless of the nature of the relationship. Holy Scripture says: "Render therefore to all their due; Wives, submit yourselves unto your own husbands; Children, obey your parents in all things;

---

[88] Groen quotes a whole host of Biblical passages together here: Matthew 22:21, I Peter 2:17, I Peter 2:16, Proverbs 24:21 and II Peter 2:9–10.
[89] II Peter 2:18–19.

Servants, obey in all things your masters according to the flesh; not with eye service, as man pleasers; but in singleness of heart, fearing God."[90] What do you think when you read these passages: is the Revolutionary doctrine biblical?

The doctrine of liberty of this age desires a kind of brotherhood, in which family ties are set aside and all dissidents are fought and killed. I highly doubt that this kind of fraternity is in accordance with the following passages of Scripture: "Add unto godliness brotherly kindness, and to brotherly kindness love. Love the brotherhood. Honor the king. Therefore, I exhort first of all that supplications, prayers, intercessions, and giving of thanks be made for all men, for kings and all who are in authority, that we may lead a quiet and peaceable life in all godliness and reverence."[91]

But what are we then to think of those who see the doctrine of the gospel as an enemy of liberty and as a proponent of slavery and suppression when they mean to grant us a better kind of liberty in terms of the relationship between people on earth? What are we to say regarding their judgment? This, namely that it is a prejudice that is directly opposed to the

---

[90] Groen quotes the following passages together here: Romans 13:7, Ephesians 5:22, Colossians 3:20 and 22.
[91] II Peter 1:7, I Peter 2:17, and I Timothy 2:1–2.

truth of the matter. Here the biblical promise is applicable: "Seek first the kingdom of God and His righteousness, and all these things shall be added to you."[92]

A proponent of slavery, they say! What revolutionary arrogance and shamelessness when they attribute this to the truth of the gospel. I would now like to proceed to call upon the witness of history.

What kind of liberty has the Revolution granted? The liberty of subjects to murder monarchs and governors and to set themselves in their place. Liberty to Robespierre to slaughter hundreds of his free and equal citizens. Liberty to Napoleon to put France and, later, a great part of the world in chains, and to satisfy his desire for power by means of rivers of blood. Liberty of constitutional governments to, under many artificial forms of government, and in the name of the rule of law, subject the fate of all to the arbitrary will of the ever-changing majority. Liberty to every government to, in the name of good politics and in the interest of the state and the common good, decide what is in the interest of all.

These are the outstanding experiments that have caused the revolutionaries to boast

---

[92] Matthew 6:33.

about their love of liberty and accomplishments over and against that of the gospel.

But let us evaluate to which degree the doctrines of the gospel have historically led to despotism. Only the new earth will have perfect justice. On this side of heaven, we have less of a permanent residence and more of a continual battle—a fight between justice and injustice, and liberty and oppression shall continue as long as sinners walk the earth.[93] In order to show the blessed, historic influence of the gospel, I, therefore, do not propose that there was no abuse of power earlier, but that the gospel had always affected right and liberty and, in many regards, opposed arbitrariness and tyranny.

How were the relationships between husbands and wives or fathers and children mitigated by true authority and love in a way that was unknown to the pagan world? To what is the abolition of slavery in Europe due? What

---

[93] For Groen, all of world history as called into existence by God is teleologically rooted in the Messianic promise of Genesis 3:15. He believed that all of history is characterized by a covenantal-historical dichotomy between faith and unbelief, in which the former represents that which is godly, good, and true, and the latter that which is evil and false. All of history, politics, and society is the battleground between faith and unbelief—a battle in which the Christian is called to engage with a confidence in the inevitability of Christ's victory over the seed of the serpent. See: Lecture XI of *Unbelief and Revolution.*

had since the very start of the medieval period and thereafter protected the common people against the tyranny of monarchs and nobles? Wherein was the sixteenth-century opposition to political and religious tyranny based? And another question: which countries were the bastions of liberty following the Reformation? These were England, the United States of America,[94] and Holland. Three countries where the strength of the pure gospel has been revealed with exceptional clarity.

England: The Constitution of 1688 has for so long rightfully been an object of veneration—sadly, just as much as it has been one that has been misunderstood and wrongfully imitated.[95] But through the mediation of William III,[96] the principles for which the godly Puritans had been persecuted and had fought, was maintained and affirmed.

America:[97] The independence of the United States—achieved by the progeny of those

---

[94] Groen writes *Noord-Amerika*, which translates as "North America," but he undoubtedly refers to the United States of America here.
[95] The Bill of Rights of 1688 was a landmark act in English constitutional history, which lays down the limits of the monarch's powers as well as the rights of parliament.
[96] William III (1650–1702) was the grandson of Prince William of Orange. He served not only as Prince of Orange in the Netherlands, but also as the King of England, Scotland, and Ireland from 1689 to 1702.
[97] Again, here Groen literally writes "North America."

who had exchanged their dear Fatherland for the unfamiliarity of an overseas territory—was the result of a fight characterized by a spirit of liberty accompanied by the fear of God and a devotion to historically acquired rights.

The Netherlands: Here, too, the duties entailed by the Christian faith have informed our society. By holding steadfast to God's Word, liberty and independence were achieved and maintained. The reliance of the Dutch virgin upon the Bible was not only an allegorical symbol of our coin; it was appropriately chosen as a true depiction of the history of our country.[98]

But let us leave history there for now and focus solely upon the contents of the gospel, also in terms of what it offers in contrast to the Revolutionary *liberty, equality, and fraternity*—namely that godliness is useful for all aspects of life and contains promises pertaining to both this life and the next.

You desire liberty. Now, do you suppose that the gospel has no principles or guarantees for true liberty in terms of the different relations in state and society? Simply look at those who live in obedience to it. This is not an obedience

---

[98] Historically, the half-guild coin in the Netherlands depicted a Dutch virgin with a spear in one hand, with the other arm placed on a Bible on top of an altar.

to the arbitrary will of man, but to the will of God. In the government, one honors God's servant. It is an obedience for the sake of conscience and for the Lord's sake: "Servants, be obedient to those who are your masters according to the flesh, as the servants of Christ, doing the will of God from the heart."[99] This obedience does not submit to earthly powers in anything that goes against the commands of the Almighty. Those who submit to government for conscience's sake would not yield to any government when that very conscience does not allow it.

No elevation of the self, but also not reducing oneself to a doormat. No service for the sake of pleasing people and no flattery. If the fear of God reigns in our hearts, we will learn to see the folly of fearing men. Then the power of the biblical admonition is felt: "I am He who comforts you. Who are you that you should be afraid of a man who will die? And of the son of a man who will be made like grass? And you forget the LORD your Maker, who stretched out the heavens and laid the foundations of the earth."[100]

Also, note the following verse: "Husbands, love your wives and do not be bitter

---

99 Ephesians 6:5–6.
100 Isaiah 51:12–13.

toward them. Children, obey your parents in all things, for this is well pleasing to the Lord. Fathers, do not provoke your children, lest they become discouraged. For the government does not bear the sword in vain; for he is God's minister, an avenger to execute wrath on him who practices evil."[101]

The Revolutionary *liberty* has time and again robbed and deceived nations of their freedoms. Would there not be a better chance of preserving liberties had the government feared the justice of God rather than the disapproval of the people? Do we not have the most powerful guarantee in the fact that men owe accountability and amenability to Him who knows all things and does not let sin go unpunished, and when the government is a servant of God rather than the people?

Those who have been initiated into the secrets of the Revolution say "No!" Their pamphlets, newspapers, and petitions all proclaim that it is in the right to revolution that the guarantee of our liberty lies. But the contrary is true.[102]

---

[101] Colossians 3:19–21 and Romans 13:4.
[102] It seems that what Groen has in mind here is the rejection of the overthrow of authority, as seen in France. This is distinct from the defense against the overreach of authority, or even the separation from a previous authority, as seen with the American War of

The possibility of true liberty lies in the durability of authority. The Revolutionary doctrine, which destroys liberty, forces the government to, for the sake of self-preservation, and under the guise of the most liberal words and political forms, strives towards tyranny. The doctrine of the gospel, on the contrary, which affirms true authority, allows those in power to truly rule with a love of liberty.[103]

But you also desire equality. Well then, let us apply the doctrines of the gospel. The relationship between the rich and the poor must be sanctified in a way that is conducive to the well-being of all.

Say unto the rich: "God loves a cheerful giver. But whoever has this world's goods, and sees his brother in need, and shuts up his heart from him, how does the love of God abide in him?"[104]

Say unto the poor: "The young lions lack and suffer hunger; But those who seek the Lord shall not lack any good thing. Behold, the eye of the Lord is upon them that fear Him, upon them

---

Independence. In other words, it seems that Groen would not have seen the American war as a revolutionary one. Edmund Burke, interestingly, never referred to it as a revolution either.

[103] This is also one of the central arguments of Groen's magnum opus, *Unbelief and Revolution*.

[104] Groen quotes from II Corinthians 9:7 and I John 3:17.

that hope in His mercy, to deliver their soul from death, and to keep them alive in famine. I have been young, and now am old; yet I have not seen the righteous forsaken, nor his descendants begging bread."[105]

Say unto the sloth: "In the sweat of your face you shall eat bread. We have commanded you this: If anyone will not work, neither shall he eat. For we hear that there are some who walk among you in a disorderly manner, not working at all, but are busybodies. Now those who are such we command and exhort through our Lord Jesus Christ that they work in quietness and eat their own bread."[106]

Say unto those who work hard but do not realize their complete and utter dependence upon God: "It is vain for you to rise up early, sit up late, to eat the bread of sorrows; For so He gives His beloved sleep."[107]

All the proposals of the wisdom of the age with regard to caring for the poor are at odds with even a single chapter of Holy Scripture—I Timothy 6.

Say unto the rich: "Command those who are rich in this present age not to be haughty, nor to trust in uncertain riches but in the living

---

[105] Groen quotes three passages: Psalm 34:10, Psalm 33:18–19, and Psalm 37:25.
[106] Genesis 3:19 and II Thessalonians 3:10–12.
[107] Psalm 127:2.

God, who gives us richly all things to enjoy. Let them do good, that they be rich in good works, ready to give, willing to share."[108]

Say unto the greedy: "But those who desire to be rich fall into temptation and a snare, and into many foolish and harmful lusts which drown men in destruction and perdition. For the love of money is a root of all kinds of evil."[109]

Say unto those that have no more than their daily bread: "Now godliness with contentment is great gain. And having food and clothing, with these we shall be content."[110]

Say unto all: "We brought nothing into this world, and it is certain we can carry nothing out."[111]

Say unto all: "But you, O man of God, flee these things and pursue righteousness, godliness, faith, love, patience, gentleness."[112]

Do you desire even more Biblical texts pointing out how the arrogance of those who trust in money and glory are thwarted, thereby mitigating inequality?

"Let each esteem others better than himself."[113]

---

[108] I Timothy 6:17–18.
[109] I Timothy 6:9–10.
[110] I Timothy 6:6, 8.
[111] I Timothy 6:7.
[112] I Timothy 6:11.
[113] Philippians 2:3.

"Let the lowly brother glory in his exaltation, but the rich in his humiliation."[114]

"Come now, you rich, weep and howl for your miseries that are coming upon you! Your riches are corrupted, and your garments are moth-eaten. Your gold and silver are corroded, and their corrosion will be a witness against you and will eat your flesh like fire. You have heaped up treasure in the last days. Indeed, the wages of the laborers who mowed your fields, which you kept back by fraud, cry out."[115]

"For there is no respecter of persons with God."[116]

"For there is no difference; for all have sinned and fall short of the glory of God, being justified freely by His grace through the redemption that is in Christ Jesus."[117]

"There is neither slave nor free, for you are all one in Christ Jesus."[118]

Most certainly, there is also an evangelical "communism."[119] You desire

---

[114] James 1:9–10.

[115] James 5:1–4.

[116] Romans 2:11.

[117] Romans 3:22–24.

[118] Galatians 3:28.

[119] It is important to read this paragraph within the context of Groen's broader argument. Groen is certainly not advocating for a Christianized kind of communism or socialism, but merely pointing to the example of the early Church in terms of the benevolence shown by the rich towards their poor brothers and sisters in the faith.

equality of goods. So did the apostle when he encouraged the faithful to give freely: "For I do not mean that others should be eased and you burdened; but by an equality, that now at this time your abundance may supply their lack, that their abundance also may supply your lack— that there may be equality."[120] Equality of goods had existed among Christians. They shared everything. Why? Because no one regarded that which he had to be his own. And why not? Was this because they were part of one state and one public treasury? No, it was because they were one heart and one spirit. And how did this unity come about? Because they had faith. In whom? In Him who "was rich, yet for your sakes He became poor, that you through His poverty might become rich."[121]

This is the equality and the fraternity of the gospel. The affirmation of true authority is the necessary precondition for true liberty. Similarly, property rights are the condition for a desirable equality. Justice and love; these are the legal and ethical teachings of Scripture.

I can continue, but then I would have to write out half the Bible. And to what avail would that be? A man can know the whole Bible, and still, if you have not accepted the shield of faith,

---

[120] II Corinthians 8:13–14.
[121] II Corinthians 8:9.

by which every fiery arrow can be extinguished, you will twist Scripture to your own demise.

I have mentioned the examples of Lamartine and Lamennais. I cannot omit this third example: A Revolutionary of whom it is said that the gospel always laid open on his desk. He claimed that the Revolution had its roots in the gospel. He claimed that in the gospel, more than anywhere else, the general will is encouraged, and the wealthy and powerful are cursed. He even claimed to adhere to the Lordship of Jesus Christ. And who was this gospel-confessor? Who was this man who honored the Savior? This friend of the people? He was a hypocrite whose thirst for blood could never be quenched. He was a man who, in claiming the cause of humanity, even suppressed the very last spark of charity and mercy within him. Robespierre could be considered kind and gentle in comparison to this man. He was—and for those who know history, he needs no introduction—he was Marat.[122]

---

[122] Jean-Paul Marat (1743–1793) was a liberal and revolutionary French political theorist and statesman. As an influential leader in the French National Convention, he was responsible for the murder (by execution) of 1,500 prisoners in September 1792—half the prison population of Paris. Many of those whom he executed were clergy and other counter-revolutionary Christians. These false

What is said about our Savior is also true with regard to Holy Scripture, namely that "it is destined for the fall and rising of many."[123]

The gospel, if man looks there for the justification of his own theories and desires, there is a smell of death unto death. But the gospel, if man looks there for the preservation of his soul through Jesus Christ our Lord, there is a smell of life unto life.

Through the distortion of the gospel, Lamartine justified revolution, and Blanc justified the disorganization of both labor and society.

On the contrary, the fullness of the gospel gave Wilberforce[124] strength to fight the evils of the slave trade for 20 years. It blessed Elizabeth Fry[125] with the strength to turn a prison into a house of prayer. It provided Chalmers[126] with

---

claims regarding Marat's own supposed Christianity can be found in de Lamartine's *Histoire des Girondins*.

[123] Luke 2:34.

[124] William Wilberforce (1759–1833) was a British Christian statesman and philanthropist and a leader in the movement that fought to abolish the slave trade.

[125] Elizabeth Fry (1780–1845) was a British Christian prison reformer, social reformer, and philanthropist. She was a major player in the process of making legislation in terms of the treatment of British prisoners more humane.

[126] Thomas Chalmers (1780–1847) was a conservative, Scottish Presbyterian theologian, minister, and political theorist. His work and ideas left a major impression upon Groen. Chalmers was a major opponent of socialism in Scotland and argued for poor relief on the basis of

the wisdom to rightly promote the Christian doctrines of the state, not only by means of his excellent writings but also in effectuating a revival of godliness, morals, and standards among the common people in the industrial cities of Scotland.

Therefore, in the midst of the heresies of our age, we will, and not only for the sake of the youth, hold steadfast unto the Psalm "How can a young man keep his way pure? By guarding it according to your Word."[127]

From the Bible, the Christian learns his duties, calculates his prospects, and appreciates his privileges.

1. The Duties of the Christian

Here I mean the duties with regard to resisting the dangers and temptations of the popular revolutionary misconceptions. I will also highlight only a few aspects thereof.

"Do not have fellowship with the unfruitful works of darkness."[128] The propagation of a doctrine which overthrows the foundations of every legitimate authority will always be a work of darkness, even if executed under the banner of enlightenment. The

---

voluntary contributions submitted privately or by means of the Church of Scotland.
[127] Psalm 119:9.
[128] Ephesians 5:11.

Christian should reject the ideas of general equality and the sovereignty of the people. While the Christian must be submissive to the rulers under any form of government, whether it be republican, monarchical, democratic, or aristocratic, we are compelled to protest any principle that seeks to overthrow the ordinances and sovereignty of the living God.

Yes, submit under any form of government. Then you also need to, in terms of your duty, make use of the rights afforded to you under that system in a way that does not force one to be disloyal to Christian principles. If, like in 1795 and later, a political confession of faith is required for obtaining civil rights, then we would be forced to object. Yes, for avoiding active participation in the political system, there is no excuse and, for our inaction, there would be no justification when we, without necessarily approving the principles behind the action, fail to make use of the existing legal framework and political means.

The appeal of the apostle in Philippi to his Roman citizenship was no approval of the political system, much less an appraisal of the tyranny within that system. Patience is a Christian virtue, but where the opportunity for action exists, passivity would be most inappropriate.[129]

But, in order to be able to live in accordance with their duty, Christians must be familiar with the form of government under which they live. Submit to the rulers that have been placed over you. Sure, but I ought to know how this rule has come to be placed over me. I must know the origin and nature of this government and know its rights as well as the rights of citizens—just as I would, in an attempt to obey the command "thou shalt not steal,"[130] carefully determine what belongs to me and what belongs to others. And in order not to err in our political theory, it is especially important not to be misled by any names of political systems.

---

[129] To Groen, the political battle for Christian anti-revolutionary principles fundamentally raged on an epistemic rather than on a systemic level. On the one hand, his perspective demanded perpetual loyalty to Christian traditionalist or conservative principles, while on the other hand remaining flexible in terms of one's strategic political engagement in what could potentially be an ever-changing socio-political landscape with its inevitable variety of political systems and governments. See: J.A. Schlebusch, "Democrat or Traditionalist? The Epistemology behind Groen van Prinsterer's Notion of Political Authority." *Journal for Christian Scholarship*, no. 56 (3–4): 113–129.

[130] Exodus 20:15.

Let us confirm the necessity of this Christian duty by means of examples. In the Netherlands, we have a king. Is that so that he "will take our sons and appoint them for his own chariots and to be his horsemen, take our daughters to be perfumers, cooks, and bakers and take the best of our fields, our vineyards, and our olive groves, and give them to his servants?"[131]

We have a Senate and Houses of Representatives. Is that so that they can, as they desire, legislate to the king and the nation? We have a constitution in which the rightful influence of the people is not completely lost and presupposes the possibility of constitutional revision. We live in a country where the entire flow of our history is, in this regard at least, in accordance with the spirit of the constitution, where the rights of citizens— although at times not sufficiently recognized— have never been forgotten, and many have at all times recognized the continual desirability and need for improvement.

Would it, therefore, be permissible to, in the name of the general will and in moments of excitement and fear, force the king, the house, and the senate into a constitutional revision that would lead straight to a republic or its equivalent? Would the submission of the

---

[131] I Samuel 8:11, 13–14.

Christian entail that he idly stands by, unconcerned regarding this change of government so that we too, like in Paris, see our streets filled with a mob of reprobates about to enter the assembly, only to force tyranny upon us tomorrow and become the legal government the day after that?

I could multiply these types of questions endlessly. And to answer them, we need knowledge, discernment, and especially a sound mind. This alone I would like to emphasize: that the duty of the Christian may vary according to the demands of the circumstances and context and also that the extent of his rights stand in direct relation to the extent of his duties.

And therefore, since we are generally required to use the rights afforded to us for the sake of our homeland, how much more important is the requirement to use these rights for preaching the Word and advancing the Kingdom of Heaven?!

We have a government. Is its purpose to govern with regard to religious doctrines? To prescribe unto the church the law? Or, to bring the church—which recognizes no other Head than its King in Heaven[132]—directly or indirectly under worldly authority? Or, to receive from

---

[132] The phrase, if literally translated, clumsily reads "no other King than its Head in Heaven."

government regulations regarding how much religion should be allowed in the education of children? Or, to force parents to send their children to schools where the biblical truths valued by all denominations are not taught or rejected outright?

Certainly not! Such a tyranny over the conscience cannot be allowed in the Netherlands, a nation that has fought against religious persecution. It is therefore opposed to both historically acquired rights, as well as the constitution.

But then it is our duty to protest, both in word and in deed, against all regulations and especially the interpretation of regulations that are at odds with the spirit of our history and politics.

Then, for example, Reformed folk must, in their request for the independence of the church and school, for protection against the unlawful deeds of unbelievers, exhibit a perseverance as well as a consciousness of their rights and duties as Christians and as Protestants. Then they may, also, when they offer modest resistance, remember that when it comes to the issue of rights, there can be no humble requests. Nothing short of justified demands will do.

Above all, it must be remembered that the greatest duty of all—one which supersedes all others—is to confess and live the gospel.

2. The Calculation of our Prospects

When it comes to the calculation of our prospects, we must base these on the Holy Scriptures. There may be nights so dark that he can hardly see his own hands in front of him. In the political domain, we are currently experiencing such a night. Guessing is allowed and everyone seems to liberally make use of this right. After all, in terms of the flow of current events, one really cannot do much more than guess. It is sure that false ideas can bring nothing other than disaster and destruction. It is sure that the so-called sovereignty of the people leads to the tyranny of those Revolutionaries who incite, flatter, and mislead the people for the sake of their own profit and glory. It is sure that the current anarchy will lead to violence, either of the radicals or communists, or the reactionaries.

But which of these alternatives has the best chance? How and when shall we return from the current chaos to a condition that resembles order and consistency?

What if tomorrow, after a new demonstration, the allies of Blanqui and

Cabet,[133] over against the desires and fanaticism of even more radical communists, are regarded as the heads of a moderate government? Or would Lamartine be able to, at some stage, ban the application of those very revolutionary doctrines which he had proclaimed with real or apparent enthusiasm? Would he also, for fear of an even worse government, for years suppress those who have, in imitating his February Revolution, attempt to do the very same that he has done? Would he reveal himself to be not only the successor but the disciple of Louis-Philippe in terms of organizing a reactionary government?

Is it not to be expected that a revolution, when considering the dangers it poses to the material interests of the middle and upper classes, and in many regards took many by

---

[133] Louis Auguste Blanqui (1805–1881) was a French socialist theorist and activist, notable for his theory of Blanquism. Blanquism advocates that the socialist revolution must secretly be carried out by a select group of organized conspirators, who only reveal their socialist agenda after seizing political power; Etienne Cabet (1788–1856) was a French, utopian socialist, who along with his followers, moved to the United States in 1848 to found egalitarian socialist communes in Texas, Illinois, Iowa, Missouri, and California. The followers of this movement were known as Icarians. Their name was derived from Icaria, the Mediterranean island which served as the scene of a socialist utopia in his allegorical novel *Voyage en Icarie*.

surprise, works to the benefit of the mob rather than the almost forgotten royal House of Orange? Would the government by its Revolutionary excitement not then be necessitated to set up a national guard which, in order to suppress the anarchists, in order to destroy their former Revolutionary allies by cannon fire, even if the death penalty is apparently abolished? And would it be possible to restore any kind of order at all, considering the pitiful condition of all the social classes, the nature of their desires, and the inevitable conflicts that have been stirred up by the indignation caused by propaganda for false theories as well as unfulfilled promises?

And how would it be in other countries where the revolutionary volcano has spewed its fiery rain or, according to Lamartine, its fiery blessings? With Prussia, where the king (in reminding us not to trust in princes),[134] in the midst of the revolutionary tumult has completely lost all direction?[135] In Austria, where the monarchy which has endured centuries of trials, is now almost completely

---

[134] Psalm 146:3.
[135] Frederick William IV (1795–1861) was King of Prussia from 1840 until his death. He was initially conservative but later turned more liberal in an attempt to accommodate the revolutionaries.

falling apart?[136] What can be expected of Great Britain? The politics of Pitt,[137] even if revived, have no cornerstones in Europe anymore; the restraint of the Chartists,[138] amid their continuous uproar, only temporarily comforting, and the cries for revolt and separation is not over in Ireland by any stretch of the imagination.

While there is much that may give us hope for international peace, Europe is certainly not immune to the danger of war. Lamartine has often declared that he has no desire for war and that as long as people do not hinder or oppose the Revolution, it generally exhibits a gentle and peace-loving nature. Of the dear Fatherland, I dare not speak, for here is uncertainty on whether a serious conflict will arise between the enemies and friends of conservation and uncertainty about how far we will be dragged along by the unconditional panegyrists of so-called progress.

And still, in the midst of all this uncertainty, there is certainty for the Christian,

---

[136] The Habsburg emperor, Ferdinand I (1793–1875) abdicated after the European revolutions of 1848 following the demands of the revolutionaries.

[137] William Pitt the Younger (1759–1806) was a Tory statesman and the British prime minister between 1783 and 1801 and from 1804 until his death.

[138] Chartism was a pro-universal male suffrage movement in nineteenth-century Britain.

security in the midst of danger, rest in the midst of tumult and light in the midst of darkness. We walk by faith and not by sight. Looking by faith enables us to see that we have a future: the second coming of Him who will return, just as He ascended into heaven.

When? When the gospel of the Kingdom is preached to the whole world as a witness to all people. When false prophets arise and deceive many. When injustice is multiplied and the love of many dies. When there is great tribulation, such as has not been seen since the beginning of the world. When you hear of wars and great earthquakes and hunger and pestilences. When the nations of the earth become anxious, when they become doubtful. When the sea and the water rise and people become frightened in expectation of the things about to happen on earth. When the injustices are revealed, and Satan performs miracles and signs of lies. Then you will see the Son of Man upon a cloud, with great power and glory.[139] When? Let us never forget in our speculations and predictions that

---

[139] Here Groen expounds a futurist interpretation of Matthew 24, which is interesting given the fact that he had expounded a preterist interpretation of this same text in 1840. See: Groen van Prinsterer, *Schriftelijke Nalatenschap: bescheidendeel I en II* 1821–1876. Ed. J. Zwaan. (The Hague: Instituut voor Nederlandse Geschiedenis, 1991), 49.

He decreed and ordained the times of all events. "But concerning the times and the seasons, brethren, you have no need that I should write to you. For you yourselves know perfectly that the day of the Lord so comes as a thief in the night. But you, brethren, are not in darkness, so that this Day should overtake you as a thief. Let your waist be girded and your lamps burning, for the Son of Man is coming at an hour you do not expect."[140] For you personally, He will come at the hour of your death, but the value of your prospect lies not in that moment, but in the certainty of His return, in the salvation of all who fight the good fight and complete the race, keep the faith and hold to the resurrection of Christ.

3. The Privileges of the Christian

Regarding the privileges of the Christian, I will, after what has already been said, write only briefly.

Who is a Christian? Is he a Christian who equates the Word of God with the word of man? Is he a Christian for whom Christ is not God to be praised forever? Is he a Christian who is offended by Christ and Him crucified? Is he a Christian who is blameless in terms of the civil

---

[140] Groen again quotes several biblical passages together: I Thessalonians 5:1–2, 4, Luke 12:35, and Matthew 24:44.

laws but indifferent to higher principles and laws and who does not know nor experience Christ? Is he a Christian who fights self-righteousness in others, but with an appeal to the righteousness of Christ sides with the workers of iniquity? Is he a Christian who knows the Bible and the Three Forms of Unity[141] and has studied the lives of both believers and unbelievers, but exhibits the thanksgiving of the Pharisee and not the begging of the tax collector? Answer these questions while prayerfully reading the Word of God.

I speak of the privileges that belong to Christians alone, but indeed to every Christian. Who would be able to name the blessings temporally and eternally bestowed upon the Christian?

Equality. Equality under the one Master: "But you, do not be called 'Rabbi;' for One is your Teacher, the Christ, and you are all brethren."[142]

Equality in love. "You shall love your neighbor as yourself."[143]

---

[141] The Three Forms of Unity are the historic Dutch Reformed confessional standards, namely the Belgic Confession of Faith, the Canons of Dordt, and the Heidelberg Catechism.

[142] Matthew 23:8.

[143] Leviticus 19:18 and Mark 12:31.

Equality with the glorified Lord and Master of all: "Who shall change our vile body, that it may be fashioned like unto His glorious body. When He is revealed, we shall be like Him, for we shall see Him as He is."[144]

Liberty. To truly understand the nature and beauty of this liberty, one needs to understand the words of the apostle when he speaks of the glorious liberty of the children of God.

Fraternity. The brotherhood of Christians among each other. The brotherhood with Him who is also our glorious Lord, but who was willing to call His brothers friends and give His life for us.

The privileges of the Christian: For us, the commands of God aren't burdensome because those who are born of God have conquered the world. For us, the theft of earthly possessions does not amount to the stealing of our joy because we have better and eternal possessions in heaven. For us, there is consolation when we have to part with loved ones in Christ because we are not depressed like those without any hope. For us, the worst kind of suffering is a light oppression because it quickly passes and ensures immeasurable rewards in heaven. For us, there is no fear of

---

[144] Philippians 3:21 and I John 3:2.

death because we can proclaim: "O Death, where is your sting? O Hades, where is your victory? Thanks be to God, who gives us the victory through our Lord Jesus Christ."[145]

I would not be able to conclude without reference to those passages from Scripture in which the promises of God are so rich and which amplify "the surpassing greatness of His power toward us who believe."[146] But I will, in the midst of the tumult and clamor of the nations and the anxiety of those whose hope is confined to this earth, limit myself to two passages, one from the Old and one from the New Testament. In considering these passages, we realize that, even in the midst of all the terrible things we currently witness, we can still follow the prescription of the apostle to "rejoice always."[147]

From the Old Testament: Even despite all the successes of the Revolution, the Christian always remains triumphantly singing:

God is our refuge and
strength,
A very present help in
trouble.
Therefore, we will not fear,
Even though the earth be
removed,

---

[145] I Corinthians 15:55, 57.
[146] Ephesians 1:19.
[147] Philippians 4:4.

And though the mountains be
 carried into the midst of the sea;
Though its waters roar and
 be troubled,
Though the mountains
 shake with its swelling.
There is a river whose
 streams shall make glad the
 city of God,
The holy place of the tabernacle of the
 Most High.
God is in the midst of her,
 she shall not be moved;
God shall help her, just at
 the break of dawn.
The nations raged, the kingdoms
 were moved;
He uttered His voice, the
 earth melted.
The Lord of Hosts is with us;
 The God of Jacob is our
 refuge.[148]

From the New Testament. Even where destruction speedily comes to nations and kings, even where they have become worn out by their perpetual deliberations, even when they search for deliverance and salvation in vain by their numerous incantations and their sorcery, even when they start to cry out to the mountains to fall upon them,[149] then, and especially then,

---

[148] Psalm 46:1–7.
[149] A reference to Luke 23:30 and Revelation 6:16.

the Christian must remember the words of Him who is our hope, our peace, and our life: "When these things begin to happen, look up and lift up your heads, because your redemption draws near."[150]

We believe, Lord. Increase our faith. Amen.

---

[150] Luke 21:28.

General Index

Scriptural Index

9 781954 504004

PITTSBURGH'S
Greatest Athletes

While Mario Lemieux (*at left*) was one of the icons of the National Hockey League on the ice, he became the first person to own a team he once played for. As an owner, Lemieux not only helped the city secure a much-needed arena but also has had a hand in making the club financially strong over a period of time for the first time in franchise history; he also brought three more Stanley Cups to the city in his role as owner. *Courtesy of David Finoli.*

· DAVID FINOLI ·

PITTSBURGH'S
Greatest Athletes

THE
History
PRESS

Published by The History Press
Charleston, SC
www.historypress.com

Cover images: Front cover, bottom, courtesy of the Pittsburgh Pirates; top, left to right, courtesy of the North Texas State University Athletics, the Rivers of Steel and the Josh Gibson family and Boston College Athletics. Back cover, top, courtesy of the Pittsburgh Pirates; bottom, courtesy of David Finoli.

First published 2019

Manufactured in the United States

ISBN 9781467141871

Library of Congress Control Number: 2019935360

To my grandson, River. Welcoming the first member of a new generation is a joy that is hard to describe. May you always understand when you read the pages of this book that dreams do come true if you believe in yourself.

CONTENTS

ACKNOWLEDGEMENTS

I've been blessed to be able to do something I've loved so much over the years: write about the history of sports in Western Pennsylvania. This project that looks over the careers of the many heroes I've had the honor to watch, read and write about could not have been done without the help of so many important people in my life.

Projects such as this are never complete without the incredible support of many, most importantly my wonderful family, including my wife, Vivian; my children, Cara, Tony and Matthew; and Matthew's wife, Chynna, and our new addition, my grandson, River.

My extended family has always been there with me over the years no matter where I've been and what I've accomplished: my brother, Jamie; his wife, Cindy; my nieces Brianna and Marissa; my sister, Mary; her husband, Matthew; my aunts Maryanne and Betty; my cousins Fran, Luci, Flo, Beth, Tom, Gary, Linda, Amy, Amanda, Claudia, Ginny Lynn, Pam, Debbie, Diane, Vince and Richard. The memory of my father, Domenic; my mother, Eleanor; my cousins Tom Aikens and Eddie DiLello; my uncle, Vince; my grandparents Inez, Thomas, Maria and Angelo and my aunts Louise, Norma, Jeannie, Libby, Mary and Evie. They have all been essential in any success I've enjoyed in my life. A thank-you also goes to my in-laws Vivian and Salvatore Pansino.

There is also my round table of Pittsburgh sports experts who provide insight both on the sports of today as well as those in the past when needed. First off there is Chris Fletcher and Bill Ranier, two friends and collaborators I have worked with on books in the past and have had the honor to know for the majority of my life. We've spent hours going back and forth with the different ratings, and they have challenged me to make sure I've done the proper research to be able to justify which athlete, game or team is better than another. There are others—including Gary Kinn, Dan Russell, Rich Boyer, Shawn Christen, Matt O'Brokta, Bob O'Brien, Gary Degnan and Robert Healy III—who have been there to bounce ideas off and give me some of their thoughts into the subjects I write about. Thanks also to the phenomenal staff at The History Press, including Banks Smither and Ryan Finn, who believed in the subject and helped make this book something I can be proud of.

Finally, a thank-you goes to those whose generous help in securing the photos for this book were most essential in the completion of this project: Dave Saba from Duquesne University; the Pirates' Jim Trdinich; E.J. Borghetti of the University of Pittsburgh; Brittany Wynne from the World Golf Hall of Fame; Melanie Root, the archivist at Rivers of Steel; the great-grandson of Josh Gibson, Sean Gibson; Boston College's Jason Baum; Aaron Chimenti of Kent State; and North Texas State University's Eric Capper.

As with all my other projects, the contributions of those here as well as the others who are too numerous to mention are most appreciated. My career would not be possible without their help.

INTRODUCTION

reatness doesn't come often. As sports fans, we spend a lifetime rooting for our favorite teams and players, but true greatness is what we look for but rarely get a chance to see. That's what makes it special. Fans of sports in Western Pennsylvania know that there have been thousands of athletes who have represented this area proudly in individual sports such as boxing, golf, swimming and track. There are thousands more who have competed for our teams wearing the black and gold of the Steelers, Pirates and Penguins; the blue and gold for Pitt; the red, white and blue of Duquesne; and the crimson of IUP, as well as the various colors of the other colleges and universities that dot the landscape in this historic area. And yet, only a very few achieve true greatness.

It's why despite the fact that Roberto Clemente tragically died almost fifty years ago, we recall so clearly his rifle arm and his unique running style as he wildly rounded second going to third. It's also why we remember so fondly the Pitt Stadium PA announcer Roger Huston scream "HUGH...GREEN" every time no. 99 stopped a running back in his tracks, the way Willie Stargell would prepare for a pitch by whipping around his bat like a windmill, Sihugo Green's amazing athletic ability playing the game in a way that wouldn't be in vogue for twenty-five more years, Mario Lemieux gliding effortlessly through an opposing defense before befuddling the goalie or Arnie Palmer's unique swing that made the everyday duffer feel like he was one of them. It's why our grandfathers and great-grandfathers marveled at the way Honus Wagner looked like a gold glove player no matter what position he took on the diamond. They've been honored with the adulation of their adoring fans, by having their numbers retired and by being voted into the Halls of Fame that represent the sports they've played.

They all played the game at a level only few have achieved and became heroes to the millions of fans who have cheered them on over the years. It's why anyone who wore a uniform wanted to be like them. The fifty men and women included in this book are truly the elite—the legends and the icons of sports in Pittsburgh history. The tale of sports in this area can't be told without including their names. They held up the trophies that have symbolized the championships we all hold so dearly; without them, they wouldn't have been won.

There were many great players who came from this area and chose to take their talents elsewhere in college or the pros—Stan Musial, Joe Namath, Jim Kelly, Joe Montana and Jack Twyman, just to name a few. As great as these players were, only stars who played at the collegiate level and above in Western Pennsylvania in team sports or those who competed in individual sports, such as boxing and golfing, and spent a significant time in the area growing up were considered. Those athletes represented the area well at the highest levels of competition in their sports, while figures like Musial are thought of more as icons in the cities where they became famous.

This book not only celebrates the careers of these extraordinary athletes but also answers the questions of who was better, Terry Bradshaw or Ben Roethlisberger...Harry Greb or Billy Conn...Dave Parker or Barry Bonds... Tony Dorsett or Hugh Green...Dick Ricketts or Sihugo Green...Jaromír Jágr or Sidney Crosby. It also includes a list of the many men and women from this area who have been inducted into the various Halls of Fame.

Truly, greatness doesn't come often. There are tens of thousands of athletes over the past two centuries who would qualify for inclusion in this book, hundreds who played the game at a special level and were stars. It's why these fifty athletes truly define what greatness is. They are Pittsburgh's greatest athletes.

Chapter 1

THE OTHER GREATS

ATHLETES 50–41

50. CHUCK COOPER

Duquesne University (basketball), 1946–50

As quickly as change was coming in professional and collegiate sports with the integration of African Americans in the 1940s and 1950s, change was still extremely difficult for those athletes who were breaking the barriers. Vulgar responses by mostly white crowds toward their efforts, being denied entrance to certain hotels and not always being allowed to eat with their white teammates were only a few of the indignities that African American athletes would experience. Men like Duquesne All-American Chuck Cooper, who became the first African American to be drafted into the National Basketball Association on April 25, 1950, endured those situations and so much more.

Born on September 29, 1926, in Pittsburgh, Cooper attended Westinghouse High School, where he became a star, leading his team to the city title while being named first-team All-City at center. Cooper was talented enough to have much more impressive scoring figures than he actually did, averaging 13.6 points per game in his final campaign at Westinghouse, but his unselfishness and willingness to pass up a shot if a teammate had a better opportunity became one of his trademarks. One of his friends growing up, Harold Brown, recalled, "He could score well. He would have scored double what he did if he wasn't so generous. That was his main fault, everyone said.

When he left Duquesne, Chuck Cooper (*no. 15, at left*) was the school's all-time leading scorer. He became a pioneer soon after he exited the Bluff, becoming the first African American to be drafted by the NBA when he was selected by the Boston Celtics in the second round of the 1950 NBA draft. *Courtesy of Duquesne University Athletics.*

He would give the ball to the man closest to the basket. They used to say 'Shoot! Shoot!' and he would say, 'Well the guy had a better shot than I did.' That was all the way to the pros."[1]

Turning down scholarship offers from some bigger New York City colleges that began to integrate in the mid-1940s, Cooper chose to join his high school teammate Bill Nunn Jr., who became an influential scout under Chuck Noll for the Steelers, at West Virginia State College. He instantly became a star, averaging almost 20 points per game, but his stay with the Yellow Jackets was short, as he left the school after one season.

With World War II still going on, he served in the navy after leaving school until the conflict came to an end. At that point, he was once again heavily recruited, including by West Coast teams this time, but Cooper wanted to return to Pittsburgh and accepted a scholarship to play at Duquesne University under Chick Davies. Even though he had played a season at West Virginia State, the young center would be allowed to play four years with the Dukes.

Life in Pittsburgh at that time wasn't as integrated as it was in some other areas in the eastern part of the United States, but an incident early in his first campaign showed that his school was firmly behind him. Duquesne had scheduled the University of Tennessee on December 23, 1946, for a game that was to be played in McKeesport. Volunteer head coach John Mauer claimed that he had sent a letter to Davies asking him not to play Cooper against Tennessee. When Mauer went into the locker room to thank the Dukes coach for agreeing to this request, Davies shot back quickly that he made no such agreement. It was still early in Cooper's career and he hadn't yet become a star, so it would have been easy for Duquesne to sit him. The freshman even insisted to the coach that he not play so the game could go on. Davies refused, telling Mauer that the only way the Dukes would play was with Cooper on the court. Tennessee refused to take the court with an African American playing on the other team. The head of the Duquesne Athletic Council, Judge Samuel Weiss, decided to back his future star and send the crowd home, which gave the Dukes a 2–0 forfeit win. The school was so angry at the situation that it canceled a January trip to Miami to play in the Orange Bowl Tournament, as there was a law in Miami prohibiting African Americans from playing sports against white athletes.

Cooper eventually became the star Davies had envisioned, but he did so under some difficult situations. Cooper stood up to the prejudice, recalling that "racism wasn't limited to the South. We were playing the University

15

of Cincinnati out in the Midwest. There was an out-of-bounds play and they were lining up to guard us. One guy said 'I got the nigger.' I walked up to him and said, 'and I got your mother in my jockstrap.' He was shocked. After the game, which I remember they won, he came over to apologize. I thought I had already said what needed to be said and I told him that. I also said 'if you can take what I said then I can take a thousand niggers.' That was the only time during my college career that I was called a nigger to my face."[2]

Averaging 10.3 points per game for his career on the Bluff, Cooper left Duquesne as the school's all-time leading scorer with 990 points. He could have scored more, but like in high school, Cooper was an unselfish player, more interested in winning than garnering more impressive personal numbers. His unselfish attitude was a pivotal part in leading the Dukes to a 78-19 record in his four seasons, with two National Invitation Tournament appearances and a sixth ranking in the final 1950 Associated Press poll his senior year. He also was selected as a first-team All-American by *Look* magazine and the *Converse Yearbook*.

The Pittsburgh native played for the Harlem Globetrotters in an eighteen-game tour after leaving Duquesne and then on April 25, 1950, etched his name in history as the first African American to be drafted in the NBA. The Boston Celtics took him in the second round with the 14th pick in the draft. There were rumors that he was to be drafted, but until it actually occurred, no one was completely sure it was going to happen. Earl Lloyd, who helped Cooper integrate the NBA as the first African American to play in a league game one day before Cooper did, thought that "I truly believe this, that if the Celtics did not draft Chuck [Cooper] in the second round, you could not tell me that the Washington Capitols in 1950 were going to make me the first black player to play in this league. No way....The Boston Celtics had a tremendous influence on my acceptance in the NBA."[3] Luckily, Walter Brown, owner of the Celtics, did make the bold move, claiming, "I don't give a damn if he's striped or plaid or polka dot, Boston takes Charles Cooper of Duquesne."[4]

Cooper, who unfortunately died of cancer in 1984, was proud of his achievement but knew that he had an advantage of coming in with two other players, which made it easier for them than it was for Jackie Robinson three years earlier. "Actually, I considered it a rather dubious achievement. So you see, I wasn't alone [coming into the league with Lloyd and Nat "Sweetwater" Clifton, who was the first to sign an NBA contract]. I didn't have to take the race-baiting and the heat all on my own shoulders like Jackie

Robinson. Besides, any black coming after Jackie, in any sport, had it easy compared to the turmoil he lived through."[5]

His historic accomplishments were finally rewarded with two impressive announcements. First, in October 2018, it was revealed that Duquesne was naming its new arena after him, the UPMC Cooper Fieldhouse. He was then given basketball's highest honor six months later when he was elected to the Naismith Basketball Hall of Fame.

While he may not have had the notoriety of Jackie Robinson, Chuck Cooper will be remembered as a pioneer in the fight to integrate sports in this country, a hero whose presence is still felt in the city of Pittsburgh with his number, 15, being retired by his alma mater, a building named after him on campus (other than the arena) and the foundation his son, Chuck Cooper III, runs in his honor that helps worthy candidates continue their education. It is an endeavor that Cooper would certainly be proud of.

49. JOSEPH "ARKY" VAUGHAN

Pittsburgh Pirates, 1932–41

There are two celebrated athletes who wore no. 21 in the city of Pittsburgh and tragically died young, Roberto Clemente and the Pittsburgh Penguins' Michel Briere, but there was a third one who wore the famed number and is mostly forgotten—one of the best shortstops the game has ever produced, Joseph "Arky" Vaughan.

Three years after he retired from the game, Vaughan was out with a friend fishing on a lake near his California home. A storm came in quickly, and the boat capsized in the chilly waters. Arky's friend, Bill Wimer, couldn't swim, and Vaughan tried to save him. They both unfortunately drowned, as their bodies were found the next day. While the end of his life came in a heroic manner and is what many remember most about Arky Vaughan, his baseball career was remarkable and deserves to be another focal point.

The clear consensus among baseball historians is that fellow Pirate Honus Wagner is the greatest who ever played the position. Afterward, names like Cal Ripken, Ozzie Smith, Ernie Banks and Derek Jeter are the ones most discussed as to who is second best. Bill James, the father of sabermetrics (the way baseball is analyzed through modern statistical means), had a different take on the matter.

Joseph "Arky" Vaughan, second only to Honus Wagner when it comes to greatest shortstops in Pittsburgh Pirates history. In 1935, he hit .385, which is a franchise record that still stands today. In 1952, he tragically drowned while trying to save a friend who had fallen into the lake after their fishing boat capsized. *Courtesy of the Pittsburgh Pirates.*

In his popular book *The New Bill James Historical Baseball Abstract*, James made the claim that it is Vaughan who should sit right behind Wagner. Despite the fact that defense wasn't necessarily Arky's strong suit, his offensive numbers are so impressive that they overcome any defensive shortcomings. James pointed out that next to Wagner, Vaughan had the most impressive three- and five-year offensive run of any shortstop in the history of the game. In a statistic he developed—win shares, which is simply the number of wins a player contributed to his team—Arky Vaughan had the second-highest figure for a shortstop per 162 games (as of 2001, when James wrote the book), 29.4; Wagner was at 38.0. His analysis sheds light on why Vaughan is one of the game's greats; it also makes one wonder why he is so underrated.

Born in 1912 in Clifty, Arkansas, Vaughan and his family eventually moved to Fullerton, California, where his friends game him his famous moniker after finding out where he was born. He was a star in many sports at Fullerton High School. A tough running back on the football squad, Vaughan was a teammate of former president Richard Nixon. In a letter to Arky's daughter after Vaughan was elected into the Orange County Sports Hall of Fame in 1982, Nixon stated, "I was a substitute tackle on the Fullerton High School championship 130-pound team and remember Arky as our star halfback—fast, hard-nosed and even then a real professional."[6] He was also an outstanding baseball player, as Pirates scout Art Griggs found out, signing him in 1931 after a neighbor of Vaughan's told the scout of his impressive potential. As it turned out, the neighbor knew what he was talking about.

Spending only one season in the minors, with the Wichita Aviators, where he hit 21 homers with a .338 average in 1931, Vaughan quickly took over the starting position at short for the Bucs from Tommy Thevenow after Thevenow broke his finger early into the 1932 campaign. Thevenow was a better fielder than the twenty-year-old Arkansas native but was struggling at the plate, hitting only .213. Vaughan proved to be vastly superior his rookie campaign with a .318 average. He followed that up hitting .314 his sophomore season, with 97 runs batted in (RBI), and was a pivotal part of a Pirate team that finished second both times.

Vaughan's third year in 1934 began the phenomenal five-year run that James spoke of in his book. Ending the campaign with a league-leading .431 on base percentage (OBP) and .333 average, Arky was selected to participate in his first of nine consecutive All-Star games. It was a great season, but it was only a glimpse of what he would achieve in 1935, one of the greatest years in Pirates history.

The only blemish on an otherwise phenomenal year was the fact Vaughan was hitting .401 by mid-September before a late-season slump plunged him under the .400 plateau. He still ended up leading the league with a .385 average and a .491 OBP; both remain club records. On top of the two record-setting statistics, Arky also topped the senior circuit in walks (97), slugging percentage (.607) and on base percentage plus slugging (OPS) (1.098) to go along with career highs in home runs (19) and RBIs (99). Despite his dominance, Vaughan was overlooked. He finished a distant third for the National League Most Valuable Player Award (MVP) to Gabby Hartnett of the Cubs, despite the fact Vaughan was superior in every offensive category, and the Cardinals' Dizzy Dean, who finished 28-12 but had a rather mediocre 3.04 earned run average (ERA). While the baseball writers didn't acknowledge Vaughan's great play, the *Sporting News* did, naming him the Player of the Year in the NL.

Missing out on the award had no effect on the shortstop, as he continued to excel during his career in Pittsburgh, never hitting below .300 in ten seasons. One of the highlights of his career occurred in the 1941 All-Star Game. Vaughan became the first player to hit two home runs in one midsummer classic. Once again, though, his remarkable achievement would be overshadowed, as Ted Williams hit a three-run walk-off homer to win the game 7–5. It is Williams's home run that is always remembered as the highlight in the '41 All-Star Game.

While Vaughan had a memorable moment, 1941 was difficult for the Arkansas native. He suffered both a spike wound and a concussion after being hit by a pitch in his head during the season, which limited him to a career-low 106 games. In the off season, the Pirates dealt him to Brooklyn Dodgers, to the chagrin of the fans. According to the great sports writer Fred Lieb, "Many of the Pirate faithful shook their heads. They didn't want to see Arky get away."[7]

Vaughan enjoyed success in Brooklyn until an argument with Manager Leo Durocher over Durocher's suspending pitcher Bobo Newsom for insubordination led Vaughan to retire at thirty-one years old. General Manager Branch Rickey would coax him out of retirement, at which time he became a valuable reserve for the team, eventually playing in his first World Series in 1947. He retired for good a year later and in 1952 met his untimely death in the boating accident at only forty.

As during his career, respect for his accomplishments after he retired were seemingly ignored. Despite his .318 career average and phenomenal peak, Vaughan garnered no more than 11.9 percent of the vote for the Hall of Fame in his first ten years on the ballot, peaking at 29.0 percent in his thirteenth and final year. Eventually, the Veteran's Committee in 1985 got it right, selecting him for baseball's highest honor. Even then, the Hall of Fame misspelled his last name ("Vaughn") when releasing the commemorative envelope celebrating his induction.

So why was respect lacking for such a great player? Most likely his quiet personality may have had something to do with it. His obituary in the *Fullerton Daily News Tribune* noted, "He lacked only one thing—a colorful personality. Those who knew him best believe he would have been one of the game's greatest heroes had he been endowed with the sparkling personality that made lesser players great."[8] His brother Bob claimed, "Sitting and talking in a one-to-one situation, he was great. He just didn't care for crowds. And he would probably avoid an interview if he could. He would just rather let his playing do the talking."[9] Regardless of his non-colorful personality, Arky Vaughan was one of the greatest to ever play the position. His inclusion in the Hall of Fame was an honor that should have come many years earlier.

48. ANTONIO BROWN

Pittsburgh Steelers, 2010–18

Being a fan of former Pittsburgh Steeler Antonio Brown is often a confusing endeavor. On one hand, there is the excitement of seeing his exhilarating play on the field; on the other, there is the frustration of his antics after the play is over. Regardless of this unique dichotomy, Brown was in the midst of a career unseen by Steeler fans in the history of the franchise before it ended in a very controversial manner.

Despite the fact that he had an exceptional career at Norland High School in Miami, Brown's life there didn't give an indication of the greatness he would eventually enjoy. The son of one of the best players in the Arena Football League, Eddie Brown, the Steeler receiver had a difficult time while growing up. His parents were separated and for a time Brown was homeless. Not ready for college academically after high school, the Miami native went to North Carolina Tech to become eligible to play for a top four-year school. At that point, it was impossible to believe that Brown would soon become arguably the greatest receiver in Pittsburgh Steelers history. It was also at this point when the fighting spirit of Antonio Brown became evident.

"When everyone turned around on me, all I had to do was rely on myself. I've got a strong spirit that I rely on and go into."[10] This spirit took him to a school in the Mid-American Conference (MAC), Central Michigan, where he began his career in 2007 without a scholarship as a walk-on. By the end of his freshman campaign, it was apparent that he was more than just a traditional walk-on. He set an NCAA football subdivision record with 2,267 all-purpose yards while being named as the MACs Freshman of the Year.

By the time his career was done with the Chippewas, Brown had rewritten the school record book. He set the Central Michigan record with 305 receptions in his career, the second most in MAC history at the time, as well as 110 in a single season. He also had the second-most touchdown receptions (22) and third-most receiving yards (3,199) for the school while playing only three seasons. The highlight of his remarkable collegiate career was his final game in a Central Michigan uniform, for which he was named Offensive Player of the Game in the 2010 GMAC Bowl, catching thirteen passes for 178 yards while scoring twice, one on a 7-yard run and another a 95-yard kickoff return in the Chippewas' dramatic 44–41 overtime victory against Troy.

After the bowl game, Brown announced that he was forgoing his senior season to enter the NFL draft; it seemed to be a mistake, as teams weren't interested in making him a high draft pick. Brown was only five-foot-ten, in a league that wanted height at receiver. He didn't have blazing speed, a 4.56 40-yard dash, in a league that desired speed, and he didn't play against elite competition in the MAC. But what he did have was an incredible work ethic and a fiery, competitive attitude. His coach at CMU, Butch Jones, said, "He's a self-made man—that's always been his edge. One of the most competitive people I've ever coached."[11] While mostly ignored, then Steeler offensive coordinator Bruce Arians saw potential in Brown and selected him in the sixth round with the 195th pick. While Arians liked him, he couldn't imagine the production he'd get out of the sixth-round pick. "You never know how hard a worker someone is until you get them in the building. Nobody works harder than Antonio Brown—to this day." His fighting attitude is even represented in the number he chose to wear in Pittsburgh, 84. He picked it because eight times four is thirty-two, the number of teams that passed on picking him in the early rounds of the draft.

He achieved so much in his nine-year NFL career to this point, much more than the twenty-one receivers who were picked in front of him that year have produced. Brown has the most receptions (526) of any receiver in their first six years in the league; the most receptions in two consecutive seasons (262), three consecutive seasons (375) and four consecutive seasons (481); and the fewest games to get to 600 receptions (96). He is also the first NFL receiver to eclipse 125 catches in two consecutive seasons, the first NFL player to have four 180-yard games receiving in one season, the first NFL player to have more the 1,700 yards from scrimmage in two consecutive seasons, the first NFL player with two games with more than 15 receptions in a game in one season and the first NFL player to lead his conference in receptions over four consecutive seasons. When he signed a four-year $68 million extension before the 2017 campaign, it was hoped that more records would drop while he's was in a Steeler uniform.

While he had been great on the field he has done some things after the play is over that have frustrated coaches, players and fans. There were some issues where he inexplicably cost his team a 15-yard penalty after celebrating following a touchdown. Then there was an incident in the Steeler locker room following an exciting playoff victory over Kansas City in 2016 when he taped Mike Tomlin's speech. Intending to inspire his team in the AFC championship game against New England, Tomlin used a few vulgarities not meant for public viewership, but Brown was in the back of the locker room showing the speech to his Facebook Live followers. It created embarrassment for the coach and another unneeded distraction before a big game. More recently, Brown went on a tirade before the 2018 campaign, taking the local Pittsburgh media to task for creating stories that put undue pressure on professional athletes.

As 2018 went on, he seemingly was in the paper as much for controversies off the field than anything on it. He was accused of throwing furniture off a hotel balcony in a Miami hotel, almost hitting a toddler. He sped along a major road in the north side of Pittsburgh at more than one hundred miles per hour. He then allegedly pushed the mother of one of his children to the ground in a dispute. All three situations took a backdrop to him missing the final game of the season against Cincinnati, a contest of critical playoff importance, after claiming to have been injured. Brown then took to social media in a barrage of criticisms leveled toward Mike Tomlin and some teammates on the Steelers. It eventually led to him being traded to the Oakland Raiders.

Even though these situations have created controversies and ended his career in Pittsburgh, on the field there is no doubt that he was remarkable. After catching 104 passes in 2018, he finished his nine years with the Steelers snagging 837 passes for 11,207 yards, including six consecutive seasons where he caught 100 or more passes. With Antonio Brown, it would be easy to push his career to the side in the midst of what happened in a twelve-month period, but in looking at his statistics and what he accomplished on the field, there is no doubt he was a tremendous athlete and arguably the greatest receiver this franchise has ever seen.

47. DICK RICKETTS

Duquesne University (basketball), 1951–55

There was a time when the men's basketball program at Duquesne University wasn't struggling; in fact, it was among the best in the country. Men like Paul Birch, Herb Bonn, Walter Miller, Ed Milkovich, Paul Widowitz, Moe Becker, Chuck Cooper and Jim Tucker kept the Dukes consistently in the hunt for a national championship, but it wasn't until a six-foot-seven center from Pottstown, Pennsylvania, by the name of Dick Ricketts came to the Bluff that the program finally was able to capture that elusive national crown.

Dick Ricketts (*no. 12, at right*) was one of the greatest players ever to don a Duquesne uniform. Today, he remains the school leader in both points and rebounds for a career. He went on to become a two-sport professional player, appearing for the NBA St. Louis Hawks and signing a contract with the St. Louis Cardinals. *Courtesy of Duquesne University Athletics.*

From his first varsity game at Duquesne, fans knew that the Pottstown native was something special. He combined with Tucker to have one of the most impressive debuts by two teammates in one game. Tucker, playing his first varsity game as a sophomore, scored 26, while the freshman Ricketts netted 23 in a 70–52 victory against Bowling Green.

Ricketts continued his impressive freshman campaign, finishing with a 12.4 points per game average, and then followed it up with a 20.9 average his sophomore year. Going into his third season, the experts were convinced that Dick Ricketts was now one of the best players in the nation and selected him as a preseason first-team All-American in a poll of more than one thousand sports writers conducted by *Dell Magazine*.

While his scoring average dropped to 17.2, Ricketts was a pivotal part of what was considered the greatest team the school had ever produced at that point. The 1953–54 Dukes finished 26-3 and attained the only number-one ranking the program has ever received following a 22-0 start. After losing consecutive games on a road trip to Cincinnati and Dayton, Duquesne entered the National Invitation Tournament (NIT) with a 24-2 mark, ranked third in the nation. They defeated St. Francis (PA) and Niagara in the first two rounds and found themselves facing ninth-ranked Holy Cross in the final. Led by future Hall of Famer and Boston Celtics great Tom Heinsohn, the Crusaders upset the favored Dukes, 71–62, as Ricketts fouled out after scoring a disappointing 13 points.

The season that had been so successful ended with Duquesne falling short of a national championship once again. It was a hard-luck program that in fourteen years had a Final Four and an Elite Eight to its credit in the NCAA tournament while garnering five semifinal appearances and two losses in the championship game of the NIT, which was of equal if not more importance than the NCAA during that era. Despite the disappointing way it ended, Ricketts was named as a first-team All-American by *Look Magazine*, the International News Service, the Newspaper Enterprises Association and Tempo, while receiving second-team status from five other organizations.

It was truly a great season, but one that looked like it would be the final chance for Ricketts to help the program win that elusive national title. He would go into his senior campaign with a less talented team. He and Sihugo Green, who also received All-American recognition, were far and away the stars on a squad that was of average talent otherwise. They were also hurt by injuries and academic issues that reduced their bench considerably. They surprised many with the campaign they produced, finishing sixth in the final Associated Press poll and receiving a bid to the NIT, but they remarkably achieved something that no Duquesne team ever had before or since, winning a national championship with a victory against Dayton in the NIT finals.

When they were both healthy and in the lineup at the same time, Ricketts and Green were a dominant duo, winning all but one game, against eleventh-ranked Dayton in the second contest of an exhausting two-day road trip. Of their other losses, two of the defeats came following an ankle injury that the Pottstown native suffered in the Holiday Festival final against LaSalle, where the Dukes defeated the defending NCAA champions, 67–65, to vault to second in the Associated Press poll. Ricketts scored a team-high 23 points in the impressive victory but twisted his ankle late in the first half. It was a lingering injury that seemed to grow worse with time. Despite the fact that Duquesne had eight days off before a matchup against local rival St. Francis, Ricketts struggled with only 13 points and was pulled by Dudey Moore with five minutes left in an 82–72 upset loss. Two days later, he tried to play against Dayton but had his worst game of the season, netting only 10 as the Dukes were defeated on their home court, 68–67.

The disappointing season that most expected seemed to be coming to fruition, but Ricketts's ankle healed and he once again became one of the best players in the country, leading his team to twelve victories in their last thirteen games and a spot as the number-one seed in the NIT.

Despite the fact there were rumors of Green's injuries, he and Ricketts dominated the tournament. Easy victories against Louisville and Cincinnati put them back in the finals—unfortunately against a team they had already lost to twice during the season, the Dayton Flyers. They were at their best, though, as the two-man team showed how effective they could be, scoring 56 of the team's 70 points in a 70–58 victory for the program's only national championship.

Ricketts was hailed as one of the best players in the country after finishing his career on the Bluff with 1,963 points and 1,359 rebounds, statistics that remain school records today. This time, he was chosen as a consensus first-team All-American after capturing the honor with such prominent selectors as the Associated Press, United Press International and the Helms Foundation. He led not only with his phenomenal statistics but also as role model for his teammates. He was an intense competitor and made sure that his teammates were properly focused on the task at hand. Then assistant coach Red Manning said, "Dick Ricketts' personality was such that when he didn't like things he was seeing on the court he would express himself. Dick Ricketts never took it easy. He played real hard in practice."[12] His intense play both on and off the court impressed the St. Louis Hawks of the NBA, who made the All-American the number-one pick in the draft.

Despite being so successful in basketball, Ricketts's first love was baseball, a sport in which he was also immensely talented. He was a first baseman and pitcher with Duquesne and made the decision to try to become a two-sport star. He not only signed a $12,000 contract with the Hawks but also received a $4,000 bonus to play in the St. Louis Cardinal farm system.

He had a solid NBA career with St. Louis and the Rochester Royals, where he was reunited with Green. The team moved in 1958 to Cincinnati, where Ricketts witnessed the tragic accident of his former rival at Duquesne, Maurice Stokes, who played for St. Francis (PA). Stokes hit his head as he fell to the floor and eventually suffered paralysis. It helped convince Ricketts, who averaged 9.3 points per game in his NBA career, to quit basketball and focus on baseball. He had some success in the minors, but his major-league career was disappointing, with a 1-6 record for the Cardinals in 1959 with a 5.82 ERA.

Retiring after the 1964 campaign, the Pottstown native became a success in business as an executive with the Eastman Kodak Company. He sadly died at only fifty-four in 1988, succumbing to leukemia. He is still remembered as one of the greatest players in Duquesne history, as his number, 12, was retired by the school. The former owner of the Royals, Les Harrison, summed up Ricketts's career succinctly after learning of his death: "He was one of the superstars of his time."[13]

46. CHARLEY BURLEY

Boxing, 1936–50

In team sports, there is almost never a situation where the great clubs aren't given a fair shot at winning a title; in individual sports, that isn't always the case, especially in boxing. Today, few fans of the sport remember the name Charley Burley. In his time he was considered a great fighter, yet he was so good champions avoided fighting him. Burley unfortunately would never be given a chance at the title, and while he is always ranked among the best middleweights to ever enter the ring, he does so without the word *champion* next to his name.

Born in Bessemer, Pennsylvania, located north of Pittsburgh in Lawrence County, to an African American father and a white mother from County Cork, Ireland, Burley moved to the Hill District section of Pittsburgh after his father, who worked in a coke oven, died of black lung disease when the young boy was only twelve. He was reportedly a baseball player of note and was considered by the Homestead Grays for a spot on their team, but his talents were stronger in boxing, which is where Burley decided to pursue a career.

He began training at Kay's Boys Club right after his father died and quickly became a successful amateur boxer. In 1936, he entered one of the most prestigious tournaments in the area, the Allegheny Mountain Golden Gloves event at the Duquesne Gardens in Pittsburgh, and won the welterweight title by easily defeating Lou Gendle from Miami Beach in the finals with a first-round knockout.

Burley had an opportunity to fight for the United States in the 1936 Olympic Games in Berlin, garnering a spot in the U.S. Olympic Trials, but chose not to participate in protest against the racial and religious discrimination being displayed by the Nazi regime in Germany. Instead, he chose to fight in an event held in Spain called the Counter Olympics. Unfortunately, the Spanish civil war began just as the boxers were arriving in the country, and they were soon escorted out of Spain and sent to Paris. Burley recalled, "When we got to Barcelona there were dead people and horses on the street. Soldiers pulled us out of our hotel before we could fight. It was too bad; we were getting five bucks a day for expenses."

The Bessemer native returned home and began his heralded professional career on September 29 with a four-round knockout of George Liggins at the Moose Temple in Pittsburgh. He went on to win his first twelve bouts before losing an eight-round decision to Eddie Dolan in Millvale one year later. It was a fine beginning to his career, but following the Dolan defeat, he decided to fight a higher level of competition.

Burley was an effective welterweight and defeated future welterweight champion of the world Fritzie Zivic in a rematch on July 13, 1938, after losing to him three months earlier. It was a prelude to a dominant one-sided fifteen-round unanimous decision over the tough Cocoa Kid at Millvale's Hickey Park for what was dubbed the "Colored Welterweight Title." By the end of the fight, it was apparent who the superior fighter was. The description in the *Pittsburgh Post-Gazette* noted that "it was not until the waning rounds that Burley really pulled away to any comfortable margin over the defender (Cocoa Kid), but at the conclusion of the final heat Cocoa was a pitiful sight. Both eyes were practically closed from incessant and effective jabs."[14] Regis M. Welsh of the *Post-Gazette* said after the fight, "Move over John Henry Lewis, move over and make room for another Negro 'champion' who calls the Hill District his home. Not a bona-fide, genuine title holder like you are, but a vigorous, willing lad, today the possessor of a rather synthetic crown labeled Colored Welterweight Champion."[15] While Welsh went on to make the claim that he would be a tough opponent for the great Henry Armstrong and the world title, the fight never took place, as this would turn out to be the only championship that the Bessemer native ever captured.

Burley fought anyone whom they put in front of him, including Zivic, whom he defeated in two out of three fights; future middleweight champion Billy Soose, beating him in a ten-round decision; future heavyweight champion of the world Ezzard Charles, losing two decisions one month apart in 1942; and Hall of Famer Archie Moore, perhaps Burley's greatest victory, defeating the future world light-heavyweight champion in a ten-round decision in Hollywood, knocking Moore down four times. Archie said after the fight, "Burley gave me a boxing lesson. He kept his punches coming at you like a riveting gun beats a tattoo on a rivet. He was the best fighter I ever fought, and the best fighter I ever saw."[16]

Over his career, he was never knocked down in 97 fights, going 83-12-2, but no one gave him a shot at the title that he deserved. There was the fact that he was one of a series of African American fighters at the time who were ducked by various champions because of race. There was also the fact that he fought during World War II when many of the champions, including middleweight title holder Tony Zale and welterweight champion Red Cochran, were on hiatus while serving their country in the armed forces. Perhaps one of the main reasons Burley never got a chance to fight for the title was that he was just too damn good.

After defeating Zivic for a second time, it was Fritzie who got the shot against Henry Armstrong for the title and upset the champion. Zivic never gave Burley the chance in a championship tilt. In fact, Zivic's manager, Luke Carney, purchased Burley's contract at one point, most likely so he could keep Zivic from having to fight him. Sugar Ray Robinson, the middleweight title holder, reportedly demanded a purse twice as high as he usually got to fight the Pittsburgh fighter, a demand that made the fight financially difficult to put together. He reportedly once said, "I'm too pretty to fight Charley Burley."[17] The Pittsburgh fighter asserted once that he could have had a three-fight series with Robinson but he would have to throw the first fight.

Eventually, Burley got tired of waiting and retired in 1950, becoming a sanitation worker in the city. It was his life that was the inspiration for the main character in August Wilson's Tony Award–winning play *Fences*.

While he never won a world championship, his career has been respected by boxing historians. Many call Burley the greatest fighter never to win a championship. The great trainer Ray Arcel said, "Charley Burley was the best fighter I ever saw who not only never won a title but never got any glory. In those days, if you were a good black fighter, nobody wanted to fight you."[18] In a ranking by *Sports Illustrated* of the greatest middleweights in the history of the sport, Charley Burley was fourth, ahead of such legends as Stanley Ketchel, Harry Greb, Marvin Hagler and Robinson. He was also elected to the International Boxing Hall of Fame in 1992, an honor that finally puts him in a place he deserves—among the sport's best.

45. ERNIE STAUTNER

Pittsburgh Steelers, 1950–63

Many legends have worn the black and gold, most of whom came after the Steelers began their era of excellence in 1972. Men like Joe Greene, Jack Ham, Jack Lambert, Mel Blount, Franco Harris and Terry Bradshaw, to name just a few, are considered among the best who ever played the game. As rich as the past five decades have been, until 2014, when Greene was accorded the honor, only one man had his number retired by the franchise: a defensive tackle from Boston College by the name of Ernie Stautner.

Unlike Greene, Stautner wasn't considered a potential cornerstone of the franchise when he was taken in the second round of the 1950 NFL draft. Born in Bavaria, he was considered an undersized defenseman lineman, weighing below 220 pounds. Starting his collegiate career at Notre Dame, Ernie was cut by the legendary Frank Leahy after the coach claimed, "You're too small. Too small and too slow."[19]

After a stint in the Marine Corps, he went to Boston College to take another shot at football. This time the experience was more positive. He was a solid two-way lineman for the Eagles and showed his versatility at BC by also handling the kicking chores. Stautner became the first Boston College player to win the Captain Edward J. O'Melia Trophy as the MVP in the Holy Cross–Boston College game and was elected to the school's Hall of Fame in 1973.

As successful as he was at BC, Stautner wasn't an All-American and not regarded among the best prospects in the 1950 NFL draft. When he was taken in the second round by the Steelers, no one took notice. The Steelers hadn't had a stellar record in drafting players in their seventeen-year history at that time, and there was no reason to think he was going to turn out any different. Pittsburgh chose Michigan State halfback Lynn Chadnois in the first round before picking Stautner with the 8th pick in the second round, which turned out to be a steal. Only 3 players of the 391 taken in the thirty-round draft went on to Hall of Fame careers: Bud Grant (chosen at the end of the first round by Philadelphia but is in Canton because of his excellent coaching career with the Vikings), Leo Nomellini and Stautner.

Steeler coach John Michelosen was one person who understood the potential of Ernie. Looking at him during a preseason practice his rookie season, Michelosen exclaimed, "Allen [the team's fifth-round pick out of Duke] and Stautner are ten strikes as far as tackles go."[20] He planned playing

Not much was expected from Ernie Stautner when the Pittsburgh Steelers took him in the second round of the 1950 NFL draft out of Boston College. He was an undersized defensive lineman whose intensity led him to the Pro Football Hall of Fame, and he also became the first Steeler to have his number retired. *Courtesy of Boston College Athletics.*

the Boston College alum both ways and considered making him his kicker, as Stautner continually was reaching the end zone with his kickoffs in training camp. Eventually, Michelosen settled on leaving him at left defensive tackle, which proved to be a fortuitous decision.

He started all twelve games that season and became a fixture there for the next fourteen seasons. What Stautner lacked in size he made up for in strength and desire. Dan Rooney recalled, "What made him was his strength. This was a time when players didn't have strength. I remember we were playing the Giants at Forbes Field one time and it was a very close game and they were moving the ball. He sacked the quarterback three times in a row."[21] Hall of Fame offensive lineman Jim Parker added, "That man ain't human. He's too strong to be human....He's the toughest guy in the league to play against because he keeps coming head first. Swinging those forearms wears you down. The animal used to stick his head in my belly and drive me into the backfield so hard when I picked myself up and looked around, there was a path chopped through the field like a farmer had run a plow over it."[22]

Stautner continued to improve as his career went on. He was selected to play in nine Pro Bowls and was chosen as a first-team All-Pro five times. As good as his career was, he never was on a playoff team during his Steeler career. The only postseason experience he had was in 1962, when the team finished 9-5, good enough for second place in the East. Back then, the two second-place squads would face off in a postseason game called the Playoff Bowl. It was nothing more than an exhibition, which Pittsburgh lost to Detroit, 17–10.

Finally, in 1963, the Steelers had a chance to win the franchise's first division title and a spot in the NFL championship game. They were 7-3-3 going into the final contest against the 10-3 New York Giants. Win and they would be celebrated as division champions, with a better winning percentage than the Giants. Lose and it would be another disappointing finish.

Stautner was slowing down in the 1963 season, starting only two games and suffering with what was described as a bad charley horse. Despite the fact that he wasn't healthy, the future Hall of Famer was still tough. He missed only one game in his career, against Cleveland in 1953, when he had an adverse effect after he was given a shot to numb the pain for a shoulder injury. Charley horse or not, he would be ready to play arguably the most important game of his career. Stautner was confident that the Steelers could beat the Giants. He told the press boldly before the game that all the pressure was on New York, claiming that they were the defending division champions and Pittsburgh had never won anything before. While his reasoning was sound, the outcome of the game showed that New York was the better team. Stautner's career ended on this day with a disappointing 33–17 loss at Yankee Stadium.

After he retired, Stautner began what would be a long career as a coach the next year. He began as an assistant coach with Pittsburgh in 1964 and then was given the ultimate honor on October 25 against the Eagles at Pitt Stadium. For the first time in franchise history and the only time in the first eighty-one years of Steelers football, the team retired a number. No one would ever wear no. 70 again. It wouldn't be the last honor he received. Stautner was named to the league's All-Decade team for the 1950s, and in 1969, he was inducted into the Pro Football Hall of Fame in his first year of eligibility.

Ernie Stautner had a long career in the NFL as an assistant coach before becoming a head coach in the Arena Football League and NFL Europe, capturing the World Bowl championship with the Frankfurt Galaxy in 1995. He unfortunately would suffer from Alzheimer's disease, and only a few days after seeing his beloved Steelers win their fifth Super Bowl championship in Super Bowl XL, he passed away at the age of eighty.

His NFL career was never supposed to be anything special, but he turned out to be one of the most dominant defensive linemen the league had ever seen.

44. CUMBERLAND POSEY JR.

Monticello Athletic Association (basketball), 1909–13
Murdoch Grays (baseball), 1911
Homestead Grays, 1912–29
Loendi Big Five (basketball), 1913–25
Duquesne University (basketball), 1916–18

The name Cumberland "Cum" Posey is remembered by baseball fans as the legendary owner of the Homestead Grays, arguably the most successful Negro League team in the history of the circuit. While he played for the club for nineteen seasons, his incredible performance as an owner was the reason he was elected into the Baseball Hall of Fame in 2006. There's more to the story though. Posey was also one of the great basketball players of his time.

Pictured in the second row, the third sitting player (*from left to right*) is Cumberland Posey. A multisport player who starred for Duquesne University in basketball as well as the great African American teams the Monticello Athletic Association and the Loendi Big Five, Posey also became a legend in baseball as the player, owner and manager of the Homestead Grays. Today, he is the only athlete to be enshrined in both the Baseball Hall of Fame and the Naismith Basketball Hall of Fame. *Courtesy of Duquesne University Athletics.*

He not only was the first African American to play at Duquesne University but also led five teams to the Colored Basketball World Championship between 1912 and 1923, making Pittsburgh the center of African American basketball in the country. His tremendous efforts would go unrecognized for almost one hundred years until 2016, when the Naismith Basketball Hall of Fame made Posey the answer to a trivia question ("Who is the only man to be in both the baseball and basketball Hall of Fame?").

Posey was innovative for sure, both as an athlete and administrator, and he came by it naturally. Born in Homestead, Pennsylvania, in 1890, his father, Cumberland Posey Sr., was believed to be the first African American in the country to be a licensed chief engineer. It was also his toughness and work ethic on top of his intelligence that he passed on to his son, two attributes that would lead the younger Posey to greatness.

Cum was not the biggest athlete there was, but his toughness was unequaled. According to Claude Johnson, who founded the Black Fives Foundation, an organization that honors the history of African American basketball in the early twentieth century, "He was extremely rugged. He would literally just charge anybody and punch them in the face." Johnson went on further to say that Posey "would walk around with a blackjack in the outer lapel pocket of his suit jacket. Partly for show, and partly for actual usage. He carried it with the handle ominously hanging out."[23]

The future two-time Hall of Famer would need to be tough, as he set out to be one of the greatest African American athletes in the country. He broke barriers at Penn State, becoming the first person of color to attend the university. He played on the freshman basketball team for the 1909–10 campaign and the freshman baseball team in the spring before playing varsity basketball a year later. In 1909, Posey also began the Monticello Athletic Association with his brother, See. It was here where he made people take notice of his immense athletic skill on a national level.

The basketball team that represented Monticello was the Monticello-Delaney Rifles. Posey wanted to take on the best competition possible, knowing that if they could defeat the better teams it would mean better pay days. In 1912, they took on Howard University, considered the best African American team at the time. Monticello was given little chance in the game, which was being billed as the "first colored game ever played in Pittsburgh."[24] The official website of the Black Five Foundation notes, "The Monticellos got no respect and were considered a 'huge joke' by Howard, who thought they would show the steel town 'just how basketball is played in polite circles'"[25] Posey didn't play basketball in "polite circles," as Howard was about to find out.

The philosophy of basketball in the early part of the century was to work the ball in until a player had a good scoring opportunity underneath. Outside shots were nonexistent; it was a strategy no one employed and certainly one Howard University hadn't seen up until this point. Posey was one of the first to embrace an outside shot and used it effectively against Howard. Posey scored 15 of his team's 24 points in the 24–19 upset victory.

The sports editor for the *New York Age*, Lester Walton, wanted to celebrate the best African American team in the land, so he and several experts from other papers would pick one team to hold the title of "Colored Basketball World Champion." With this impressive win, Monticello was given the title in 1912.

One year later, Cumberland renamed the team the Loendi Big Five after the sponsor of the team, the Loendi Social and Literary Club. Cumberland would not only be the team's star player but also do the scheduling and run every aspect of the business. With Posey leading the way, the Big Five became iconic among African American teams, capturing four consecutive Colored Basketball World Championships between 1920 and 1923. His intensity led to his success. W. Rollo Wilson of the *Pittsburgh Courier* said, "Giants crumpled and quit before the fragile-looking Posey. He was at once a ghost, a buzz saw, and a 'shooting fool.' The word 'quit' has never been translated for him."[26]

In the midst of building a professional powerhouse with Loendi, Posey decided to go back to school. In 1915, he decided to attend the Pittsburgh Catholic College of the Holy Ghost, eventually renamed Duquesne University, and went in under the name Charles W. Cumbert, becoming the first African American athlete in school history. Many thought that he went in under an assumed name because of his race, but Rob Ruck, a history professor at the University of Pittsburgh who is an expert on the Negro Leagues, thought it was to hide the fact that he was making money playing basketball outside of college. Nonetheless, Posey was as much a star at Duquesne as he was with Loendi, leading the Dukes in scoring in each of the three seasons he was there.

While he was getting paid as a basketball player, in his quest to become the finest African American athlete in the country Cum also was getting paid in another sport, baseball. He joined the Murdock Grays in 1911. One year later, they changed their name to one more recognizable to baseball fans as one of the best franchises ever assembled, the Homestead Grays.

Posey was a center fielder for the team, with incredible speed that made him a natural for the position. He was a solid player, but his future would be in the front office. His leadership skills were soon on display, first as a captain and then as manager, which he became in 1917. Then he became the secretary in charge of the business dealings of the team. Eventually, in 1920, he bought the team with the help of his father, who had bought a shipbuilding business and then founded the Diamond Coke and Coal Company and was one of the richest men in the area, as well as Charlie Walker, who at one time was a batboy for the Grays and was now a businessman.

Cumberland Posey's reign as owner of the team, from 1920 until he died from lung cancer in 1946, was legendary. The Grays won ten league titles and two Negro League World Series championships under his direction. The fine sports writer for the *Pittsburgh Courier*, Wendall Smith, said, "Some may say he crushed the weak as well as the strong on the way to the top of the ladder. But no matter what his critics say, they cannot deny that he was the smartest man in Negro baseball and certainly the most successful."[27] It was what led Posey to his deserved election to the Baseball Hall of Fame. For basketball, though, it was his innovative play on the floor that helped him achieve what no other athlete, coach or owner has done, becoming a member of both the basketball and baseball Hall of Fame. It's what makes him one of the great icons in Western Pennsylvania sports history.

43. TROY POLAMALU

Pittsburgh Steelers, 2003–14

The Pittsburgh Steelers rarely make trades to move up in the NFL draft. They generally have a list they stick to and take the top player left by the time their turn comes around, especially when in the first round. In 2003, moving up in the first round was something the franchise had never done, which is why it stunned most general managers in the league when Pittsburgh GM Kevin Colbert started calling around to inquire about moving up. This was not necessarily a permanent change of philosophy for the team but rather an opportunity to pick a player whom they felt could help their anemic pass defense. As it turned out, it was a once-in-a-lifetime choice, a player who helped change the way safeties played the game. His name was Troy Polamalu.

Pittsburgh paid a high price for the opportunity to choose Troy, giving the Kansas City Chiefs their first, third and sixth choices. In the end, it was well worth the price. The Steelers received a player who most likely will end up in the Hall of Fame, while Kansas City received Penn State running back Larry Johnson, cornerback Julian Battle and quarterback Brooks Bollinger. With Polamalu anchoring their impenetrable defense, the Steelers won three AFC championships and two Super Bowl titles.

He was certainly an enticing pick, blessed with 4.4 speed in the 40-yard dash and an instinct to know where the ball was being thrown. He was also a hybrid of sorts, being able to play from almost any position, as fast as any running back and as tough as any linebacker. He was a two-time All-American at USC who won the team's Most Inspirational Award. He

Sitting to the left on a car during the Steelers' Super Bowl XVIII celebration parade is Troy Polamalu. Coming out of USC, Polamalu helped changed the way that the safety position in football was played. A magnificent athlete, the USC alum played twelve seasons with Pittsburgh. *Courtesy of David Finoli.*

obsessively watching game film and seemed to be a natural early first-round choice, but his aggressive, no-holds-barred philosophy of playing made him susceptible to injuries and concussions. Some teams also wondered if that aggression would hurt him in deep pass situations, which is an area where safeties needed to be sound. That kind of overanalysis is common in the NFL draft and causes otherwise higher picks to fall. Luckily for the Steelers, they looked at him differently—he was a new type of player who gave offenses something new to worry and think about. Troy did fall to the middle of the round and was still available when the Steelers traded for the 16th pick. While he struggled for most of his first season, eventually he began to be the player the team had hoped for.

The All-American had a unique outlook that eventually endeared him to Steeler fans. His ponytail coming halfway down his uniform; his deep, philosophical way of looking at life; and his aggressive, wild, "I can come from anywhere" approach to the game made him a legend in Western Pennsylvania.

Drafting both Polamalu and Ike Taylor in 2003 gave hopes that the Steelers could turn their lackluster pass defense into one of the best in the league. Early on that season, it looked like it hadn't improved at all. While Polamalu was effective on special teams early in his rookie year, he didn't start off looking like an All-Pro when he was on defense. People began to question the thought process of giving up so much to acquire the USC All-American. By the end of the season, those doubts were being erased, as Pittsburgh fans began to get a glimpse of the future when he was awarded the Joe Greene Trophy, given to the team's Rookie of the Year.

Two years later, his potential was in full bloom. After snatching five interceptions his sophomore campaign, he was a driving force in 2005 to the team's spectacular playoff run that culminated with a trip to the Super Bowl. Perhaps the most memorable moment in the postseason was when the referees inexplicably overturned his spectacular game-clinching interception in the divisional round against the Colts. The next day, the NFL concluded that the officiating crew was incorrect to overturn the interception ruling on the field. It was a call that almost cost the team the game, but thanks to a fingertip tackle by Ben Roethlisberger on a fumble return and the luck of a missed Colts field goal, the Steelers were on their way to finally capturing the elusive fifth Super Bowl championship.

Troy was named to his initial first-team All-Pro selection that season and, three years later, would be honored again. Ironically, 2008 was also a year when the Steelers were on their way to Super Bowl victory number six. Before the season began, Pittsburgh signed Troy to a new contract that made him the highest-paid safety in the league; it would prove to be a wise investment. Polamalu showed his worth with a phenomenal season that was highlighted with an interception in the AFC championship game at Heinz Field against bitter rivals the Baltimore Ravens. With time running out and the Ravens with the ball and a chance to take the lead, Polamalu showed his superb instinct and athleticism as he read quarterback Joe Flacco's play call, stepped in front of the receiver for a spectacular interception and then ran through the Baltimore offense into the end zone for the touchdown that helped give the Steelers the victory.

The USC alum would continue to show his incredible skills as the years went on, being named to two more first-team All-Pro squads in 2010 and 2011 and being named the AFC Defensive Player of the Year in 2010, a year when the team went to a third Super Bowl in Polamalu's career. As the mid-2010s were approaching, it was apparent that his aggressive style of play was wearing down this superstar. Injuries limited him to five games in 2009 and seven in 2012. Five times in his first eleven seasons he was unable to complete a full campaign. Finally, after the 2014 campaign concluded, he decided to retire—more than likely, the Steelers helped him with that decision.

His final season was one filled with injuries, and reportedly, Pittsburgh let him know that they had no plans to bring him back for 2015. He was left with the choice to sign with another team and hope he could recapture the success of past seasons or retire. While he still seems bitter that the franchise did not re-sign him and hasn't returned for any team celebrations in recent years, he also seemed to realize that retiring was the right choice:

> I had talked to a lot of people about what I should do with my situation, and what they kept saying back to me, and which was not a sufficient reason, was, "Troy, you played 12 years in the NFL, you won Super Bowls, won individual awards. You have a legacy." And I just kept saying, "First of all I don't care about a legacy. Second of all I play the game because I enjoy it." But when I started this process and started to debate whether I should come back or should I play, that was kind of the sign for me to say "Whoa, if you're just even debating it maybe you shouldn't play anymore," because what I do know about this game is it takes a lot—a lot—of commitment just to be an average player.[28]

So, Polamalu reluctantly retired after twelve seasons, but his place in league and team history is certainly secure. He along with the Ravens' Ed Reed redefined the position, one that has been largely ignored by Hall of Fame voters over the years. His dynamic and athletic style was hard to ignore, especially with the fact that he almost single-handedly changed the offensive game plans of opponents to try to keep Polamalu from beating them. While it's not certain he will be a first-ballot Hall of Famer, his spot in Canton is almost secure. It shows that perhaps the Steelers should trade up more often in the first round.

42. JAMES "COOL PAPA" BELL

Homestead Grays, 1932, 1943–46
Pittsburgh Crawfords, 1933–37

When speaking of the fastest men in baseball history, the all-time stolen base list is usually where one goes to compile the roster. Men like Rickey Henderson, Lou Brock, Ty Cobb, Max Carey and Honus Wagner are among the leaders in that category. Then there are the baseball historians who dig deeper and also look outside the major leagues. It's there they find one of the greatest players the Negro Leagues ever produced, a man many feel was the fastest of all time—a player who was a star for both Negro League franchises that represented the Steel City, the Crawfords and the Homestead Grays. His name is James Thomas "Cool Papa" Bell.

The stories of Cool Papa are timeless. The great Satchel Paige once said of him that he "was so fast he could flip the light switch and be in bed before the room got dark."[29] Or that "one time he hit a line drive right past my ear. I turned around and saw the ball hit him sliding into second."[30] Now the thought of a player running from home to second and being hit by his own line drive is obviously an exaggeration, but it was Paige's way to describe just what impressive speed Bell had.

The name "Cool Papa" is one of the legendary nicknames in all of sports. It came about not because of anything the speedy outfielder did on the base paths, but rather what Bell did on the mound. Born in Starkville, Mississippi, in 1903, Cool Papa came up in the Negro Leagues as a pitcher. He had a repertoire that included a knuckleball, a curve and a screw ball. Like the great Juan Marichal, who threw his pitches from all different angles, Bell could throw his pitches from three different angles. In 1922, Hall of Famer Oscar Charleston came to bat against Bell with men on base, and the young nineteen-year-old hurler struck him out. His manager, Bill Gatewood, thought he was cool under pressure. To give the nickname more flair, he added "Papa" to the end of it, thus one of the most famous monikers in baseball history was born. He would be forever known at that point as "Cool Papa" Bell.

Two years after his impressive beginning as a professional pitcher, his days on the mound were over. An arm injury reduced his velocity and forced a move to center field, where his speed would hopefully be an asset. He had a quick release, which helped overcome his throwing issues, and worked on becoming an effective switch-hitter. Changes from pitcher to everyday

There were few if any baseball players in the history of the game who were as fast as James "Cool Papa" Bell. Elected to the Baseball Hall of Fame in 1974, Bell was an incredible player on the Pittsburgh Crawfords between 1933 and 1938, playing center field in Pittsburgh for some of the greatest Negro League teams of all time. *Courtesy of the Pittsburgh Pirates.*

player rarely have such results, but the Negro Leagues soon found out that pitching was not his strongest position.

Bell was magnificent. Playing for the Grays and the Kansas City Monarchs in 1932, he hit .326 while posting an .803 OPS, remarkable for a man who didn't hit a home run during the season. In 1933, he was lured to the Pittsburgh Crawfords by owner Gus Greenlee, along with several other all-star Negro League talents. The group that included Bell, Josh Gibson, Oscar Charleston, Judy Johnson, Satchel Paige and Leroy Matlock would form one of the great dynasties in the circuit's history. While the franchise's stay in Pittsburgh was short, eight seasons, it was impactful, winning three Negro National League championships in 1933, 1935 and 1936. Many Negro League historians considered the 1935 squad as the strongest team the circuit ever produced. Bell was certainly a pivotal part of those championship squads.

He played with the Crawfords for five seasons during their peak in the Steel City, hitting under .300 only once with a .279 mark in 1936. Other than that subpar campaign, Cool Papa was phenomenal. With batting averages of .300, .332 and .321 his first three seasons at Greenlee Field with Pittsburgh, Bell finished his career with the legendary club posting a .362 average and career high .966 OPS.

Following the season, Cool Papa went to Mexico, where he played the next four years. In 1940, he broke the .400 plateau, hitting .437 with Tampico. He came back to the United States in 1942 and signed with the Chicago American Giants at thirty-nine years old before coming back to Pittsburgh to play with the Homestead Grays his final four seasons.

Despite the fact that the fleet center fielder was now in his forties, Cool Papa Bell wasn't slowing down. In the last four years of his remarkable career in the Negro Leagues, Bell was still one of the best players in the circuit. He hit .334 between 1943 and 1946, including a .393 mark his last campaign, once again eclipsing .900 in OPS at .903, again while, incredibly, not hitting a homer.

After that, he played four more seasons in the Negro minor league and was offered a shot to play with the St. Louis Browns in 1951. He was forty-eight years old at the time and had to know that he wouldn't be an effective player at the major-league level, instead becoming a scout for the club until it moved to Baltimore in 1954. Bell became a security guard and custodian in St. Louis until retiring in 1970. Four years later, he was given the game's highest honor when he was elected to the Baseball Hall of Fame. Cool Papa Bell stayed in St. Louis until he passed away in 1991 at eighty-seven years old.

He was truly one of the baseball's most extraordinary players, being ranked as the ninth-greatest Negro League player in an ESPN.com poll in 2015, and those who saw him run could attest to his incredible speed. He reportedly rounded the bases astonishingly in only twelve seconds, and it was said that he would beat out throws to first on two-hop infield hits, something that is rarely accomplished. There were legends that he scored on a sacrifice bunt and would often turn singles into triples with two stolen bases. Bell was the kind of player who could change the course of a game with his speed. While he was definitely one of the fastest players the game has ever seen, there are some who question the legend that he was the fastest.

Glen DuPaul of the website Behind the Box Score pointed out that while certainly fast, Bell was only credited with having 132 stolen bases in 3,672 plate appearances, approximately 22 per year over six major-league seasons—good, but not to the level of the game's best. Seamhead.com, considered one of the authorities on Negro League statistics, has him with 141, a 28 per season average over the course of a 162-game season. While DuPaul uses sabermetrics to rate the game's all-time fastest players, bringing Bell in at sixth behind Cobb, Charleston, Carey, Wagner and Pete Hill, the inconsistencies of Negro League statistics would bring into question any such analysis.

Look at any two sites that carry Negro League statistics and you will find varying numbers. In the great book by James Riley, *The Biographical Encyclopedia of the Negro Leagues*, he credited Bell as having 175 stolen bases in under 200 games, a feat that certainly would put him among the best.

Regardless of the various opinions of how fast Cool Papa Bell was, he was one of the best players the Negro Leagues produced and a worthy Hall of Famer. While he may have not made it to his bed before the room got dark after turning off the light switch, people who saw him play attest, almost to a man, to how his speed could dominate a game—a talent that baseball fans in Pittsburgh were lucky enough to see in his prime.

41. SIHUGO "SI" GREEN

Duquesne University (Basketball): 1953–56

When you speak of the greatest players who ever donned a Duquesne basketball uniform, usually the conversation veers toward Dick Ricketts and a man from Brooklyn, New York, who played by his side for two seasons—two campaigns where the program reached heights it never had before or since. His name is Sihugo Green.

Recruited for Duquesne by Dudey Moore out of Boys High School in Brooklyn, where he averaged 25 points per game and was named to the All-Metropolitan New York team while leading his squad to the city championship, Green arrived in the Steel City in a unique way. It was very different when compared to the celebratory atmosphere that a five-star recruit comes to college in the twenty-first century.

Marino Parascenzo, a writer with the *Pittsburgh Post-Gazette*, told a story the day after Green's death in 1980 about his first trip to the Bluff to meet his new coach when he found no one on campus. He was instructed to go to a bank in the Hill District if no one was at the school and see a man named Buck Gefsky. According to the story, Green went into the office. "He was carrying a cardboard box. It was his suitcase, turned out. High-cut tennis shoes were slung over his shoulder, the laces tied together. He had just arrived from Brooklyn and said and he was supposed to see Coach Dudey Moore but there was no one at the college."[31] Gefsky called the coach, who asked him what the player's name was. When he responded that it was Green, Moore screamed, "What! Well chain him to the gawddam desk 'til I get there!"[32]

Moore was so excited because he knew just what kind of talent Green had. After a season on the freshman squad, he became a star on varsity his sophomore season. Averaging a team second-best 13.5, Green had a breakout contest in an exhibition against the Quantico Marines in Monessen on February 6, 1954. That night, he led all scorers with 25 points and played well defensively in the 81–68 victory. The school's media guide in 1954–55 exclaimed that it was "one of the greatest exhibitions of basketball ever seen." The sophomore was named by several organizations as the national Sophomore of the Year, as well as a third-team All-American.

Green was described as quirky by some and a hypochondriac by others. He said that he couldn't jump unless he had his jumping socks on, and legend had it that a game they were playing had to be delayed until he found his proper jumping socks.[33] Often he would complain of one malady or another, but many said that when he was suffering the most he would play his best. It was a claim that was on display many times in the team's NIT championship season. In the tournament's final contest against Dayton, he netted 33 points after complaining of a stomach flu before they left for New York. He also had his foot stepped on in the quarterfinal and a bad toothache in the days before the semifinal.

Driving to the basket to the right in the Duquesne uniform is Sihugo Green. Green was a two-time consensus All-American while with the Dukes and helped the school become the only one in NCAA history to have two players in two consecutive years be the the 1st pick in the NBA draft when he was chosen by Rochester in 1956. *Courtesy of Duquesne University Athletics.*

Assistant coach and future Duquesne head man Red Manning described the Brooklyn native this way: "Si never said a word. He always wore his jumping socks, those thick gray ones with a green trim. The kind hunters wear. That was his superstition. Si's touch outside with a line-drive jumper was pretty good, but he could tell you he was going around you and he'd still get around you. He would give you a fake and a real big first stride. Si was his own man. He would play hard against tough teams; ease up on teams he knew he could beat."[34]

As a junior, Green was selected to seven first-team All-American squads and joined his teammate Dick Ricketts on the consensus first team. It was an amazing season that was a prelude to a senior campaign that was filled with superior individual performances, although it was disappointing from a team standpoint. The Dukes slipped to 17-10, losing in the second round of the NIT. He was without Ricketts for the first time, and it showed. It was a duo that Coach Dudey Moore claimed "were both real All-Americans, neither went for personal glory but instead always was ready to help the other get a score."[35]

There just wasn't enough depth for them to seriously think about defending their national championship. Green averaged a career-high 24.5 points per game and a team-high 13.5 rebounds while being named as a consensus first-team All-American for the second consecutive season. He also had the honor of making the cover of *Sport Magazine* that year, but it was a disappointing season for the program, which hoped to capitalize with more success after its long-awaited national title.

Sihugo graduated with a business degree and wanted to go into advertising, but his plans were diverted when he was the first player selected in the NBA draft. It is the only time in the history of the sport that players from the same school had that honor in two consecutive years, Dick Ricketts being the top choice the year before.

The Rochester Royals took Green, hoping to take advantage of his all-around skills that included good quickness, a great outside shot and his ability to play defense. That same jumping ability allowed Moore to use him against players much taller, including seven-foot center Bill Uhl of Dayton, whom he so aptly guarded in the NIT final, even blocking one of his shots.

Green went on to have a solid NBA career, although somewhat disappointing considering his lofty draft status. In the midst of a fine rookie campaign, when he averaged 11.5 in thirteen games, Green was drafted into the armed forces and missed the entire 1957–58 season. When he returned, the team had moved to Cincinnati, and Green suffered through many bouts of dizziness that kept him out of the lineup. There were fears that he had a brain tumor, but it turned out to be a contusion on the brain. With the team fearing that he would not ever be the player originally envisioned, Green was dealt midseason to the St. Louis Hawks for Med Park, Jack Stephens and cash.

The Brooklyn native ended up playing nine seasons with the Royals, Hawks, Chicago Packers and Zephyrs. He also wore the uniform of the Baltimore Bullets and Boston Celtics, with whom he won his lone NBA championship before retiring following the 1965–66 campaign. The greatness predicted ended up in mediocrity, as he averaged 9.2 per contest during his career. A collegiate contemporary and opponent, Tom Heinsohn, said of the Duquesne alum, "He wasn't much of an NBA player; he had all this hype because he came out of New York."[36]

While he was a better player than Heinsohn's evaluation indicated, Green's career was not befitting of a number-one overall pick. When his name is mentioned in NBA circles, it's usually when discussing the mistake Rochester made in passing on Bill Russell to draft the Dukes All-American.

Green's life after basketball was filled with both success and tragedy. Achieving the position of vice-president of Operations for Associated Textile Systems Inc. in Lawrenceville, Pennsylvania, Green found himself in trouble in 1968 when he was shot by a woman after an argument. He suffered wounds to his shoulder and legs. Surviving the incident, the Brooklyn native continued his career with the textile company. Twelve years later, suffering from lung cancer, Green passed away at forty-six years old. A scholarship in his name was set up soon after his death that benefited troubled teenagers in Pittsburgh.

The effect Sihugo Green had on Duquesne University basketball was resounding. Green cemented himself as one of the true icons in school history, scoring 1,605 points, still the eighth-best mark, good for a 19.8 career average, which is second behind Wille Somerset's 22.7. The university gave him the ultimate honor by retiring his number, 11, in 2001. His NBA career may not have been what he expected, but when it comes to Duquesne basketball, he is the school's only two-time consensus All-American and a man who helped give it its only national championship.

Chapter 2

THE CLASSIC WARRIORS

ATHLETES 40–31

40. LAURYN WILLIAMS

Track and Field, 2002–13
Bobsledding, 2013–15

When Lauryn Williams was a student at Rochester High School in Rochester, Pennsylvania, a small community in Beaver County about twenty-five miles outside the city of Pittsburgh, a spot in the Summer Olympics with the United States track team was certainly something within her reach. After all, she had won state titles her junior and senior years and was named an All-American as a junior in both the 100- and 200-meter dash. She received a scholarship offer to the University of Miami, Florida, where she won several Big East titles and was a gold medalist in the 100-meter dash at the 2002 World Junior championships. While being a track Olympian was a realistic goal, there was more to the story of Lauryn Williams that put her in rare company. Before the 2014 Winter Olympic Games in Sochi, only one American athlete in Olympic history had medaled in both the Winter and Summer games. After Williams made the USA bobsled team that year, that number would double.

Williams was ten years old when the young prodigy seemingly became enamored of track and field after a visit to the Carnegie Science Center in Pittsburgh with her father. At that point, there was a ten-meter-long display where people were challenged to defeat a likeness of the great Florence

Griffith Joyner in a short race, presumably to show just how fast Joyner was. Williams spent a good portion of the day trying to defeat Joyner and impressed all who witnessed her efforts. It was a moment that ignited her competitive spirit. "I was just being competitive at anything. I wanted to be the best at everything."[37] Her life was not easy, as she spent part of the year with her mother in Detroit and the rest with her father in Rochester, who was an integral part of her success and was battling leukemia. "He never let it [his illness] get him down. He always kept the burden on himself. It was definitely sad on his bad days, but he was always a positive person. He kept going."[38]

Despite the issues, Williams was already making a name for herself when she graduated from high school in 2001. At Miami, she continued her ascent as a track star, winning the 60- and 200-meter dashes in the indoor championships and the 100-meter on the outdoor. Williams was named the outstanding athlete at the indoor meet and an All-American for the 100-meter in the NCAA outdoor meet. A year later, she won three Big East indoor titles and achieved All-American status three more times, garnering a spot on the USA team in the 2003 Pan-American Games in Santo Domingo. She surprised the track world with an impressive gold medal performance there.

The year 2004 would prove to be a banner time for Williams as she not only graduated from Miami with a degree in finance while being a member of the Iron Arrow Honor Society, the highest honor a student can attain at the university, but also became a national story in track and field. That year, she became the first woman to win the Big East 100-meter title three consecutive years and won the NCAA 100-meter dash. Lauryn finished her collegiate career with eleven Big East championships and was a nine-time All-American.

With her impressive collegiate career behind her, in 2004 she was invited to the Olympic Trials and garnered the last spot in the 100 on the track team by finishing third. Her father now had kidney complications and needed dialysis, so he couldn't afford to make the trip to Athens to see his daughter run at the Olympics. When word of this came out, donations started coming in to help her father and her family make the trip to Greece—$20,000 was raised, including the $10,000 necessary for the six dialysis treatments David Williams would need while there. The efforts were well worth it, as they got to see Lauryn win a silver medal in the 100. The success continued a year later with two gold medals in the 100 and 4x100 relay at the world championships.

Much was expected from Williams in the 2008 Olympics at Beijing, but a dropped handoff between teammate Torri Edwards and herself resulted in the team being disqualified in the semifinal. It was a repeat of her performance in the 4x100 in Athens four years earlier, when she took off before securing the baton. Lauryn recalled the 2004 situation: "We got off to a great start. I saw [my teammate] coming down the straightaway. I turned, I took off, and thought, 'Hey where is this stick?' And the next thing I knew, the opportunity had come and gone. I just embarrassed our whole country; this is all my fault."[39] Williams went on to finish fourth in the 100-meter and left China without a medal.

Four years later, Lauryn Williams got a final chance in the 4x100 relay and made the most of it, helping the team to the gold medal. In 2013, she retired from competition, finishing her career with an Olympic gold medal and a silver. A fine career for most, but Williams wasn't finished.

In the bobsled event, arguably the most important part of the race is the start, and a strong sprinter could be the difference between just finishing and medaling. In 2013, Williams wanted to put that theory to the test, so she took on the challenge of medaling in the Winter Olympics.

She went to a rookie camp in 2013 and teamed up with Elana Meyers Taylor, who had won a bronze medal in the two-women event at the 2010 games in Vancouver. Williams's sprinting talent proved to be very effective, as six months later, the two qualified for the 2014 games in Sochi. Lauryn was not the only sprinter competing in the women's bobsled event in 2014, as fellow sprinter Lolo Jones was teamed with Jazmine Fenlator, but Williams and Meyers Taylor seemed to be the superior team, coming into the games ranked number one in the World Cup point standings. After setting a track record in the first heat, Williams and Meyers Taylor sat in first after the first two runs. They slipped a little in the final two runs, finishing second by a tenth of a second.

With their finish, they secured a silver medal, giving Lauryn Williams her place in history. Only Eddie Eagan had won a medal in both the Summer and Winter games for the United States, capturing a gold as the light-heavyweight champion in boxing at the 1920 Antwerp games before winning another twelve years later in Lake Placid in the bobsled. Williams became the first American woman to do so and the fifth Olympian overall to win a medal in the Winter and Summer games. It was a moment that began many years before at the Pittsburgh Carnegie Science Center with a ten-year-old challenging a cutout of Florence Griffith Joyner.

39. AARON DONALD

The University of Pittsburgh (Football), 2010–13

The history of football at the University of Pittsburgh is a rich one. Ninety-two times a player has been designated as a first-team All-American, twenty-four have been elected to the College Football Hall of Fame and eight found their way into the Pro Football Hall of Fame, but only one has captured four major collegiate awards in a single season—the most decorated athlete in the program's history, Aaron Donald.

While Pitt football has struggled on the national level for the better part of the past four decades, there have been some memorable players who have worn the blue and gold, with Donald being one of the best. Recruited by former coach Dave Wannstedt, the All-American was considered one of the most dominant defensive players to come out of Western Pennsylvania in the twenty-first century. A two-time All-State defensive lineman out of Penn Hills, Donald was a member of the *Pittsburgh Post-Gazette*'s "Fabulous 22." *Scout* rated him as the twenty-fifth-best defensive tackle in the country and the eighth-best overall player in the state. It ended up being quite a recruiting coup for Wannstedt.

Even though he was a decorated recruit when he came to Pitt in 2010, he was considered small for the position at six-foot-one, 285 pounds. What he lacked in size, Donald made up for with an incredible work ethic and determination: "[When] you've got older siblings to look up to push you and motivate you, that makes my job a lot easier. When I wanted to sit down and watch TV and those guys are outside doing extra work, I'm like, 'Let me get up, let me do some extra work too.' That's how it's always been in my household, you know we always fed off each other, pushed each other so my family is definitely a huge part of my success and where I'm at today because of the way they pushed me and who they made me as a person and as a football player, I give a lot of credit to them."[40]

The inspiration from his family paid off. After playing as a reserve in his first nineteen games for the Panthers (eleven as a freshman and the first eight contests his sophomore season), he burst on to the scene, quickly starting the final five games at defensive end that second campaign. Despite the fact he spent most of the season as a reserve, he became the fifth Pitt player in twenty years to garner more than ten sacks in a season, finishing with eleven. Fox Sports was able to look past the fact he only

No. 97, Aaron Donald of the University of Pittsburgh, became the most decorated single season player in the football program's history. In 2013, he was a consensus All-American as well as the best defensive player in the country, winning the Bronko Nagurski Award, the Chuck Bednarik Award, the Outland Trophy and the Lombardi Award. *Courtesy of the University of Pittsburgh Athletics.*

started five games and named him to the Foxsportsnext.com second-team All-American squad.

Donald moved to defensive tackle in 2012 and continued to excel, being named first-team All–Big East and setting a career high with 13 tackles against UConn, but his sack total dropped, finishing with only 5.5. His senior campaign, though, would be special. With the Big East deteriorating, Pitt decided to end its long relationship with the league and move up to one of the power five conferences, the Atlantic Coast Conference. The year 2013 marked the Panthers' initial campaign in the circuit, and Aaron Donald was the face of the program as it entered ACC play. The league learned quickly that he was the best defensive player in the country.

After making an inauspicious debut in the ACC with a 41–13 loss to Florida State, the Panthers settled down as Donald became a problem for opposing offenses. He was named as the Chuck Bednarik Defensive Player of the Week with two sacks in a 14–3 win over Virginia and then completely dominated the Georgia Tech offensive line in what some considered the most dominant defensive effort of the year with eleven solo tackles, six for losses, two forced fumbles and a sack. For his efforts, he was named Defensive Player of the Week by many who choose the award.

He continued his tremendous season and finished the campaign with several impressive stats—11 sacks while leading the nation in tackles for loss with a 2.2 per game average, incredible for a defensive tackle. He was unblockable for most of the season, and most coaches who faced him felt that Donald was the most intimidating force in college football. He was a unanimous first-team All-American, and on the evening when college football announces its major awards, the honors kept coming in. He was named the Bronko Nagurski Award winner, given to the Defensive Player of the Year by the Charlotte Touchdown Club; the Chuck Bednarik Award, which is the Maxwell Football Club's version of the best defensive player in Division I; Pitt's second Outland Trophy winner as the nation's best interior lineman (Mark May won the trophy in 1980); and the school's second Lombardi Award recipient as the nation's top defensive lineman or linebacker (Hugh Green captured this award also in 1980).

When the awards were over, he had four major national awards; only Tony Dorsett and Hugh Green came close, winning three in 1976 and 1980, respectively. To go along with his consensus All-American status and the four trophies he won, Donald was also named the Athlon Sports National Defensive Player of the Year, CBSSports.com National Defensive Player of the Year, Lindy's Sports National Defensive Player of the Year, ACC Defensive Player of the Year, Athlon Sports ACC Defensive Player of the Year and first-team All-ACC.

Even though he was considered the best defensive player in the country, Donald went into the NFL combine feeling as if he was still not respected for his talent by the media. He was confident, though, that when NFL scouts saw the film, they would make him a high draft pick. "I feel like I'm more underrated when it comes to TV coverage. I don't get talked a lot about as far as the draft or top players at the position, but I feel like at the end of the day scouts know who I am. Teams know who I am. They watched the film and that's what it's about. It's about what the teams like. I feel like they watch film and they know what they want. As far as everything on TV talking about the draft and my name not being involved in it very often, that doesn't get to me at all. It's about what these teams want. There's 32 teams that are picking, so the moment I get picked by one of those teams the other stuff doesn't matter."[41]

His confidence paid off, as he was selected in the first round with the 13th pick by the St. Louis Rams (now the Los Angeles Rams). Donald has been as impressive in the NFL as he was at Pitt, being named first-team All-Pro four times in his first five seasons and winning the NFL Defensive Rookie of the Year in 2014 and the NFL Defensive Player of the Year in both 2017 and 2018. In 2018, he signed the richest contract ever given to a defensive player in NFL history. He proved to be well worth the money, as he garnered 20.5 sacks after signing the pact, the seventh most in NFL history for a single season. With all his success in one of America's biggest cities, he still considers himself a Pittsburgher through and through. "That's where blue-collar football comes from in my eyes...the city of Pittsburgh, so I'm just happy to be a guy that was born and raised in a great city."[42]

38. CARLTON HASELRIG

The University of Pittsburgh–Johnstown (Wrestling), 1986–89
Pittsburgh Steelers, 1989–94

The story of Carlton Haselrig is as impressive as it is tragic. At its best, it's about an athlete who achieved something that no one had in the past and, ironically, because of his incredible efforts, no one will ever do again. It's also about a man who, with no prior experience, became an NFL All-Pro—a player whose coach felt would end up in Canton and then had it all come crashing down, the victim of addiction. In the end, it was a story about a man who has seemingly found himself and was given the honors he so richly deserves.

It started in 1984, when Haselrig was a student at Johnstown High School. The school had no wrestling program, and the future Pittsburgh Steeler wanted to wrestle. The Pennsylvania Interscholastic Athletic Association (PIAA), the organization that runs high school sports at the state level in Pennsylvania, allowed schools to have students not part of a program participate in championships in swimming, golf and tennis, but not wrestling. His uncle, Brice Haselrig, who was a wrestling coach at the University of Pittsburgh at Johnstown, and a man named Damian Zamias, who would become the coach for a one-man wrestling team, persuaded the Johnstown School Board to sponsor a team made up of just Carlton Haselrig. They had six matches, with Haselrig winning each one before he won the heavyweight title at the Northeast Regional Tournament. Remarkably, he went on to win the PIAA heavyweight championship by decisioning Joe Smith of Northern, 10–7.

While he eventually became an All-Pro with the Pittsburgh Steelers, Carlton Haselrig was a legendary wrestler at the University of Pittsburgh–Johnstown. While at UPJ, he did what no other wrestler had done before or since: capture six championships, three in Division II and three in Division I. *Courtesy of the University of Pittsburgh–Johnstown Athletics.*

The state champion wanted to play football in college while also wrestling, so he accepted a scholarship to Lock Haven University, which while a Division II school in football wrestled at the Division I level. A knee injury in football that necessitated surgery kept Haselrig off the gridiron as well as the mat. He was also having trouble in the classroom and becoming homesick, so he decided to transfer to his hometown school, the University of Pittsburgh–Johnstown (UPJ). NCAA rules would force him to sit out a year after transferring, but it was time he needed to adjust to collegiate academics.

He didn't want to play anything at UPJ, just study. "My original plan was to come home and just go to UPJ and not play sports. I figured I would do therapy on my knee, take classes and then maybe transfer somewhere to play football. However, UPJ felt like such a good fit."[43] The knee injury proved to be fortuitous, as he eventually decided to wrestle with the Mountain Cats. Pat Pecora, who as of 2019 remains the wrestling coach at UPJ and is the first Division II coach in NCAA history to record 500 victories, tutored his new heavyweight to help him adjust. "He worked on academics as hard as he ever did on wrestling. It's like being an athlete. You have to believe you can do it."[44]

Finishing an impressive third in the 1986 NCAA Division II championship his freshman year, Haselrig set his sights on winning the DII title the next year—a goal he achieved. In the 1980s, the Division II and III champions automatically qualified for the Division I tournament. While this was an honor, no one in the lower divisions had ever actually captured the Division I crown. That streak ended in 1987.

After being named the outstanding wrestler in the Division II Eastern Regional, where he led UPJ to the region championship while winning the heavyweight title, he captured the Division II national championship, which sent him to the Division I tournament. He fought his way through the tournament and advanced to the final, where he went against Edinboro University's Dean Hall, who was coached by world champion wrestler Bruce Baumgartner. In a close match, Haselrig took down Hall in the final five seconds of the match to make history with the NCAA Division I title.

One year later, Haselrig wouldn't sneak up on anyone, as he now was the favorite to repeat his performance. The heavyweight defended his Division II title and was named the NCAA Division II Wrestler of the Year. Becoming the first lower-division wrestler to win a DI championship was hard enough—doing it twice certainly would be a challenge. Focused, Haselrig was up to it. He once again advanced to the championship, facing Dave Orndorff of Oregon State in the final. While it took an exciting move in the final seconds in 1987, he would need no drama in 1988, winning a decision easily, 12–2.

He was now a legend on campus, with a year to go in his career, matching the NCAA record with four championships. Carlton had a chance in 1989 to do what no other wrestler had: win a fifth and hopefully sixth title. He won his 117th consecutive match to capture his third Division II title in a row and with it the record for most NCAA championships at five. In the Division I tournament, he once again advanced to the final, facing Joel Greenlee of Northern Iowa. He had won a record 121 matches in a row at this point, and no. 122 may have been his toughest. The two combatants were in a close match, but the defending heavyweight champion was determined not to lose and won title number six, 1–0.

Haselrig had done what no one had done in the past, winning six championships, three in each division in three consecutive years. Haselrig finished with a 143-2-1 mark, including his then NCAA record 122 in a row, with an NCAA Division I tournament record of 15-0. While his goal was to win Olympic gold, his plans quickly changed one month later. The NFL had shown interest in him, and the six-time champion was determined to be a defensive tackle. He ran a 4.8 40-yard dash, and there was talk that he might be a late-round draft choice. Pittsburgh talk show legend Myron Cope thought that drafting Haselrig would be the smart thing for the Pittsburgh Steelers to do and spent most of his time on his show before the draft promoting his thoughts in hopes the Steelers would take notice. While most likely Cope's impassioned stance had no effect on the team's front office, they nonetheless decided to take the UPJ alum in the twelfth round.

He was moved from nose tackle to the offensive line, and by his third season, Haselrig was a starting right guard. One year later, he became the first Steeler guard in eighteen years to be selected to play in the Pro Bowl. His ascent in the NFL was remarkable, especially considering he had no practical college football experience. But his downfall would be just as dramatic. He became a victim of substance abuse. In 1991, he was arrested for drunk driving, and two years later, he drove his Jeep up the steps of the Pittsburgh Theological Seminary. His days with the Steelers were over, but he was given a chance to play with the Jets in 1995. After a good start, he disappeared after finding out that he would be suspended by the league for a year after a failed drug test.

His days in the NFL came to an end, but his issues unfortunately didn't. He went to jail in 1996 and was shot in a dispute a year later. In 1999, he went to jail on a disorderly conduct charge, and in 2003, after a dispute with his wife, he spent time in jail again. Finally, after all the altercations, Haselrig began to turn his life around. He spent some time in the MMA in 2008 and went back home to become an assistant football and wrestling coach at his high school in Johnstown. In 2016, with his troubles seemingly behind him, Carlton Haselrig was given an honor he richly deserved. After being named as one of fifteen wrestlers to the NCAA's seventy-fifth-anniversary team in 2005, he was elected to the National Wrestling Hall of Fame and given a day in his honor in his hometown.

With his life turned around and able to call himself a Hall of Famer, Carlton Haselrig owns an NCAA record that will never be broken. The year after he graduated, the NCAA voted not to give the Division II and III champions a spot in the Division I championships anymore, a rule most likely passed because of Haselrig's domination in both tournaments. His successes were unbelievable, and his decline was truly tragic. In the end, his story was remarkable and ended the way it should, with honors he deserves.

37. MIKE WEBSTER

Pittsburgh Steelers, 1974–88

It would have been nice if Mike Webster's contribution to the history of football was that of one of the greatest centers ever to play the game. A seven-time first-team All-Pro and a member of the All-Decade teams for the 1970s and 1980s, as well as a member of the NFL's seventy-fifth-anniversary squad, his achievements were many and his play impeccable. Unfortunately, Mike Webster is remembered most for his tragic post-career situation. After his death at fifty years old, an autopsy performed showed that the former star center suffered from chronic traumatic encephalopathy (CTE), a degenerative brain disease caused by brain trauma due to a history of repetitive hits to the head.

Dr. Bennet Omalu did the autopsy, and what he found was startling. The brain damage was extensive, the first discovery of CTE. It showed just how devastating the game of football is on the brain. There are lawsuits by many former players afflicted by the disease. A book was written about the shocking findings, and a movie was made. The league is still wrestling with the conflict of making the game safer in the future and keeping the sport America's pastime. While the findings were tragic and the end of Webster's life was heartbreaking, when it came to his play on the field, they were few if any centers who matched his excellence.

A part of arguably the most magnificent draft in history of professional sports in this country, Webster was chosen by the Steelers in 1974. He was taken after Lynn Swann (first round), Jack Lambert (second round) and John Stallworth (fourth round), giving Pittsburgh four Hall of Famers in their first five picks.

Coming out of Wisconsin, he was not only the captain of the Badgers in his senior season but also voted as team MVP, a spectacular achievement for a position that is rarely recognized for such awards. A third-team All-American his senior season, Webster was known for the strength he possessed with his intense year-round workouts, but he was considered undersized at only 225 pounds. He put on 30 pounds after being drafted and backed up Ray Mansfield at center as well as at guard his rookie season, but he showed enough potential to be named to the NFL All-Rookie team by the Pro Football Writers Association. After spending one more season as a reserve, he became a starter in 1976, splitting time between center (eight starts) and guard (six starts). A year later, Mansfield retired and Webster became the starting center.

The honors began in 1977 with a second-team All-AFC selection, and in 1978, the football world would know who the best center in the league was, as Webster made his first Pro Bowl and was selected first-team All-Pro for the first time. A pivotal part of the Steelers' third and fourth Super Bowl championship squads, the Wisconsin alum repeated both honors every year from 1979 to 1983, being named to first-team All-Pro and selected to play in the Pro Bowl each season. He showed his leadership in 1980 when he was selected as the team's offensive captain despite having Hall of Fame talent at almost every skill position. That year, he entered the NFL's Strongman Competition, where his incredible strength was on display as he won the event.

Mike Webster was as durable as he was strong. Going into the 1986 campaign, he stood only 5 games short of Mansfield's team-record 182 consecutive games. He dislocated his elbow in the final preseason game of the year against the Giants and sat out the first four contests of the regular season. He was named first-team All-Pro by the Newspaper Enterprise Association in 1987 and played his last game in a Steelers uniform in 1988, finishing his career in Kansas City in 1990.

The records were impressive, as he still holds the franchise mark for seasons played (tied with Ben Roethlisberger at fifteen) and games played (220). While not officially retired, his number, 52, has never been worn by another Steeler, and in 1997, he was elected to the Pro Football Hall of Fame. His actions in the months leading up to his induction showed the severe issues that Webster was dealing with after his retirement.

Following his election to Canton, it was reported that Webster was homeless, heavily in debt, ill without health insurance, about to be divorced and was in a lawsuit over a real estate investment. Webster responded to the accusation: "Because of all this publicity over my situation, people treat me like I'm dying or something. And I don't want their pity. Things in general, they're getting a lot better. I don't think it's anybody's business. I'm not destitute. From time to time, yes, I did sleep in my car and stay in my car. There's a broad definition of what living out of your car is. And yes, I slept in a train station one time. I had some things to think through. I wasn't broke. I wasn't in danger. I was just out of gas, tired and exhausted, and that's as far as I got that day."[45]

Despite suffering with his condition, his speech at Canton was inspirational: "You only fail if you don't finish the game. If you finish, you won. You have to measure by what you started out with, by what you overcame. Who wants to get to the end of their life and find out they haven't lived at all? You're going to fail—I did—but that's O.K. because in your life no one is keeping score. Just finish the game."[46]

As the years went on, the situation got worse. Two years after his induction, he fell into legal troubles by forging nineteen prescriptions to obtain Ritalin in the hopes that the stimulant could help control the symptoms of his brain injuries. He bought a taser gun and used it on himself to try and knock himself out so he could sleep. His memory was diminishing, and this once proud athlete seemed just a shell of himself.

There were lawsuits before he died. He and a lawyer named Bob Fitzsimmons, who was trying to help the former All-Pro, filed a disability claim with the NFL in hopes of getting Webster $12,000 per month in assistance. They felt that they had enough medical evidence to show that he deserved the award to help with his living and medical expenses. Instead, the NFL insisted on Webster seeing its own doctors. Then the NFL pension board unanimously awarded him the lowest amount it could, partial disability for $3,000 per month.

Sadly, the Hall of Famer died in 2002 at fifty years old. Following his death, Dr. Omalu, who was working for the Allegheny County Coroner's Office, did the aforementioned autopsy. Through his research, Dr. Omalu discovered extensive damage to Webster's brain and found things in his brain no one had before. He called the disease chronic traumatic encephalopathy and went to the NFL with his findings, thinking that its doctors would be appreciative. Instead, they questioned the existence of CTE. Their response upset Dr. Omalu. "I was naïve. There are times I wish I never looked at Mike Webster's brain. It has dragged me into worldly affairs I do not want to be associated with. Human meanness, wickedness, and selfishness. People trying to cover up, to control how information is released. I started this not knowing I was walking into a minefield. That is my only regret."[47]

The research spawned a book, *League of Denial*; a movie, *Concussion*; and a lawsuit by former players, in which the NFL agreed to pay $1 billion to those affected by brain injuries throughout their career. When he played the game, though, he was a beloved figure in the Steelers locker room. Terry Bradshaw remembered after his death, "I couldn't have been the player I was without him. He was so smart, so prepared for everything we would face in a game. We all worked hard, but none as hard as Mike did."[48] Bradshaw's words were perhaps the legacy that Webster would have wanted to be remembered for, but unfortunately his struggles and the autopsy that revealed CTE are Mike Webster's legacy in the game.

36. EVGENI MALKIN

Pittsburgh Penguins, 2006–19

The Pittsburgh Penguins were going through a losing era after the franchise was purchased by a group that included its greatest player, Mario Lemieux. They were coming through bankruptcy and knew that the only way to properly rebuild the club was through the draft. It was important that they not be wrong about the type of players they picked with high draft picks they would receive. Not only did General Managers Craig Patrick and Ray Shero not miss, they actually hit home runs in three consecutive drafts. In 2003, Patrick traded up from third to first to nab future Hall of Fame goalkeeper Marc-Andre Fleury. Coming off the lockout in 2004–5, the NHL had a drawing to determine who got the top draft pick. Luckily, the Penguins won the lottery and selected Sidney Crosby. Two draft picks, two Hall of Fame talents. There was a third draft that was in between these two in 2004. That year, Alexander Ovechkin was considered the top talent by a slim margin over a fellow Russian player. The Washington Capitals had the first pick and expectedly took Ovechkin. Pittsburgh had the second pick and chose his fellow countryman. While not as heralded as the top pick, they ended up doing okay. The player they chose was Evgeni Malkin.

Malkin didn't have the scoring prowess of Ovechkin, but as it turned out, they got a player who arguably is a better all-around talent. With three potential superstar players in the fold, the Penguin front office had two big challenges ahead of it: surround them with good enough players to win another Stanley Cup and figure out a way to get Malkin into the country.

After being drafted by the Pens, the NHL shut down in 2004–5 due to the aforementioned lockout, so Geno, as he is known in Pittsburgh, stayed to play with his hometown team, Metallurg Magnitogorsk. He wanted to take his immense talent to the NHL after playing one more season in Russia. There was one issue though: he had just signed another contract with Metallurg.

According to the young star, he signed the contract at three o'clock in the morning after hours of being persuaded by Metallurg management. He felt that signing the contract was a mistake and wanted to know how he could get out of it, so he called agent J.P. Barry. He faxed a resignation letter to the front office, which allowed him to leave under Russian law. Then, after his team flew to Helsinki for training camp, Barry met Malkin at the airport and hid him in a hotel until the 2004 first-round pick could secure a visa to the United States.

Evgeni Malkin was to Sidney Crosby what Jaromír Jágr was to Mario Lemieux, a Hall of Fame talent who combined with one of the game's greatest players to win Stanley Cups for the Pittsburgh Penguins. Malkin broke the 1,000-point barrier in 2019 for his career. He also captured the Conn Smythe Trophy in 2009 as the NHL's postseason MVP. *Courtesy of David Finoli.*

Once the visa was in hand, he met with Penguin officials and signed an NHL contract. Malkin was excited and relieved that he could now live his dream. He was a little concerned how Metallurg and their fans would react. "I definitely was a little concerned. But knowing him [Metallurg general director Gennady Velichkin] for so many years, I had to believe that he wouldn't go for any harsh measures toward me. After I had my visa obtained, I called my parents and informed them that everything was fine and I was doing great. They contacted Mr. Velichkin, and actually now they are doing well and Mr. Velichkin doesn't have any hard feelings against me."[49]

With the third of three stars now under contract, Pittsburgh immediately went from doormats to Stanley Cup contenders. Geno quickly showed his potential, scoring against Hall of Fame goalie Martin Brodeur in his first NHL game, and then he became the first player in eighty-nine years to score in each of his first six career contests. Both he and the Pens were successful that year, as Pittsburgh finished Malkin's rookie season with 105 points, good enough for their first playoff appearance since 2001, as the rookie had thirty-three goals and 85 points to capture the Calder Memorial Trophy as the league's Rookie of the Year. Safe to say that his magnificent career was starting off well.

The Penguins went to the Stanley Cup final his second campaign, and one year later, the seventeen-year wait for another Stanley Cup was over. Malkin had a wonderful season, winning the Art Ross Trophy as the league's leading scorer. Then he joined Mario Lemieux, Wayne Gretzky, Guy Lafleur and Phil Esposito as the only players since the expansion era in 1967 to win the regular season and the postseason scoring titles, amassing 36 points in twenty-four postseason games, including his first hat trick in a game against the Carolina Hurricanes in game two of the Eastern Conference final. Pittsburgh defeated the Detroit Red Wings to win the cup, and Malkin was awarded the Conn Smythe Trophy as the playoff MVP.

He continued his solid play, but on New Year's Day 2011, as the Penguins were taking on the Washington Capitals at Heinz Field for the Winter Classic, he would be thrust in a new role, that of team leader, as Crosby suffered a severe concussion that kept him out the better part of the next season and a half. Unfortunately, Geno also would miss the remainder of the 2010–11 campaign after tearing both his anterior cruciate ligament (ACL) and medial collateral ligament (MCL) in his knee. It was a tough situation for the franchise, but after successfully recovering from the surgery, Malkin responded to his new role in an amazing fashion. He won his second scoring title in 2011–12 and broke the fifty-goal plateau for the only time in his career as he was named the winner of the Hart Memorial Trophy, given to the league MVP.

The NHL once again went on strike in 2012–13, canceling half of the season. Malkin returned to his hometown and rejoined Metallurg until the lockout was over and was exceptional there, with 65 points in thirty-seven games. He came back when the NHL was ready to play but wasn't able to recapture the success he had been having up to that point. In the four seasons that followed, injuries began to mount as the former league MVP was unable to finish a full season during this period.

Both he and the team as a whole had a disappointing few years, Malkin with his injuries and Pittsburgh unable to win another Stanley Cup despite having so much talent. Finally, in 2016, the Penguins found the right mix as General Manager Jim Rutherford transformed the team from one that looked like it was about to end its successful era to a younger, quicker team that won back-to-back Stanley Cups in 2016 and 2017. In the latter cup run, Malkin found his touch, scoring 28 points in twenty-five games. In 2017–18, he continued the momentum, having his best year since his MVP campaign, playing in seventy-eight of the team's eighty-two games while netting 42 goals, the third-highest total in his career, as well as 98 points. A year later, he became only the eighty-eighth player in NHL history to eclipse the 1,000-point plateau when he accumulated two assists against Ovechkin and the Capitals on March 12, 2019.

Evgeni Malkin is universally considered one of the franchise's greatest four players—along with Lemieux, Crosby and Jaromír Jágr. He has been everything the franchise hoped he would when he was signed after hiding in a Helsinki hotel in 2006, and without him, Pittsburgh would most likely not have captured three Stanley Cups in a nine-year period.

35. JOHN WOODRUFF

Track, 1936–40

There were many obstacles for African American athletes in the 1936 Summer Olympics in Berlin. They were not wanted in the country by Hitler and his Nazi regime, and every time one would win a gold medal, it would anger the Fuhrer, as he considered it a slap in the face to his perceived philosophy of Aryan supremacy. Despite the challenges, many African Americans crossed the finish line first, the most famous being Jesse Owens with four gold medals. There was a less publicized victory that was as impressive as any of the others achieved by African American athletes, when a young twenty-one-year-old freshman at the University of Pittsburgh by the name of John Woodruff made one of the boldest maneuvers in Olympic history to capture the gold medal in the 800-meter run.

Woodruff was born in 1915 in Connellsville, Pennsylvania, which is located fifty miles southeast of Pittsburgh, and track and field wasn't the sport he intended on playing when he came to Connellsville High School. He wanted to play football but didn't make the team, which was okay with his mother because practice conflicted with his home chores. With the country in the midst of the Depression and the family needing money, John dropped out of school to try to get a job in a glass factory. They told Woodruff that they weren't interested in hiring an African American, so he decided to go back to school. At that point, an assistant coach on the football

A Connellsville, Pennsylvania native, John Woodruff took his track talent to the University of Pittsburgh. In 1936, he made headlines winning the gold medal in the 800-meter run at the Berlin Olympics in one of the most exciting races in the history of the event. Woodruff was one of a group of African American track athletes who won gold medals at the games, angering Adolf Hitler, who felt it was a slap in the face of his dream of Aryan supremacy. *Courtesy of the University of Pittsburgh Athletics.*

team who was also the head track coach, Joseph Larew, remembered the speed of Woodruff and talked the future gold medalist into trying out for the team. After failing at the shot put and the discus, he was persuaded into trying the half mile. He had misgivings at first but eventually gave it a try. As it turned out, he was perfect for the event. He had a long nine-foot stride, which prompted the nickname Long John, and his career in track soared, setting school and state records.

With the help of a local businessman, Woodruff secured a track scholarship to the University of Pittsburgh. There were twelve thousand students attending Pitt, and Woodruff would be one of only twelve African Americans on campus. He stayed at a YMCA in the Hill District of the city and worked cleaning Pitt Stadium as well as a basketball gym. His coach with the Panthers, Carl Olsen, and the editor of the *Pittsburgh Courier*, Robert L. Vann, also helped John with his living expenses. Their generous help was rewarded, as the Connellsville native would bring honor to his city, school and country just as his freshman season was finishing.

Woodruff finished second in a national Amateur Athletic Union (AAU) race and qualified for the Olympic Trials in the 800-meter run. The Connellsville native won that race impressively, only 0.1 second off the world record, and was headed off to Berlin as a favorite in the event.

The games had been awarded to Berlin in 1931, two years before Hitler took over. By the time they were to take place, there were calls from the United States and Europe to boycott the games for the reported human rights abuses that were going on in Germany. There were legitimate concerns, as his Nazi regime was promoting Aryan supremacy and the party's newspapers called for the exclusion of Jewish and black athletes. The Nazis demeaned the African Americans, calling them "black auxiliaries." It marked the first time the games were subjected to the political pressure that became more commonplace more than forty years later. The political pressure failed, and forty-nine nations sent their contingents to Germany for the event.

Black athletes would be successful and thwart Hitler's propaganda efforts. When Woodruff had his chance in the 800, he took advantage. He won his semifinal race impressively, starting out of the gate in a fast manner for the first lap. In the final, he was forced to run a different kind of race, one that included a bold strategy that most of the time is doomed to failure.

No American had won the event since Ted Meredith in 1912, and after the first 300-meter in 1936, it looked like the streak would stay intact. Woodruff would later recall, "Phil Edwards, the Canadian doctor, set the pace, and it was very slow. On the first lap, I was on the inside, and I was trapped. I knew that the rules of running said if I tried to break out of a trap and fouled someone, I would be disqualified. At that point, I didn't think I could win, but I had to do something."[50] Those who were there recall the American runner almost stopping, a tactic that most times would lose the race. Woodruff remembered it being a bolder move: "I didn't panic, I just figured if I had only one opportunity to win, this was it. I've heard people say that I slowed down or almost stopped. I didn't almost stop. I stopped, and everyone else ran around me."[51]

Falling to the back of the pack, the Pitt alum dashed by the competition with his legendary long strides, pulling to the front as he headed into the stretch of the final lap. He lost the lead but then regained it as he sprinted to the finish line. Woodruff held off Italy's Mario Lanzi at they hit the finish line. The final time was slow, slower than any 800 Olympic final since 1920, but it didn't matter. The man whom few considered an Olympic gold medal threat only a few months earlier was now an Olympic champion.

While there was prejudice all around him in Berlin, he rarely took notice. "The [German] people were very, very cordial. They just crowded around us and asked for autographs. It seemed like they were very anxious to be friendly."[52]

They weren't all friendly of course. Hitler and his Nazi Party were furious at the success of the African American athletes, and when Woodruff returned home, he found he wasn't always welcomed with open arms here either. The Connellsville native stayed at Pitt instead of traveling to a meet against the U.S. Naval Academy because the navy didn't want to run against a black athlete. In 1937, he broke the world record in the 800-meter at a meet in Dallas, only to have the record disqualified by the AAU later on, claiming that the track wasn't of regulation—despite the fact that a leading engineer at the time guaranteed the track was of regulation to within one thousandth of an inch. Later in life, Woodruff contended that "they just weren't going to give the record to a black man."[53]

Regardless of the way he was treated, his career was still phenomenal. He reportedly lost only one race in his career, in 1935 at West Virginia University, and was undefeated after winning the gold at Berlin. His track career ended prematurely, as World War II forced the cancelation of the 1940 and 1944 games. Woodruff served his country proudly in the Pacific during this war and then in Korea, eventually achieving the rank of lieutenant colonel. Before he went into the service, he received his masters at New York University and afterward worked in several capacities in New York, including as a teacher in the public school system.

Woodruff would be the last living medalist from the 1936 games, eventually passing away at ninety-two in 2007. His hometown still remembers the champion fondly. At a popular restaurant in the city of Connellsville, Bud Murphy's, there is a display on the wall that celebrates his achievements, while at the high school stadium there is a sixty-foot oak tree grown from an oak sapling awarded to Woodruff in Berlin with his medal. He gave the sapling to a friend after he returned from Berlin, who nursed it back to health and planted it, becoming the tree that honors him today. He is also remembered as a great ambassador to the University of Pittsburgh. At the time of his death, former Pitt chancellor Mark Nordenberg summed up his life: "John Woodruff's story was indeed a remarkable one. The people in our University community loved and respected John Woodruff. We stood in awe of his athletic achievements, but we also admired him as a human being who helped advance humanity's cause through the values he held and promoted. His lifetime and lifeline of achievements placed him and Pitt in the embrace of the vast and eternal."

34. BARRY BONDS

Pittsburgh Pirates, 1986–92

There are few who remember Barry Bonds's time in a Pirate uniform with the respect that is warranted for a two-time MVP. Instead, most recall his cantankerous demeanor, his public berating of team director of publications and special projects Jim Lachimia at Bradenton or the way he left the team following the 1992 debacle in game seven of the National League Championship Series (NLCS). All his challenges aside, Bonds was a spectacular all-around player who, even considering the accusations of heavy steroid use later in his career with San Francisco, is one of the greatest talents in the game's history. In Pittsburgh, his prime was short, but it's still one of the best that the fans of baseball in this area have ever witnessed.

The son of former Giants great Bobby Bonds, Barry spent his youth among baseball royalty. He hung around some of the game's greats and has the honor of having Willie Mays as his godfather. Bonds was a three-sport star at Serra High School in San Mateo, California, and decided to follow his father's footsteps in the national pastime when he accepted a baseball scholarship to Arizona State University. Barry started his collegiate career in a very successful manner, as the Sun Devils reached the College World Series his freshman season after Bonds was named MVP of the NCAA West II Regional Tournament. At the World Series, he made the All-Tournament team in both his freshman and sophomore campaigns, tying a record by collecting seven consecutive hits in 1984. He showed at ASU that he had elite potential, hitting .347 in his career, with 45 home runs and 175 RBIs

Barry Bonds went on to produce the greatest home run numbers in the history of the game, hitting a record 762 in a career and 73 in a season. Unfortunately, it was done under the suspicion of steroid use. Before the accusations, he was a star left fielder with the Pittsburgh Pirates until 1992, winning two MVP awards in three seasons. *Courtesy of the Pittsburgh Pirates.*

while being named to the All-Pac-10 team for each of his three years; he was also a first-team All-American his junior year.

When the future great was available with the 6th pick in the first round, the Pirates didn't hesitate to choose him. After a short year-and-a-half stay in the minors, Pittsburgh was convinced that Barry was ready for the majors and called him up on May 30, 1985, to begin one of the most dominant yet controversial careers in the sport's history.

The Scouting Report: 1987 analyzed Bonds's potential and predicted that he'd be a star. It claimed that he would be an excellent base runner, being tutored by the all-time stolen base leader Rickey Henderson and his father, and he had the speed and instinct in the field to be an elite defender, although the strength of his arm was questioned. Offensively, the analysts felt that his biggest challenge was hitting the inside fastball, claiming that his swing was too long and looping. Former Pirate Jim Rooker, who was a contributor to the book, summed up his potential: "Barry has a chance to become as good as his father, maybe even better...and he knows it. Bonds is thoroughly confident in his skills, so much so that some think its arrogance." He finished his assessment by noting, "He should become one of the game's brightest stars."[54]

Barry Bonds quickly fixed his swing deficiency, which allowed him to become a fearsome hitter. The skills he learned running the bases were apparent, as he did become one of the great base stealers of his era, and his defense was exceptional, allowing him to win eight gold gloves. But his less-than-average arm necessitated a move from center to left field. He also did become one of the game's brightest stars, and he did know it.

After struggling his rookie year with a .223 average, although he led the rookies in the National League in homers, RBIs and stolen bases, the Arizona State alum improved to .261 in 1987, smacking 25 homers and stealing 32 bases before hitting .283 his third campaign. Unfortunately, he hurt his left knee in June 1989 and struggled for most of the season, with a .248 average, hitting only .211 with men in scoring position. He eventually had arthroscopic surgery as the season was coming to an end. Through four seasons, he had shown potential but was not the star that some had projected. The team was young and exciting, but no one would have guessed what was ahead for Bonds and his teammates over the next three seasons.

With the Bucs picked fourth before the season began by *The Complete Handbook of Baseball*, claiming that the team was falling back to a second division team after a surprising 1988 campaign, the Bucs started quick, winning 22 of their first 33 games and 95 for the year, holding off the Mets to win their first division title in eleven years. Bonds was their best player, becoming only the second man in major-league history to hit 30 or more homers in a season while stealing 50 or more bases. For his efforts, he won his first National League MVP award and finally looked to become the player many experts thought he would.

The California native was in the beginning of what would be one of the great three-year stretches in franchise history, during which he would win two MVP awards and arguably should have won all three. His restlessness with Pirate management was also beginning to show. There was bitterness over his salary, as instead of negotiating for a contract they took Bonds to arbitration. He asked for $1.6 million, and the Pirates offered $850,000. The Bucs won the case, and the reigning MVP felt slighted. "We were both [he and teammate Bobby Bonilla, whom they also took to arbitration] really upset. Not about losing. Our feelings were hurt more than anything else. They had told us that Andy Van Slyke, Jose Lind and we were going to be the franchise players, then they won't even talk to us. It was like they lied to us."[55]

He also brought his surly attitude to spring training before the 1991 campaign. Once again he lost an arbitration case, being paid $2.3 million instead of the $3.25 he asked for, and he was not happy. An angry Bonds said that it didn't matter what Pittsburgh offered him when he was to become a free agent—he wouldn't sign with them. His anger was still apparent in the famed argument with Lachimia over a dispute about getting his picture taken by the media. Pirate manager Jim Leyland had had enough of his attitude and confronted his star in front of the players and the media, exclaiming, "One player's not going to run this club. If you don't want to be here, get the hell out of here. Let's get the…show over with or go home. If guys don't want to be here, if guys aren't happy with their money, don't take it out on everybody else."[56]

While the irascible star never seemed to forgive the team, it didn't affect him on the field. He led the league in on base percentage (OBP) and on base plus slugging (OPS) the next two seasons and eclipsed 100 RBIs each time, all while leading the Bucs to their second and third straight eastern division title.

Unfortunately, Pittsburgh was never able to win the National League Championship Series (NLCS) and advance to the World Series. It especially hurt when they blew a 2–0 ninth-inning lead against Atlanta in game seven of the 1992 NLCS, losing 3–2 as Bonds's throw to home plate was off line as the winning run scored.

He kept to his word and didn't sign with the Pirates when he became a free agent following the bitter loss to the Braves. The team seemingly had no interest in signing him either. Bonds inked a contract with San Francisco, where he spent his final fifteen years in the majors, and amassed figures that no one had ever seen in the history of the game, including 762 home runs in his career (73 in one season in 2001) and seven National League MVP awards. Instead of being adored and revered by fans across the country, he was accused of taking performance-enhancing drugs (PED), and many seemed to discount his achievements because of it. In 2007, he was indicted by a grand jury in San Francisco for four counts of perjury and one of obstructing justice, as he was accused of lying about his steroid use. He was convicted of obstructing justice in 2011, but in 2015, his conviction was overturned.

Bonds did admit to taking steroids, claiming that he thought they were flaxseed oil and arthritic balm and not PEDs, and despite the fact that his conviction was overturned, he still has not been elected to the Baseball Hall of Fame. As of 2019, he garnered no more than 59.1 percent of the vote in seven attempts (75 percent is needed for election). While many fans still hotly dispute his inclusion in Cooperstown, one thing is for certain when it comes to his days in Pittsburgh. He is one of the greatest ever to put on a Pirate uniform.

33. DAN MARINO

University of Pittsburgh (Football), 1979–82

There are few people who dispute who the greatest quarterback ever to take the field at the University of Pittsburgh was. Dan Marino's accomplishments are many while he played at Pitt. He was part of a team that went 42-6 in his four seasons, including three consecutive 11-1 marks in his first three campaigns. His junior season in 1981 garnered him first-team All-American status and is considered the finest season a quarterback ever had at the university. Through all the school marks he set when he left Pitt in 1982, some of which still remain in the record books today, it is the controversy and rumors that some claim led to his disappointing senior season that cloud his legacy at the school.

His decision to stay home to play for the Panthers was something that had all the earmarks of an inspirational movie. Growing up only a

When talking of the greatest quarterbacks ever to play at the University of Pittsburgh, the conversation usually begins and ends with the name Dan Marino. He was an All-American in 1981, breaking just about every Pitt passing record at the time. His thirty-seven touchdowns that year have never been surpassed. Also one of the greatest NFL quarterbacks of all time, Marino is enshrined in both the College and Pro Football Halls of Fame. *Courtesy of the University of Pittsburgh Athletics.*

few blocks from Pitt Stadium, Marino was a star at Pittsburgh Central Catholic in high school and walked through the campus every day on his way to school. While he excelled at football, he was also a star on the baseball team, earning four letters at Central on the diamond and being drafted in the fourth round by the Kansas City Royals. Marino and his family thought there was an NCAA rule saying he could play professional baseball while also accepting a college football scholarship, since it's what John Elway did at Stanford, signing a contract with the New York Yankees while playing football, and Danny Ainge was doing accepting a contract from the Toronto Blue Jays while also playing basketball at BYU. However, the NCAA insinuated that the star player at Central had to choose one or the other. According to Marino's father, Dan:

> I wanted to know why, if the rule read this way, other kids were getting both. I didn't get definite answer at first. Every time called I got someone else, and I was getting a run-around. Evidently they were saying Dan could not have both. Once the N.C.A.A. told me my son should make up his mind and decide which he wants—professional baseball or college football. At 17, a kid doesn't have to make up his mind. That's why he's going to college. Then they told me that if he accepted a bonus from the Royals he would no longer be in need, and thus that was why the N.C.A.A. did not permit him to also have a scholarship.[57]

To make matters worse, Kansas City apparently wasn't interested in having a high draft pick play both sports. Marino recalled, "They had me projected as a third baseman. What I wanted to do was what John Elway did. I don't think Kansas City wanted to spend the money for me to play baseball just three months a year. I hit near .500 in high school and I used to hit home runs like Reggie Jackson. When I hit them, they'd go a long way and I'd stay and watch them, then wave to the crowd. I had the home run trot down in Little League."[58]

Marino, of course, was also one of the best football players in the country. He was a Parade All-American and was named to just about every other All-American list there was. As he was considered the premier player coming out of football-rich Western Pennsylvania, Pitt heavily recruited the quarterback, wanting to make him the central piece of their recruiting efforts in 1979. It was a tough decision he would have to make between the two sports, but luckily for Panther fans, he chose to stay home and try to keep Pitt among the elite teams in college football.

His new coach, Jackie Sherrill, was thrilled with his choice, saying, "His commitment not only means a lot to our program but also to the city of Pittsburgh. During his prep career, Danny developed a following who want to see him develop."[59] It was a quick development his freshman season. Junior Rick Trocano began the year as the starting quarterback and led the Panthers to a 5-1 start. Against Navy, he pulled his hamstring, and the heralded freshman moved into the starting lineup. He was spectacular, going 6-0 as a starter, including a Fiesta Bowl victory over Arizona.

In 1980, the team finished 11-1, second in the nation, which was a prelude to 1981, when Marino was about to finally reach his massive potential. The team was incredible as Pitt stood at 10-0, ranked first as they entered a season-ending game against Penn State. Marino had been equally stellar in leading his team to the undefeated record. Against South Carolina, in a regionally televised 42–28 rout, he threw for 346 yards, breaking the then-school record with six touchdown passes, which gave him a two-consecutive-game school record of eleven touchdowns.

They were flying high and broke out to a 14–0 lead against the Nittany Lions, threatening to make it a rout as the star quarterback was leading them in for another score in the second quarter. Unfortunately, he tossed an interception, and then Penn State's defense began to confuse Marino as they rushed two players and dropped nine into coverage. Their rivals scored 48 consecutive points to upset the number-one team in the nation, 48–14, and end their championship hopes. Not wanting to let the entire season get away, Marino rebounded with arguably the top play in school history, tossing a 33-yard touchdown to tight end John Brown on fourth down late in the game to defeat Georgia in the Sugar Bowl, 24–20.

It was a phenomenal year for the junior, setting school records for yards in a season, 2,876, which as of 2019 is still seventh, and touchdowns with 37, a record that while equaled by Rod Rutherford in 2003 still remains the school mark. Marino was named as a first-team All-American and finished fourth in the Heisman Trophy race. Much was expected of both him and the team in 1982, but Sherrill left for Texas A&M and the expectations proved to be too much. After being ranked first with a 7-0 mark, they lost to Notre Dame, 31–16, and were defeated in three of their final five games to finish a disappointing 9-3.

The All-American's play suffered in 1982. He still threw for an impressive 2,432 yards but had a less than stellar 17-to-23 touchdown-to-interception ratio. As the NFL draft was approaching, rumors were going around about the Pitt quarterback. There was a rumor that he had flunked a physical with the New York Jets because of his injured knee, and other rumors of drug use seemed rampant. His coach in 1982, Foge Fazio, discounted the notion that Marino had been on drugs. In an article in the *New York Times*, he claimed that it was angry gamblers who were at the root of the rumors. "A lot of it was disappointment we didn't beat the point spread. That's where the viciousness came out. It's only a college game. But there was an NFL strike and no pro games, and a lot of people focused their attention on the colleges."[60] Even though they were unfounded, the rumors persisted, and he surprisingly was unselected as the Steelers' turn was coming up at number 21 in the first round. Dan Rooney and his father, Art, really wanted to select Marino at that point, but Noll went for defense by taking Gabe Rivera from Texas Tech. While Noll claimed that he thought Bradshaw still had a few years left, years later in 1992 he said on a talk show it might have been because of the rumors of recreational drug use that incensed Marino. "Those rumors have always been totally false and I'm extremely disappointed that Chuck Noll would even bring them up. I feel Noll has been irresponsible to comment on something that in fact has no truth to it."[61]

The Miami Dolphins selected Marino with the 27th pick in the first round, and it turned out to be one of the best late first-round picks in the history of the draft. He finished his NFL career in 1999 as the all-time league leader in attempts, completions, yardage and touchdowns and is enshrined in both the Pro and College Football Halls of Fame. He also was given the ultimate honor by his alma mater when his number at Pitt, 13, was retired. It may have been a bumpy end of his career at the University of Pittsburgh, but in retrospect, arguably their most heralded high school recruit lived up to his potential. He is the finest ever to play the position at Pitt.

32. DAVE PARKER

Pittsburgh Pirates, 1973–83

When it comes to rating the best players ever to don a Pittsburgh Pirates uniform, two players come together in the ratings and form the great debate: does one choose a player based on a great peak performance or for the complete time he was with the franchise? The two players in question are Barry Bonds and Dave Parker, Bonds having the incredible peak seasons while Parker had more sustained success. They are two players who share more than just their names close together in these rankings. While they both had talent rarely seen in Major League Baseball, both ended their time in the Steel City experiencing an intense bitterness from the fans.

Born in Grenada, Mississippi, in 1951, Parker's family moved to Cincinnati when he was five. They lived close to Crosley Field, where Parker became a Reds fan. He attended Courter Technical High School, where he was the three-sport star, playing basketball, football and baseball, but it was on the gridiron where he truly excelled. After his junior season, more than sixty schools were recruiting him to play college football, but an unfortunate knee injury in the first game of his final high school season ended his season and his football career.

The injury also ended his high school baseball career, but future Pirates general manager Harding Peterson liked what he saw out of Parker before the injury, and when it came the Pirates' turn in the fourteenth round in the regular phase of the 1970 draft (at that time MLB had a January draft made up of players who were previously drafted but didn't sign, with the regular phase in June), they made three-sport star out of Cincinnati their pick. It turned out as a fortuitous pick for Peterson as the Pirate draft was poor otherwise, only generating three major-league players: Parker, catcher Ed Ott (twenty-third round) and a pitcher named John Caneira, who was chosen in the eleventh round but didn't sign with Pittsburgh. Caneira had an abbreviated career on the mound, pitching eight games for the Angels in 1977 and 1978.

While Parker seemed like an impressive physical presence, he was not considered much of a major-league prospect at the time he was drafted. Scouts questioned whether he could hit the ball consistently in the air. He also had a reputation of being difficult with coaches.

With all the criticisms of his play before he was drafted, Parker quickly moved up the Bucs' system, hitting .319 with the Pirates' Gulf Coast League team and their AA team in Waterbury in 1970 before a .358 average with the Western Carolina League Monroe Pirates in 1971. After an impressive 22 home run/101 RBI campaign in Salem the following season, his minor-league days would soon come to an end.

Parker had been invited to the major-league camp in 1971 and 1972, acquitting himself nicely. In 1973, he was brought in again, but this time it was a different atmosphere. Their leader, Roberto Clemente, had recently been killed in a plane crash that put a pall over camp. Parker recalled, "Roberto Clemente was more than a humanitarian, more than our spiritual team leader, more than a baseball angel. Roberto was our brother, and I

For a period of time in the late 1970s, there was one name that always came up when you thought of the best players in Major League Baseball: Dave Parker. The Cobra, as he was called, could hit and had a rifle arm in right field that helped garner him the MVP of the 1979 All-Star game. Named the National League MVP in 1978, Parker signed the first contract in league history that averaged $1 million per year. *Courtesy of the Pittsburgh Pirates.*

never experienced a life shock this close to me. I started getting phone calls from friends and family, asking whether I heard what happened. Sometimes people want to connect with you over a tragedy, be there for you, and it's genuine and all, but sometimes you just need to sit down by yourself and process what happened."[62]

He would soon have the unenviable task of replacing a legend. He began 1973 in AAA at Charleston, being brought up in July to replace an injured Gene Clines, and spent some of 1974 on the injured list with a bad hamstring. He showed his potential both seasons, but in 1974, Murtaugh rarely played him against left-handed pitching. In 1975, the Pirates' legendary manager decided to begin the Dave Parker era by giving him the starting spot in right field.

The Cobra, as he was called, hit over .300 in his first two seasons as a regular, finishing third in the MVP vote in 1975, and by 1977, he had become arguably the greatest player in the game. He led the league in hits (215) and doubles (44) and won his first batting title with a .338 average but finished third once again in the MVP vote behind George Foster and Greg Luzinski. He captured the batting title in 1978 with a .334 mark and the slugging and OPS crowns while knocking in 117. This time it turned out different, as he won the MVP award decisively over Steve Garvey and Larry Bowa.

One year later, the Pirates made Parker's ascension as the best player in the game complete, signing him to the first contract in baseball history to average more than $1 million per year. Although the base was $775,000, with incentives and bonuses it reached the $1 million level. The Cobra was confident that he deserved the money and was indeed the best on the game. "There's only one thing bigger than me, and that's my ego. Take Willie Mays and Roberto Clemente and match their first five years against mine, and they don't compare with me. When I have trouble with a girlfriend or there's something else I need to push aside, I say, 'Wait 35 years and see if anybody comes along like me.'"[63]

He proved worthy, with a solid season in the Bucs' 1979 world championship campaign, hitting .310 with 25 homers and a .345 World Series average. Dave also won the MVP in the All-Star game with two outstanding putouts from right field. It would be the last superstar season for him in a Pirates uniform. The fans wanted perfection from a man making $1 million to play baseball and felt that his 1979 output wasn't good enough. His attitude certainly wasn't helping the situation. An angry Parker skipped the series parade, as his relationship with the city of Pittsburgh was strained. It got to the point that one fan threw a nine-volt battery at him during a game in 1980.

Knee, wrist and thumb injuries, combined with the fact that he had gained weight, were factors in Parker struggling at the plate over the next four seasons, as he fell under .300 for the first time in his career as a regular, hitting .295, .258, .270 and .279, respectively. At that point, it seemed like it would be best for all if Parker left, so he signed with his hometown Reds.

While his play on the field improved in Cincinnati, his reputation in Pittsburgh continued to slide as he admitted in testimony at the Pittsburgh drug trials in 1985 that he used cocaine on a consistent basis between 1979 and 1982 while in a Pirates uniform.

Even though he was a controversial figure in Pittsburgh, his career rebounded. Eventually, his nineteen-year career came to an end in 1991 after stints with Oakland, California, and Toronto, finishing with a .290 average, 339 homers, 1,493 RBIs and 2,712 hits. As the years went on, the animosity between Pittsburgh and Parker healed, as he has been welcomed back to the city by the fans. While he now suffers from Parkinson's disease, he has traveled back for various Pirate events over the last few years.

In 2017, he was considered for the Baseball Hall of Fame by the Modern Era Committee but fell short of the necessary twelve votes for inclusion. Despite the fact that he wasn't elected to Cooperstown, it showed that the negative incidents of his past were seemingly forgotten, and people were looking at Parker's résumé on the field while considering his career.

31. TERRY BRADSHAW

Pittsburgh Steelers, 1970–83

Terry Bradshaw had many ups and downs in his fourteen-season career as quarterback for the Pittsburgh Steelers. He was selected with the first pick in 1970 NFL draft with the hopes that he could do what no other quarterback in franchise history had done and lead Pittsburgh to their long-awaited first championship. By early 1974, he had struggled to the point that many felt he was nothing more than another Steeler first-round bust. Eventually, one year later, he discovered the talent many had projected for him and not only led the team to four Super Bowl titles but also, until Ben Roethlisberger came to town, was considered the undisputed best Pittsburgh Steeler quarterback of all time.

Bradshaw didn't have the pedigree of a potential Hall of Famer coming out of college. He did not play at a power five conference school, instead playing quarterback for Louisiana Tech. On top of being a talented quarterback, the Shreveport, Louisiana native was an incredible athlete, setting the national high school record in the javelin. He led the Bulldogs to a 17-4 mark and their first two bowl appearances in his final two seasons while breaking every passing record and total offense record in school history. Named as a first-team All-American in the college division (what the minor colleges were referred to before the division system began in the NCAA), his arm was incredibly strong and he had mobility that was rarely seen for a quarterback in the era.

While Bradshaw had all the apparent attributes to be a successful NFL quarterback, it wasn't until his performance in the 1969 Senior Bowl that the Steelers were convinced that the young quarterback was their pick. Despite the fact that he had a pulled hamstring and a rib injury going into the game, Bradshaw outplayed the power five conference prospects in the Senior Bowl and was named the game's MVP. Legendary Steelers coach Chuck Noll noted, "Terry is an extremely accurate drop back passer and he can take off and run with the ball if necessary....You have to get closeups to judge accurately. Terry convinced me that he was the most valuable piece of property in the college ranks."[64]

Even though the Steelers wanted to draft the young quarterback, it wasn't completely in their control, as they had to flip a coin with the Chicago Bears to determine who got the first pick. In 1969, the two iconic NFL franchises were suffering with the worst seasons in their respective histories, finishing with 1-13 marks. There were no tie-breaker systems then to determine draft order, so it was done via the flip of a coin. It was an unlucky franchise at the time, but this year their luck would change, as they won the flip and, with it, the 1st pick in the draft.

Before Noll took over as coach and Dan Rooney as president, the Pittsburgh Steelers were among the most laughable NFL franchises in the history of the league. By the fate of winning the coin flip with the Bears, the offensive cornerstone of the team was now theirs, if they wanted it. Dan Rooney said, "We had numerous trade offers for the No. 1 pick but most of them were for a lot of junk. But three or four were legitimate and we considered them carefully. However, we felt none offered us enough talent to equal the worth of Bradshaw."[65]

They decided to keep the pick and chose the Louisiana Tech alum, who was the first number-one pick in the draft from a small college school.

Perhaps his inexperience led to a difficult rookie campaign, during which he threw 24 interceptions with a 38.1 completion percentage. While interceptions were still an issue in 1971, he started thirteen of fourteen games and completed 54.4 percent of his passes for 2,259 yards, a vast improvement over his rookie campaign.

The team climbed to 6-8 in Bradshaw's second campaign, and a year later, with the young quarterback at the controls, the Steelers finally captured their first division championship in 1972. While he wasn't as effective in most categories as in 1971, he cut his interception almost in half as the team went 11-3 and faced the Oakland Raiders in their first playoff game in twenty-five years. The Hall of Fame quarterback didn't have his best of days against the Raiders, but on the Steelers' last offensive play of the game, he heaved up a Hail Mary pass with Pittsburgh down 7–6. The ball bounced off Jack Tatum (or the Steelers' John Fuqua, if you believe what Tatum had to say, which in 1972 would have made the play ineligible) and into the hands of Franco Harris for the game-winning score in a 13–7 victory; the play has been known since then as the "Immaculate Reception."

A shoulder separation curtailed his 1973 season, and in 1974 the league went on strike. Bradshaw stayed out of training camp with most of his teammates, but rookies and some of the veterans crossed the picket line to train. When the strike was settled, Bradshaw came back to camp and eventually lost his job to Joe Gilliam in what must have been the low point of his career. It highlighted the tough relationship between Noll and Bradshaw, Noll being a tough disciplinarian and Bradshaw needing encouragement. The Louisiana native was upset by being benched and wanted to be traded. He sat while Gilliam had two phenomenal games to start the season, but eventually Joe started to struggle. While the team stood 4-1-1, Noll felt it was best to insert Bradshaw back into the starting lineup. Not wanting to give the position back to Gilliam, he began to play like the quarterback everyone thought he could be.

He led Pittsburgh to back-to-back Super Bowl victories in 1974 and 1975, being named the NFL Player of the Year in the latter season. Bradshaw went on to become the only quarterback to lead his team to successive Super Bowl victories on two occasions, as Pittsburgh won their third and fourth in 1978 and 1979. It was in the final two championships that Bradshaw showed his ability to be at his best when the games mattered most, throwing for more than 300 yards in both Super Bowl XIII and Super Bowl XIV while being named the game MVP both times.

Terry began to realize that perhaps the way Noll pushed him was best for his career. While talking to Bradshaw in the team weight room, Art Rooney Jr. told him, "You may have gone somewhere and struggled and played for years and then got traded somewhere else, or been somewhere they brought a new coach in. Both of us, he made us look like we're something special. You actually are special." To which Bradshaw responded, "Aw, dammit, you're probably right."[66]

The Louisiana Tech alum continued to excel until injuries began to take their toll. He injured his thumb and broke his hand, which caused him to miss games in the early 1980s, and in 1983, he underwent surgery for torn muscles and tendons in his right elbow. He appeared in only one game in 1983, against the Jets in the season's next-to-last game, when the team was struggling and desperately needed a win to clinch their first division title in four years. His ability as a big-play quarterback was on display here, throwing for two quick touchdowns as the team took a 14–0 lead. He was taken out in the second quarter, as his arm proved not to be fully healthy, but his start led them to a 34–17 victory. It turned out to be Bradshaw's final game.

Six years later, the quarterback taken because of a lucky coin flip was enshrined in Pro Football's Hall of Fame. While he still seemingly has hard feelings toward Noll, saying recently that he respected him but didn't like him, and he is often critical of the Steelers' Ben Roethlisberger and Coach Mike Tomlin, the NFL legacy that is Terry Bradshaw rests in a black and gold uniform.

Chapter 3

THE STORIED COMPETITORS

ATHLETES 30–21

30. RALPH KINER

Pittsburgh Pirates, 1946–53

Ralph Kiner was a rock star in Pittsburgh when the athletic landscape of the city had few. The Pittsburgh Steelers, for the most part, were a struggling franchise, and many assume that the worst era of Pirate baseball was between 1993 and 2012. It was actually in the late 1940s and most of the 1950s when they produced some of the poorest teams ever to play the game. Kiner was seemingly the lone bright spot. Leading the league for seven consecutive years in home runs, dating some of the most beautiful actresses in Hollywood, being the player Pirate fans would come to see every day, as fans emptied out of Forbes Field after Kiner's last at bat, Ralph was everything a franchise legend should be. While he would be traded away after General Manager Branch Rickey came to town, Kiner nonetheless has a résumé that still makes him elite when talking about the greatest players the franchise has ever produced.

Born in Santa Rita, New Mexico, in 1922, Kiner was raised in California, where he became a professional baseball player. He played for a semipro team that was sponsored by the New York Yankees and was being courted by the Bronx Bombers to sign with them. Pirate scout Hollis Thurston was also interested in the slugger and not only convinced him that he would be stuck in the Yankee farm system for an extended period of time but also promised

Pictured is the Pirates' Ralph Kiner (*left*) and the Giants' Johnny Mize (*right*). After Kiner captured the 1946 home run title by one over Mize, the two tied in 1947 with fifty-one apiece. Kiner went on to win a record seven NL home run championships in a row and hit .301 in his eight-year career with the Bucs. *Courtesy of the Pittsburgh Pirates.*

him an invite to the major-league camp with the Bucs. He also gave him a $3,000 signing bonus and a promise of $5,000 if he made the Pirate roster. It was an impressive deal at the time, so the future Hall of Famer decided to sign with the Pittsburgh organization.

The team kept that promise and brought him to the major-league camp in 1941. He played in Albany of the Eastern League in 1941 and 1942, leading the league with 14 homers the latter season but struggling with Toronto in 1943, hitting only .236 in 144 at bats at the time he joined the navy. He was a pilot in the service, flying almost 1,200 hours while stationed in Hawaii. Unlike the many other players who entered the service during World War II, he played little baseball during his time in the navy. To Kiner it wasn't a big deal for him to come back and prepare himself to play again after missing so much time away from the game. "But luckily, I was young enough to handle my time in the service and then come right back and play. I always get a kick out of young guys these days missing a small amount of time and then talking about having to get back in shape. When you are young, you can get back in shape in a week, tops!"[67]

He returned to the club and was so impressive at spring training that the Pirates had no choice but to add him to the roster in 1946 instead of sending him to their top affiliate in Hollywood. He was bigger now, having added almost thirty pounds, and instantly became their biggest home run threat, leading the National League with twenty-three, tying Johnny Rizzo's team record that he set in 1938.

Pittsburgh had never been known as a team with much power, as evidenced by Rizzo's meager team record as well as Paul Waner's all-time career franchise mark of 109. That's the way former owner Barney Dreyfuss wanted it, never doing anything to promote the long ball during his tenure at the cavernous Forbes Field. In 1947, that would all change, and Kiner would be the main beneficiary.

The team had new owners, led by the Galbreath family, and they wanted to push the Bucs back to their championship ways. They purchased one of the game's great sluggers, Hank Greenberg, from the Detroit Tigers and made the future Hall of Famer the first player to make $100,000 in National League history. As part of the deal to entice him to come to Pittsburgh, they made a change to the configuration of Forbes Field, decreasing the distance of the fence in left field from 365 feet to 335 feet and calling the new area "Greenberg Gardens." While Greenberg would eclipse the team home run record in 1947 with twenty-five, he became a mentor to the young Pirate slugger who obliterated the mark the same season.

Greenberg helped bring Kiner along and convinced management not to send him down to the minors after the New Mexico native struggled early on in 1947; it was a decision that would prove to be very fortuitous. Greenberg helped refine his protégé's swing, and the results were incredible. "[Johnny] Mize and I tied for the lead in home runs [in 1947]. We were the second people to hit over 50 home runs in the National League, and that was really a tremendous accomplishment. At the time only six people had hit 50 or more. On top of that I only had three at the end of May. I hit 48 from June 1 through the end of the season. I really exploded with the help of Greenberg."[68]

It was a spectacular season indeed. He hit four home runs in a doubleheader, five in two consecutive games (on two occasions), six in three games and eight in four games. When Greenberg retired following his lone season in a Pirates uniform, they renamed Greenberg Gardens Kiner's Korner. The slugger used Kiner's Korner to his advantage, leading the league in long balls a record seven consecutive times in each of his first seven major-league seasons. He also eclipsed the fifty–home run plateau a second time in 1949 with fifty-four.

He was an immense star in Pittsburgh as well as the rest of the country. Kiner dated such Hollywood luminaries as Elizabeth Taylor and Janet Leigh and had friendships with the likes of Jack Lemmon, James Garner, Lucille Ball and Desi Arnaz. Unfortunately for Kiner, Branch Rickey took over as general manager in 1950, and Rickey was intent on building a winner in Pittsburgh through a strong minor-league system. While his relationship with Kiner got off to a good start, it grew more adversarial as time went on. In 1951, the team finished 64-90 and attendance dropped by more than 200,000. Rickey wasn't intent on cutting player salaries but wasn't going to give any increases either. Kiner went behind his back to Galbreath and received a $25,000 raise. This incensed Rickey, who began to criticize his star, saying that he was slow, couldn't field and didn't have power to all fields, claiming that he needed Kiner's Korner to secure his home runs.

After a 42-112 mark in 1952, with attendance dropping another 300,000 to 686,673, Rickey negotiated a cut in Kiner's salary, making the famous statement that they could finish last with or without him during the negotiations. He was traded to the Cubs midway in 1953 and lasted only two more seasons before back issues forced him into retirement at only thirty-two years old.

Eventually, Kiner became the beloved voice of the New York Mets and found his way into the Hall of Fame in 1975. While he hit only 369 homers in his short career, his 14.1 at bats per home run is still the sixth-highest mark in major-league history as of 2018.

Kiner was beloved in Pittsburgh throughout his life, and his trade out of the Steel City remains one of the most quizzical moves in baseball history. The great sabermetrician Bill James wrote, "Rickey [made] one of the oddest moves of his career, systematically destroying Kiner's reputation as a player so he could trade him, it's nuts."[69] To remove a franchise icon at his height for such reasons can be described as nothing but.

29. FRANCO HARRIS

Pittsburgh Steelers, 1972–83

As the Pittsburgh Steelers were going through another rebuilding process in the early 1970s, they finally seemed to be putting the young pieces together to become a formidable team. They had a quarterback and several pieces of a solid defense but lacked the type of running back who could help the offense dominant their opponents. John "Frenchy" Fuqua and Preston Pearson were good, but not to the level that Head Coach Chuck Noll was looking for. When it came time for the team to choose the first pick in the 1972 NFL draft, the legendary coach wanted to pick Robert Newhouse, the All-American from Houston. The scouting department was convinced that a power back out of Penn State by the name of Franco Harris was the way to go. Luckily, the scouting department was able to convince Noll that its assessment was correct. Newhouse ended up being a solid back with the Dallas Cowboys, while Harris was a Hall of Fame running back who would lead the Steelers to greatness.

A six-foot-two, 230-pound fullback, Harris was not considered an elite running back at State College; he wasn't even the best running back on the team. Lydell Mitchell was a first-team All-American who rambled for 1,567 yards his senior campaign, leading the Nittany Lions to an 11-1 record. Harris had a solid season with 684 yards rushing but didn't seem to be of the quality of Mitchell or Newhouse, who had 1,757 yards for the Cougars. Nonetheless, when the 13th pick in the first round came up, it was Franco Harris the Steelers took, while the other two dropped to the second round.

Even with the lack of statistics, it wasn't a surprise choice. If a team was looking for a prototypical bruising running back, Harris was the man. He had a relatively good 40-yard dash time for a big man at 4.7 seconds and was considered a good blocker and solid receiver. As impressive as the scouting reports were, not many could have expected the impact he would have on his team, as well as the league as a whole.

His rookie year didn't get off to a phenomenal start. After four games, he only had 69 yards, hardly a statistic that would justify the team taking Harris over the more celebrated backs. With the team sitting at 2-2 in 1972, the Penn State alum got his opportunity at home against the Houston Oilers and showed why the team scouts believed so much in him. The running back ran for 115 yards in a 24–7 victory. After thirty-nine mostly frustrating seasons, the Steelers' fortunes turned. Over the final nine games of the regular season, Harris ran for more than 100 yards in six consecutive games as the team went 8-1 to capture the initial division crown and a spot in the playoffs for the first time since losing the eastern division title game against Philadelphia in 1947.

The power back finished the year with 1,055 yards and a 5.6 yards per carry average, becoming only the second Pittsburgh back to break the 1,000-yard plateau in a single season, joining Hall of Fame back John Henry Johnson, who did it twice. Harris was voted Rookie of the Year, became a second-team All-Pro and was the only rookie in the American Football Conference (AFC) to be selected to play in the Pro Bowl. As good as a season as it was, the moment for which Franco Harris will be remembered in perpetuity came at the end of the team's first-round playoff game against the Raiders. It was the moment he went from just a good rookie to a Steeler legend.

With under thirty seconds left and Pittsburgh trailing 7–6, Terry Bradshaw threw a fourth-down pass downfield that appeared to bounce off Oakland's Jack Tatum high in the air. (Tatum knocked down Fuqua; at the time, an offensive player couldn't catch a deflection that went off another offensive player, and had the ball bounced off Fuqua, the play would have been nullified.) Franco caught the ball out of midair, running for a touchdown in a play that became known as the "Immaculate Reception," giving Pittsburgh a 13–7 victory.

After such a phenomenal season, injuries would curtail Harris's 1973 campaign, forcing him to miss two games and fall significantly short of 1,000 yards with 698. The question now was whether 1972 was a fluke. The Fort Dix, New Jersey native answered that emphatically in 1974 with a resounding *no*. He matched Johnson's Steeler mark of running for more than 1,000 yards twice in a career before having the game of his life in the franchise's first Super Bowl encounter. After rambling for 111 yards against

Pictured here is the plaque commemorating Franco Harris's "Immaculate Reception" in the 1972 playoffs against the Oakland Raiders. With the Steelers down 7–6 and time running out, Harris pulled in a Terry Bradshaw pass after it presumably deflected off Oakland's Jack Tatum and ran it in for the game-winning score. The plaque is located outside Heinz Field on the spot where the play occurred. *Courtesy of David Finoli.*

Oakland in the AFC championship, Harris set a Super Bowl record with 158 yards in the 16–6 win over the Minnesota Vikings, giving the team its first NFL title. For his efforts, he was named the game's MVP.

Now that he had matched Johnson's feat in 1974, he would go on a streak that obliterated it. Franco eclipsed the 1,000 barrier five consecutive times, starting in 1975 with arguably his greatest NFL season with a career-high 1,246 yards, once again helping Pittsburgh to a world championship.

One year later, he had another solid season, as the team won its final nine games of the season after a 1-4 start. In the playoff game against Baltimore, Harris was magnificent, running for 132 yards in the first half and 153 in the game before a rib injury not only put him out of the contest but also prohibited him from playing in an AFC championship loss to the Raiders.

As Noll unleashed Bradshaw and the Steelers passing game in the late '70s, Harris was still an effective part of the offense, helping this once beleaguered franchise to two more Super Bowl victories. Injuries prevented Franco from taking his 1,000-yard streak to seven consecutive seasons in 1980, while an injury to Bradshaw in 1981 prompted defenses to stop the run by stacking the line and kept Harris 13 yards short of breaking it once again.

At thirty-three years old, Franco once again ran for more than 1,000 yards with 1,007 in 1983 and was only 362 yards short of Jim Brown's NFL career rushing mark. The record was well within his sights, and to have a Steeler break such a treasured mark held by a Cleveland Brown would have been something special. It was at that point that one of the most troubling moments in Steeler history occurred.

Franco wanted a two-year contract and a raise from his $385,000 salary. He decided not to attend training camp until a new deal was done. Noll was not a coach who put up with such things. When asked in a press conference where Harris was, Noll just uttered, "Franco who?"[70] The comment irritated the Hall of Fame running back, but perhaps not as much as the fact the team settled the matter by releasing Harris. He ended up signing with the Seattle Seahawks. He was a shell of himself in Seattle, running for only 170 yards in eight games before retiring, falling short of breaking Brown's mark, an achievement that looked so certain only months earlier.

The shock of being cut eventually wore off, and he was elected to the Pro Football Hall of Fame in 1990. Franco remains a cherished icon in the city of Pittsburgh, where Steelers fans still rejoice that Noll relented to picking a big back from Penn State instead of two other elite running backs.

28. BEN ROETHLISBERGER

Pittsburgh Steelers, 2004–18

When it comes to playing quarterback with the Pittsburgh Steelers, it was universally thought that Terry Bradshaw was the best to ever wear the black and gold, while everyone else was fighting for second place. In 2004, things changed. Coming off a disappointing 6-10 campaign, the Steelers had the 11th pick in the first round of the NFL draft and chose the man they hoped would lead them back to an NFL championship. His name was Ben Roethlisberger.

Out of Miami (OH), Roethlisberger was a unique blend of power and finesse. He had the size of a linebacker, six-foot-five and 241 pounds, but had incredible touch on his passes. In three years as a starter for the Red

Hawks, he complied impressive numbers while holding just about every school passing career mark. In only thirty-eight games, he threw for 10,829 yards, averaging 285 per game, while also tossing 84 touchdowns. His ability to throw on the run was what impressed NFL scouts.

The draft in 2004 was deep in elite quarterbacks. Along with the man Pittsburgh now refers to as Big Ben, there was Mississippi quarterback Eli Manning, Phillip Rivers from North Carolina State and JP Losman, who played at Tulane. Manning was the first player taken in the draft by San Diego, and the New York Giants selected Rivers with the 4th pick (eventually the two would be dealt in a trade that saw Manning go to New York and Rivers end up in San Diego). Losman wasn't the man the Steelers wanted, so the choice came down to whether or not the Steelers would take a quarterback.

They had an incumbent, Tommy Maddox, who had been very successful, throwing for more than 6,000 yards in two seasons as a starter, but he was going to be thirty-three years old when the season began. There was also the issue of Steeler president Dan Rooney remembering the team passing on drafting hometown hero Dan Marino twenty-one years earlier. "I couldn't bear the thought of passing on another great quarterback prospect the way we had passed on Dan Marino in 1983, so I steered the conversation around to [Ben] Roethlisberger."[71] The team heeded the owners' wishes and drafted the Miami quarterback. As it turned out, the owner knew what he was talking about.

The intention was to bring Roethlisberger around slowly, but injuries made that impossible. Backup Charlie Batch was lost for the season with a knee injury, and Maddox hurt his elbow in the team's second game of the season. Ben came into his first NFL contest down 20-0, and while he rallied the team, leading them to two touchdowns, most thought the season was over, as thoughts turned to another potential high draft pick in 2005. Instead, Roethlisberger showed that perhaps he was the most talented quarterback in the draft.

Starting with a 13–3 win at Miami in a driving rainstorm, the impressive rookie led the team remarkably to thirteen consecutive victories, becoming the first quarterback in NFL history to start a career with a 13-0 record his rookie season. He also broke the league rookie records of the man Pittsburgh passed on in 1983, Marino, by connecting on 66.4 percent of his passes and finishing with a 98.1 rating. Pittsburgh fashioned an AFC record with a 15-1 mark but fell short in the playoffs by losing to New England in the AFC championship game. Roethlisberger struggled in the postseason with a 61.3 quarterback rating and was disappointed that the team didn't win an NFL championship for legendary running back Jerome Bettis, who was considering retirement. Bettis chose to come back, and both the team and the rookie quarterback would have the opportunity to make amends.

With the season coming to a close, the team went into a late-season slump, losing three in a row. They stood at 7-5 after a December 4 38–31 loss at the hands of the Bengals and needed to win their last four games to secure a playoff spot. Despite the fact that it wasn't an easy chore, the team did just that, sneaking into the playoffs with an 11-5 mark. In the divisional series against the high-powered Colts, Pittsburgh decided to forsake the run early on and unleash their second-year quarterback. He played spectacularly in the upset at Indianapolis and was even better in defeating the Denver Broncos at Denver with 275 yards passing and a 124.9 quarterback rating. While he had a less than stellar performance against the Seattle Seahawks in Super Bowl XL, Roethlisberger made a couple clutch plays in leading the team to their long-awaited fifth Super Bowl title and sending Bettis into retirement as an NFL champion.

It was after the season that Roethlisberger's off-the-field issues began to occur. He was involved in a serious motorcycle accident in the off season where he wasn't wearing a helmet. It took a team of five surgeons to repair the injuries he suffered to his face. Then, in July 2008, he was accused of raping a woman at a Lake Tahoe hotel-casino. While he was never convicted of the charges, a civil lawsuit she brought against him was settled in 2012.

The Steelers quarterback seemed to put the issues behind him in 2008 and led the team to a 12-4 mark despite the fact the team played an extremely difficult schedule. He played well in the playoffs, leading the team to an appearance in Super Bowl XLIII; unlike in 2005, he was at his best in the championship affair, throwing for 256 yards and a game-winning touchdown in the last minute of the contest to Santonio Holmes to give Pittsburgh an exciting 27–23 victory.

Roethlisberger was now considered only behind Bradshaw when talking of the best all-time Steeler quarterbacks. He had become the fifth Pittsburgh quarterback to eclipse 10,000 passing in his career and stood second with 14,974 yards. Two years later, his off-the-field issues reappeared when he was accused of raping a woman in Milledgeville, Georgia. The woman didn't want to speak with the police and didn't want to pursue the case, so the district attorney decided not to prosecute the All-Pro quarterback. Even though he escaped having charges brought against him, the NFL decided to suspend him six games for violating the league's personal conduct policy, a decision that Rooney seemed to support. It also ordered Roethlisberger to undergo a behavioral evaluation. The Miami alum chose not to appeal and eventually had his suspension reduced to four games. He had a solid season in 2010 after coming back, tossing only five interceptions in twelve games, and once again took the Pittsburgh Steelers to a Super Bowl. Unfortunately, they lost to the Green Bay Packers as Ben tossed two interceptions against the Packers.

In the years since this situation, Roethlisberger has put the off-field issues behind him and has also arguably surpassed Bradshaw as the team's best quarterback. As of 2019, he is far ahead of anyone else in team history in just about every category, including 56,194 yards, the sixth-highest figure in NFL history and almost twice what Bradshaw produced in his career. He also has the only three 4,000-yard campaigns a Steeler quarterback has ever enjoyed and in 2018 became the first to break the 5,000-yard plateau with 5,129, the seventh-highest single-season total in NFL history. Roethlisberger has thrown for more than 300 yards fifty-seven times, including two 500-yard games. The second-highest total of 300-yard games by a Steelers quarterback is six by Maddox and Neil O'Donnell. Ben also has the ten-highest single seasons in franchise history for both completion percentage and passer rating.

The only thing Terry Bradshaw has over Roethlisberger is his four Super Bowl championships and his ability for playing his best in those championship encounters. While those are important attributes to have, Roethlisberger's phenomenal career and dominant regular season stats have finally allowed him to do what no quarterback had come close to since Bradshaw retired in 1983: become the greatest Steeler to ever play the position.

27. CAROL SEMPLE THOMPSON

Golf, 1965–2018

As her days as one of the top amateur golfers in this country's history were coming to an end, Carol Semple Thompson stood at the eighteenth hole at the Fox Chapel Golf Club near Pittsburgh, Pennsylvania, in 2002 looking at a difficult twenty-seven-foot putt. If she made the putt, it would complete an incredible comeback against Vikki Laing, to whom she was down three holes after the seventh, and give the United States a victory in the Curtis Cup, women's amateur golf's version of the Ryder Cup. The

Carol Semple Thompson is arguably the greatest women's amateur golfer in the history of the sport. She won three different USGA champions, a feat matched by only JoAnne Carner, Jack Nicklaus, Arnie Palmer and Tiger Woods. She won sixty-two championships over the course of her career and was elected to the World Golf Hall of Fame in 2008. *Courtesy of the World Golf Hall of Fame.*

fifty-three-year-old amateur legend, who was on the U.S. team with seven collegiate players, sunk the long putt to win the match and give her country its ninth point in the competition, good enough to keep the Curtis Cup for the United States. It was truly a fairy tale ending to one of the most decorated amateur careers in golf.

Looking for a starting and ending point for her magnificent career is tough, but in 1965, as a sixteen-year-old, Thompson advanced to the Women's Golf Association of Western Pennsylvania championship match against a woman who was an accomplished amateur golfer in her own right, Phyllis Semple, her mother. Thompson defeated Phyllis, a victory that must have come to a shock to many, but not her mother. "I knew she was going to win. She has a much better swing than I have—period. And she always had the best timing."[72] As far as the end, in an interview in the *Beaver Valley Times* in May 2018, Thompson admitted that while she hadn't played in a tournament for a while, she wasn't ready to say that her career playing tournaments was over.

Thompson was born into a golf family. Of her mother, Phyllis, Carol said she bribed her into playing at twelve and felt that "a pushy mother is better than a college education,"[73] and her father, Harton "Bud" Semple, was president of the United States Golf Association (USGA). The trophy that is given to the U.S. Women's Open champion is named after her father, who died in 1990 at sixty-nine years old.

Seven years after her WGA title, she became a national figure when she finished ninth in the 1972 U.S. Women's Open at Winged Foot Golf Club in Mamaronek, New York. After shooting matching seven-over-par 79s in the first two rounds, the twenty-three-year-old settled down with a 74 and 73 the final thirty-six holes to finish tied with former champion Carol Mann for ninth, ahead of every former U.S. Open champion in the field except for Mann, Mickey Wright and the eventual winner, Susie Berning. The finish would mark her only top ten finish in the most prestigious event in women's golf.

Her performance in 1972 was a prelude to Thompson's finest moment in her career. The 1973 U.S. Women's Amateur championship was played at the Montclair Country Club in New Jersey. Carol advanced through the tournament and faced Anne Quast Sander in the final. Quast was one of the premier amateur players in the country at the time, winning the U.S. Amateur title three times, the last in 1963. In the thirty-six-hole final, Sander was one up at the end of the first eighteen holes in the morning round. While Thompson scrambled to tie the match on the first hole in the afternoon round, she lost three of the next four to fall three down with fourteen holes left. It was at this time that the Sewickley native made her first run into greatness. Winning the seventh, eighth and tenth holes, she quickly tied the match going into the eleventh. Thompson bogeyed that hole to drop one down again, but she would win the fifteenth to tie the match with three holes remaining. Sander double bogeyed the seventeenth to give Thompson the lead, and then the two halved the final hole with pars to give the twenty-four-year-old her first USGA title.

She was thrilled with the victory. "I can't believe it. It's fantastic."[74] Her proud father stated, "I'm numb. Among the three of us, Carol, Phyllis and myself, this is something we've waited twenty-five years for, and it took Carol to do it."[75]

Semple Thompson had another impressive campaign a year later, returning to the U.S. Women's Amateur championship, losing this time to Cynthia Hill 5 and 4, but was victorious in the British Women's Amateur championship, defeating Angela Bonallack 2 and 1. The victory over Bonallack made the Western Pennsylvania native the first American since Louise Suggs in 1948 to capture both the U.S. and British Women's Amateur titles.

While she never won those elite titles again, Carol had a career that few if any amateur golfers ever came close to. She's won sixty-two championships over the course of her career, including two U.S. Women's Mid-Amateur championships and four U.S. Senior Women's Amateur titles. By winning three different USGA tournaments, she put herself in rare company, as only JoAnne Carner, Jack Nicklaus, Arnie Palmer and Tiger Woods have achieved that distinction. It was the one accomplishment she is most proud of. "Tiger did his on the way up. He won the Junior Amateur, the Amateur and the U.S. Open. With me, I started at the top by winning the Women's Amateur and, as I got older, the Women's Mid-Amateur and then the Women's Senior Amateur. So I was kind of on my way down. But it's still three different championships. I'm not complaining. It is select group, a very select group."[76]

Semple Thompson appeared in a record twelve Curtis Cups before becoming the U.S. non-playing captain two times; played in a record thirty-two U.S. Women's Opens; was given the 2003 Bob Jones Award, the highest award presented by the USGA, given to the golfer who demonstrates distinguished sportsmanship in the game; was given the PGA of America's First Lady of Golf Award; and was voted into the National Golf Coaches Association Hall of Fame.

In 2008, Carol Semple Thompson received the highest honor a golfer can hope for: election into the World Golf Hall of Fame. Even in her proudest moment, Thompson was humble. "Well, it's very humbling, and I'm honored that each of them would even consider me. Each of them means so much to me. Of course, the World [Golf Hall of Fame] is the big one. It doesn't get any better than that. Really, I don't know what I'm doing in there. You know, all the great names in golf are in there. I sort of snuck in."

In her mind, she may have snuck in, but to the rest of the golf world, it's an honor well deserved.

26. WILBUR "PETE" HENRY

Washington & Jefferson College (Football), 1915–19

When coming to Pittsburgh, it seems like the first place people want to visit is a restaurant that is most associated with the city, Primanti Brothers. The original restaurant is located in the strip district of the city, and one of its most memorable features is a wall with caricatures of some of the town's greatest heroes. From Willie Stargell to Terry Bradshaw to Fred Rogers, they're seemingly all there. There is one picture that most don't recognize, a football player from early in the twentieth century. The patrons try to guess who it is but often are unable to come up with the proper name. While they may not think he belongs with the collection of Pittsburgh icons, the player in question is Wilbur Francis Henry, more commonly known as Pete Henry, and when it comes to sports icons in the Steel City, the two-time All-American from Washington & Jefferson College more than belongs among the area's iconic figures.

Currently, W&J fields one of the most successful NCAA Division III programs in the country, but in the first three decades of the twentieth century, the program was among the best in major college football. A top rival of the University of Pittsburgh during the period, W&J had many successful seasons, the most successful of which was in 1921 when the team finished 10-0-1, a year that included one of the greatest games in Western Pennsylvania collegiate sports history, a scoreless tie in the Rose Bowl against heavily favored California. They had many great players in the era, such as Ed Garbisch, Russ Stein and Dan Towler, but the best player ever to take the gridiron for the Presidents was Henry.

Born in Mansfield, Ohio, Henry was a star fullback and lineman on the town's high school football team. As a freshman at Mansfield, Henry weighed 215 pounds, which was extremely large for the time. He was a rare combination of speed and power, and while he was an incredible defensive lineman, he also turned into an effective fullback. Nicknamed "Fats" because of his weight as well as his hearty appetite, Henry's powerful running style caught the attention of many colleges, including W&J coach Bob Folwell, who went on to become the first head coach of the New York Giants and convinced him to continue his career with the Presidents in 1915.

Besides being a great football player, the Mansfield native was a successful all-around athlete. Aside from football, Pete also played baseball, basketball and track while at the school, accumulating eleven letters in his four years at Washington and Jefferson. Even though he was proficient in the other three, it was football where the lineman truly excelled. Despite the fact that Henry was a great fullback, Folwell put him in as a tackle, as Henry played on the freshman team that first season. It was on the line where Henry would forge his way into football history. He had an exceptional burst off the line and was very efficient at blocking punts.

After starting on the varsity line in 1916, where he received All-American mention, Pete was named as a first-team All-American one year later. It was a season where the Presidents went 7-3, losing three consecutive weeks to Pitt, Notre Dame and West Virginia by a combined 13 points. Much was expected from the team in 1918, but that season would be a unique and somewhat tragic one.

It was Pete Henry's senior campaign, but with World War I going on in Europe and the flu pandemic striking the country, it was a trying season for all. More than 675,000 American citizens would die during the pandemic, and many professional and collegiate athletes were fighting in the war, so the college football schedules were drastically reduced. W&J only played four games, finishing at 2-2, but Henry was spectacular, garnering consensus All-American status for the season.

While 1918 should have been Wilbur Henry's final collegiate season, because of the issues during the 1918 campaign that forced the team to play such a reduced schedule and the fact that Henry was in an army training group on campus, he was permitted to play a fifth season. The Presidents had gotten off to a spectacular 4-0 start in 1919 that included an impressive 20–0 victory over Carnegie Tech and a 13–0 upset at Syracuse, a game in which Henry, now weighing 250 pounds, played so well that some were referring to him as one of the best ever to play the game.

It seemed like W&J had a legitimate chance at some national honors, but those would come to an end when their next opponent, the University of Pittsburgh, questioned Henry's fifth year of eligibility and decided to refuse to play the Presidents if Henry was in the lineup. The Western Conference (what the Big Ten conference was called in the early 1920s) and most other conferences had decided not to count the abbreviated 1918 campaign against a player's eligibility, but Pitt refused to acknowledge this decision. The administration at W&J offered to settle the matter through an independent arbiter, but again their opponents refused to budge. Finally faced with the option of canceling the game, Presidents team manager John Murdoch Jr. announced that Henry would sit for the contest. Without their star lineman in the game, the Panthers handed Washington & Jefferson their first loss of the season, 7–6.

As it turned out, there was more to the controversy than just an extra year of eligibility; there were rumors that Henry had played a game professionally for the Massillon Tigers, a fact he vehemently denied. "Apparently someone has tried to put me in the wrong at Massillon. Not only did I not play with Massillon on Sunday, but I have no intention of playing professional football before I am through my college course. I will admit that flattering offers have been made to me to play on a number of professional teams, but I have rejected all of them and certainly will maintain my amateur standings while I am in college."[77]

Henry went on to play the remainder of the schedule in 1919, being named as a consensus All-American for a second consecutive season. True to his word, he turned down the pro football offers that came his way after the Presidents' season concluded so he could remain eligible for the school's spring track season. After he graduated, he signed with the Canton Bulldogs and embarked on a professional career that saw him become one of the greatest players in the early days of the NFL. Eventually he was elected to both the College and Pro Football Halls of Fame (as a charter inductee in both museums), making Henry one of only eight, and the only lineman, to be so honored.

After retiring from the game, he went on to serve his alma mater proudly as both a football coach and the athletic director, a job he had for ten years until he passed away in 1952. He suffered from diabetes, which was the cause of infections that spread to both his legs, necessitating the amputation of one in 1949 and culminating with his death three years later.

While Henry is relatively unknown in the area today, the *Canton Repository* summed up his career best in 1922: "Tackles will come and tackles will go, but never will professional football enthusiasts of Canton [Ohio] ever see the peer of Wilbur Henry, 247-pounder, resident of Mansfield, graduate of Washington-Jefferson College at Washington, Pa., and a member of Canton Bulldogs teams for the last three campaigns in which he has played every game. Though he never would be able to qualify as a matinee idol, the Richland-co. individual stands out as the greatest tackle in football today—bar none, as the prohibitionists say."[78]

25. MARSHALL GOLDBERG

University of Pittsburgh (Football), 1936–38

When speaking of the most prolific running backs in the history of football at the University of Pittsburgh, the conversations usually steers to the school's only Heisman Trophy winner, Tony Dorsett. While Dorsett is the greatest running back in the program's history, for thirty-eight years there was another man who was the unquestioned king of backs at the school. His name was Marshall Goldberg.

A multisport star from Elkins, West Virginia, Goldberg was considered one of the greatest athletes the town had ever produced at the time. Nicknamed "Biggie" due to his small size, which saw him weigh only 110 pounds as a sophomore at Elkins High School, as well as the immense intensity he showed on the field of play, the future Pitt star was named All-State in football, basketball and track in his high school career. While he was successful at the other two sports, it was football that made colleges take notice of his athletic ability.

During his senior season for Elkins in 1934, Goldberg was named team captain while scoring seventeen touchdowns. College football coaches pursued the young running back, including national powers such as Notre Dame. While it was tempting to continue his career at the school Knute Rockne turned into a legendary program, Goldberg decided to play a little closer to home for another iconic coach by the name of Jock Sutherland at the University of Pittsburgh. Later on in his life, the Elkins native kidded around saying he chose Pitt because "in those days a Goldberg at Notre Dame would have been a big thing,"[79] referring to a Jewish running back playing at a Catholic college.

Despite his small stature, Marshall Goldberg showed quickly that he could be a force on the college football gridiron. As the team prepared for their opening contest against Ohio Wesleyan University, lineman Steve Petro looked over at the diminutive sophomore running back and said that "he was there about two or three days [at training camp] before I realized he was a football player. I thought he was a manager he was such a small person."[80] As Petro and the Panther faithful soon found out, he was in fact a football player.

Like Dorsett would thirty-seven years later when he opened his college career by breaking the 100-yard plateau against Georgia, Goldberg would have a similar day in his first game against the Battling Bishops. It was a game where the Panthers didn't expect much difficulty and were never threatened, winning 53–0 while outgaining their opponents 801 yards to 44. The most impressive part of the contest was the performance by Goldberg. He scored the game's opening touchdown on a short run before breaking off a 76-yard touchdown romp to make it 14–0. By the time the dust had settled on the big victory, the Elkins native had run for 203 yards in his first varsity game.

Marshall had been an integral part of the team in his first season as they finished the year 7-1-1 and accepted a bid to the Rose Bowl to play the University of Washington. The Rose Bowl had not been kind to Coach Jock Sutherland and his team during the previous few years, losing all three times they traveled to Pasadena, including two routs at the hands of the USC Trojans. The team would be prepared this time, as Pitt's exceptional backfield, led by Goldberg, dominated the Husky defense, shutting out Washington 21–0. With the victory they earned the school's seventh national championship.

Marshall Goldberg (*far right*) is taking instruction from his legendary coach, Jock Sutherland (*far left*). Before Tony Dorsett, the greatest running back the University of Pittsburgh ever produced was Goldberg. The team captured two national championships in his three seasons, as the two time All-American twice finished in the top three in voting for the Heisman Trophy. He was elected to the College Football Hall of Fame in 1958. *Courtesy of the University of Pittsburgh Athletics.*

While the team should have been in a celebrative mood, they were anything but, as a controversy regarding the expense money the Panther players received versus what their opponents got struck a nerve with the Pitt players. Goldberg remembered years later, "We got nothing, except a sweater and a pair of pants. When we showed up for a reception with them [the Washington players, who received $100 in expenses plus new suits for the reception], imagine how we felt. Jock sold some bonds he had, and the other coaches threw some money into a pool. They gave us each $2, all they had. Then the bowl people took us out to the Santa Anita racetrack for an outing. Big deal. Two dollars at a racetrack. So we all threw in a dollar to make pools to bet. And tapped out quickly. You know what it's like to stand around a racetrack with no money?"[81]

Despite the controversy, the team came back in 1937 and had one of the great seasons in the program's history with a 9-0-1 mark while being selected as an almost unanimous choice for national champions. Goldberg continued to show he dominant he was, running for a team-high 698 yards, and was named as a consensus All-American while finishing third in the Heisman Trophy race behind Clint Frank of Yale and future Pittsburgh Steeler and Supreme Court justice Byron "Whizzer" White. Remembering the issues from the season before at the Rose Bowl, Goldberg and his teammates voted to turn down a bowl bid following the campaign, a controversial move that irritated the school administration, which was threatening stronger academic requirements and a reduction in stipends for the football players. It eventually enacted these requirements, which ended the championship era at Pitt.

With the stressful situation between the program and the administration still going on, the team would have one more successful season in 1938, Goldberg's senior campaign. Sutherland had put together a phenomenal backfield that would be dubbed the "Dream Backfield." To get Dick Cassiano and Curly Stebbins on the field, Goldberg had to agree to move to fullback. The senior running back was a great leader and unselfishly agreed to move so the team could be more successful. They got off to a great start, winning their first six games as they were on the verge of winning a third consecutive national title. Pitt unfortunately lost two of their last four to finish 8-2, but the Elkins native still had a phenomenal year, being selected as a unanimous All-American and becoming the only Panther in the history of the program with two top-three finishes in the Heisman Trophy vote, finishing second behind Davey O'Brien of TCU.

After his career at Pitt had ended, Marshall Goldberg embarked on a successful NFL career that was interrupted by a stint in the navy during World

War II, during which he eventually became a lieutenant. The Cardinals eventually retired his number, 99, and the University of Pittsburgh followed suit, making sure that no one would ever wear 42 at Pitt again. He was selected by the Pro Football Hall of Fame as a senior candidate for election twice, in 1972 and 2008, but never received enough votes for selection into Canton. He was deservingly elected to the College Football Hall of Fame in 1958 and was a great ambassador for the university until his death at eighty-eight in 2006.

Pitt's former sports information director and popular ESPN analyst Beano Cook put it best when he said, "Tony Dorsett was Pitt's greatest runner, but Marshall was one of the greatest football players."[82]

24. ROGER KINGDOM

University of Pittsburgh (Track), 1981–84
University of Pittsburgh (Football), 1981–82
Track, 1981–99

When Roger Kingdom came out of Vienna High School in Unadilla, Georgia, the last thing University of Pittsburgh football coach Jackie Sherrill thought was that Kingdom would end up being a Hall of Fame hurdler and an Olympic champion. After all, while Kingdom was a star on the track at Vienna, setting state high school records in both the high jump and high hurdles while being named the Middle Georgia Track Athlete of the Year, he was coming to Pitt because of his proficiency on the gridiron. In his senior season, he ran for more than 1,000 yards with a 7.0 yards per carry, and Sherrill thought that he'd be explosive in the Panther backfield, as did Tennessee and Clemson, who also recruited him before the six-foot-two, 175-pound back decided to come to Pitt. Funny how things turn out. Kingdom never amounted to much on the football field, lettering only once in 1982, but on the track he continued to excel, eventually becoming arguably the greatest track star the school ever produced.

Coming to the university with such lofty credentials, Kingdom had a successful first season at Pitt on the track, but his statistics at running back were limited to nine yards on four carries for a Pitt team that finished second in the nation following an exciting 27–23 victory over Georgia in

While he came to the University of Pittsburgh as a running back, Roger Kingdom (*far left*) became arguably the school's greatest track athlete. He won the 110-meter hurdles in the 1984 Los Angeles Summer Olympics amid controversy when several Eastern Bloc countries boycotted the games. Four years later, in 1988, when the world was at the Summer Olympics in its entirety, Kingdom successfully defended his title, winning his second gold medal. *Courtesy of the University of Pittsburgh Athletics.*

the Sugar Bowl. The coaches decided to switch the young back to safety before his sophomore season to backup incumbents Tom Flynn and Rick Dukovich. According to his position coach, Anthony Folino, "Roger has outstanding speed and is very tough. We expect that he will fit in very well into our secondary."[83]

Even though he struggled in football, the Georgia native continued to be an important part of the track team, eventually becoming a national champion for the Panthers and capturing both the 110-meter hurdle NCAA outdoor championship in 1983 and the 55-meter indoor NCAA championship a year later. With his running success, Kingdom decided to take a red shirt in football for the 1983 campaign and wanted to switch to wide receiver if he was to return to the team in 1984.

After winning the indoor title, Roger Kingdom received an invite to the Olympic Trials for the 1984 Los Angeles Summer Olympic Games. The United States had quite a few quality athletes in the 110-meter hurdles. Renaldo Nehemiah had dominated the event in the early 1980s but had signed to play wide receiver with the San Francisco 49ers and wasn't available for the '84 games. Despite the fact that Kingdom had captured the gold medal at the Pan-American Games in 1983, Greg Foster, who had run in Nehemiah's shadow, was now the favorite, and Tonie Campbell was considered second best. While not considered one of the top two, Kingdom came up with an outstanding effort in the finals at the trials, tying his personal best at 13.36 seconds to finish third and qualify for the team.

It was a great moment in his career but also caused some eligibility questions at Pitt. He had resisted signing a track endorsement contract, which would have negated his college eligibility. There were other issues such as the post-Olympic tour of Europe by the USA track team that would have kept him out of spring practice with the football team once again, as well as the fact that he cut his class schedule back to part-time status so he could train for the trials and the games, all of which brought up questions of his outdoor eligibility in the fall. Kingdom accepted a red shirt so he could stay eligible and intended on returning not just to run but also to finish his degree.

He was proud of the work he had done not only to prepare for the games but also to remain on schedule for his degree. "In an Olympic year, going through what I've been through, it's a hassle. I feel a lot of other people would have cracked. It was a lot of pressure. But I am still determined to get this degree."[84] While it may have been difficult getting to this point, he was about to succeed beyond his wildest dreams.

Questions as to who was the best in the world became an issue at these Olympics. In response to the United States leading a boycott of the 1980 Moscow Olympics, fourteen Eastern Bloc nations, including the Soviet Union, boycotted these games. Knowing that he could only beat the runners who came, Kingdom won his preliminary heat and then set a personal record in winning his semifinal race at 13.24 seconds to qualify for the finals. He had a poor lane assignment, running in the eighth lane, and was facing great opposition, including Foster, who was a heavy favorite, and Campbell.

As the race began, Foster thought that he had a false start and slowed just for a bit, expecting it to be restarted, which it was not. The favorite was in the first lane, far apart from Kingdom, so each couldn't easily tell where the other stood during the sprint. Kingdom was a powerful hurdler and overtook Campbell following the first four hurdles despite a poor start himself. Foster, who was the defending world champion and had the second-fastest time in the history of the event, had a small lead as the two were coming to a finish line. He took a look over to see where Kingdom was just as the Pitt alum surged past him for the gold medal, tying the Olympic record at 13.20 seconds. Roger had no idea he won, thinking he finished with the silver, and looked over at Campbell, who informed him that he won the close race over Foster.

The young runner was ecstatic, but he was humble, claiming that it was just one race and didn't make him a better runner than Foster. Between winning this medal and what would happen four years later, Kingdom could soon make that claim as the world's best.

His career at Pitt was all but over at this point, but his standing in the world for the 110-meter hurdles was just beginning. He was ranked number one in the world in 1984 and 1985 in the event and captured many major titles, including the 1985 U.S. Outdoor championship. At that point, he pulled a hamstring and struggled for the next few years, eventually enlisting the help of orthopedist Dr. Freddie Fu, who put Kingdom on a program that helped him recover. In 1988, he looked like he was regaining his form as he captured his second U.S. championship before winning the Olympic Trials with a 13.21 mark. He came into the Olympics as a favorite to defend his title and knew that to be taken seriously as one of the all-time greats he would have to capture the gold in an Olympiad where all the nations were competing for the first time in eight years.

Only Lee Calhoun had ever won consecutive 110-meter hurdle gold medals, and Kingdom now had the chance to join him. Unlike 1984, when he won the gold in a close race by .03 seconds, there would be no such tension in this final. The defending Olympic champion dominated the field, breaking the 13-second barrier with an Olympic-record 12.98 seconds while easily defeating Great Britain's Colin Jackson and Campbell to defend his title.

Now considered among the all-time greats in the event, Roger Kingdom went on to break Nehemiah's long-standing world record in 1989 with a 12.92 mark. While he damaged his knee in 1991 playing in a pickup basketball game, Kingdom went on to win his fifth U.S. outdoor title in 1995 and his second Pan-American Game gold medal that same year.

He retired for good in 1999 and was elected to the USA Track and Field Hall of Fame in 2005, as well as was selected in the initial Hall of Fame class at the University of Pittsburgh in 2018. After becoming a legend in the track and field world, the two-time gold medalist had stints as head track coach at California (PA), a speed coach for the NFL's Arizona Cardinals and interim director of the track and field team at Central Florida. Kingdom has had an incredible career, one that Jackie Sherrill never would have expected when he recruited the speedy running back so many years ago.

23. JACK LAMBERT

Pittsburgh Steelers, 1974–84

When the Pittsburgh Steelers made Kent State linebacker Jack Lambert their second-round choice in the 1974 NFL draft, Steeler fans throughout the Western Pennsylvania area weren't excited. He was an undersized linebacker, weighing only 215 pounds, and didn't have an All-American résumé to brag about. In Mid-American Conference circles, though, he certainly was well thought of. Being named first-team All-Conference twice, Jack Lambert was also the circuit's Defensive Player of the Year in 1972. Still, Pittsburgh fans as well as his new teammates had no idea of the passion and intensity their new middle linebacker possessed. He played mostly with an aggressiveness and toughness that made this small linebacker one of the most feared players in the history of the National Football League.

Born in Mantua, Ohio, Lambert was a quarterback in high school and was only 185 pounds when he was recruited to Kent State as a safety. In the middle of his sophomore year, he was converted to a middle linebacker, where the man they would soon call "Count Dracula in cleats" took advantage of his intensity to become a star with the Golden Flashes. Drafted in the second round of arguably the greatest draft in North American sports history, where Pittsburgh took four Hall of Famers Lynn Swann, Lambert, John Stallworth and Mike Webster, in four of the first five rounds, Jack had other options to continue his pro football career at the next level. He was also taken in the sixth round of the World Football League draft by the Philadelphia Bell. The linebacker considered offers from both the Bell and the Canadian Football League before opting to sign with Pittsburgh. Securing him was a priority for Noll despite his size, as the iconic coach stated, "He's a lot like Ted Hendricks of Baltimore. He's a mean, tough, hard hitting, skinny kid."[85]

Jack came to training camp at St. Vincent College in Latrobe, Pennsylvania, with his rookie teammates and had a tremendous opportunity to show his talent. The NFL was in the midst of its first player strike in 1974, and most of the veterans were on the picket line. Lambert took advantage as Noll noticed his exceptional potential. "We're running a play where the flow goes right. Only the quarterback fakes the handoff, bootlegs the ball and throws to his left. Lambert goes with the flow, catches himself, goes the other way and dives in the air and takes that ball out of the receiver's hands. Fantastic play."[86]

Pictured while playing at Kent State is Hall of Fame linebacker Jack Lambert. He was undersized when taken in the second round of the 1974 draft, but what Lambert lacked in size he made up for in intensity. Considered one of the most aggressive linebackers in the history of the game, he set a record when he was named to nine straight Pro Bowl games. *Courtesy of the Kent State University Athletics.*

It was rare for Noll to praise a rookie in training camp, but Jack Lambert was no ordinary rookie. When he came in, he was third on the depth chart behind the incumbent starter Henry Davis and third-year backup Ed Bradley. Before too long, he would vault up the depth chart two spots, taking over the starting role for the season opener against the Baltimore Colts. It was a position on the depth chart he would not relinquish.

Lambert was the only rookie in the starting defensive lineup. He picked off two passes in a 34–24 defeat of the Kansas City Chiefs and was named the Associated Press NFL Defensive Rookie of the Year while being named to the first-team All-NFL Rookie squad by the UPI, *Pro Football Weekly* and the Pro Football Writers. It was a great season that got even better in the postseason.

At that point, the Pittsburgh Steelers had never won an NFL championship in the history of the franchise, often languishing in the bottom half of the standings. This was a different team led by an exceptional defense, of which Jack Lambert was becoming a significant part. The running games of the Oakland Raiders and Minnesota Vikings were rendered useless in the AFC championship game and Super Bowl IX, as the Pittsburgh defense held both teams to a combined 41 yards in 46 carries rushing as the team captured the world championship. While Lambert did a significant job shutting down the running attack of both teams, he showed his versatility against the Raiders, making a great open field tackle to stop speedy wide receiver Cliff Branch from tying the game. As great a rookie season as he had, he showed that there would be no sophomore jinx, as the young linebacker became a team leader in 1975.

The star of the defense at that point was undoubtedly Joe Greene, one of the greatest defensive players in the history of the game. Greene was slowed down in 1975, first by a sprained knee and then a pinched nerve in his left shoulder. Lambert picked up for the injured star and had a remarkable campaign, leading the team in tackles and assists, as he had done his rookie season. He was named as a first-team All-Pro and once again took his game to the next level in the postseason with a record three fumble recoveries in the AFC championship game victory against the Raiders on an icy-cold day in Pittsburgh.

Pittsburgh took on the Dallas Cowboys in Super Bowl X trying to defend their title, and the situation was looking dire when Lambert showed the nation that it's not a good idea to screw around with the Pittsburgh Steelers. Roy Gerela was the team's kicker and had a difficult game that afternoon after bruising his ribs on the opening kickoff while making a touchdown-saving tackle against Thomas "Hollywood" Henderson. With

Dallas up 10–7 in the third quarter, Gerela missed a game-tying field goal. Dallas defensive back Cliff Harris then mocked Gerela and patted him on the head. Jack Lambert took exception, grabbing Harris and throwing him on to the ground. Even though he was undersized, no one wanted to go after Lambert. A tough reputation was born, and an inspired Steeler team came back for a 21–17 victory.

His continued to excel in 1976, as the Kent State alum once again was named to the first-team All-Pro squad while being named the Associated Press NFL Defensive Player of the Year. In 1977, the season began with controversy when Lambert sat out the beginning of training camp in a salary dispute, as he was looking to sign a new contract for close to $200,000. After his contract situation was resolved, a knee injury curtailed his season. When healthy, Lambert, who was named defensive captain for the first time, still played to his outstanding level.

He continued his path to Canton afterward, being named first-team All-Pro at least once every year between 1978 and 1983. In 1979, he was named the AFC Defensive Player of the Year while becoming the first Steeler to lead the league in interceptions since Jack Ham in 1974. That year, he had his first and only postseason interception, coming late in the fourth quarter of Super Bowl XIV against the Rams to clinch the franchise's fourth Super Bowl title in six years.

In 1983, he broke Jack Ham's record of eight consecutive Pro Bowl games when he was voted to play in his ninth in a row. Ironically, that would be the end of the glory days for the iconic linebacker. Of all things, it would be turf toe that ended the career of one of the toughest NFL players ever to take the field.

He hurt the toe in the second game of the 1984 campaign, and the chief himself, Art Rooney Sr., warned him to take time off. Not wanting to stay off the field, he played against Cleveland and San Francisco, aggravating the injury each time. They finally put him on the injured reserve, but he came back against the Dolphins in the AFC championship game. It would be the last contest he would play, as the damage was too severe. According to Rooney, "This is second-guessing, but when he got his toe hurt…I think it would've been fine to go on the [injured reserved list]. I knew if he wasn't on it, he would always be trying to play. Whether or not just staying out 30 days would've cured him, I don't know.…I believe if it wasn't for the toe, he could've played four or five more years of top-notch football." Lambert disagreed, claiming, "There's no way of telling. It's all hindsight now."[87]

There is no way of knowing for sure, but what is known is that Lambert was one of the all-time greats, as his selection to the NFL's seventy-fifth-anniversary team signifies, as does his selection to the Hall of Fame in 1990. It was an exceptional career for a linebacker who was undersized, showing that grit and a fierce attitude can overcome physical shortcomings.

22. LARRY FITZGERALD

University of Pittsburgh (Football), 2002–3

In college football, when you are considered one of the sport's all-time greatest talents, it doesn't take long to ascend toward the top of a list such as the one that is found in the pages of this book. For wide receiver Larry Fitzgerald of the University of Pittsburgh, it was apparent from the beginning that the star recruit was better than the rest. With so little time to make such an impact, Fitzgerald couldn't waste a second. By the time his short two-year career was done with the Panthers, he was among the most decorated collegiate receivers in the history of the game. His talent was such that he continued to excel with the Arizona Cardinals after being selected with the third overall pick in the 2004 NFL draft. His career started at the Academy of Holy Angels in Richfield, Minnesota.

He was a star for both sides of the ball at Holy Angels. As a top-five recruit at receiver who caught 127 passes for 2,602 yards and 28 touchdowns his final two seasons and was named to *Prep Star Magazine*'s Dream Team, Larry was heavily recruited. Fitzgerald traveled to Penn State to see what the Nittany Lions had to offer with his coach, Mike Pendino. On the way back from State College to catch a plane home from the Pittsburgh International Airport, Pendino talked his top recruit into taking an impromptu stop at the University of Pittsburgh to meet Coach Walt Harris. While Fitzgerald wasn't happy at first to be taking the detour at Pitt, he fell in love with the city, school, coaches and players after the visit. He then decided that this is where he wanted to be. As it turned out, there was also another reason he wanted to play at Pitt. When he was originally being recruited on the aforementioned trip to Penn State, Joe Paterno wanted him as a linebacker, as did almost 70 percent of the offers he received, according to Fitzgerald. He had been a star linebacker in high school and playing at a school often referred to as "Linebacker U" was tempting, but in the end Harris swayed him to play receiver at Pitt; as it turned out, it was the perfect position for him.

Unfortunately, academics were an issue, and his college career was diverted to the Valley Forge Military Academy in Wayne, Pennsylvania. After a year at the academy, Fitzgerald decided to open his recruiting once again to make sure he was making the right decision in going to Pitt. There were other influences that made him want to reaffirm his decision, as he was dating someone who was attending Michigan State and had a close friend who was playing for Tom Izzo on the basketball team for the Spartans. He also wanted to see Ohio State one more time, the school he was originally considering before deciding on Pitt. Eventually, his relationship with Harris, plus one he had forged with a quarterback who was another Panther commit, Tyler Palko, pushed Fitzgerald back to his original plan to become a Panther.

After starting his career at Pitt unassumingly with a catch against Ohio for 11 yards, Pitt hosted Texas A&M in the season's second game. That day, Larry Fitzgerald became a star. He caught ten passes for 103 yards, including a spectacular 8-yard grab late in the game for a first down, leaping up as a defensive back was draped all over him. His play helped Pitt rebound from an early 14–0 deficit, losing the contest 14–12 though it was now clear that opponents would have to come up with a game plan to stop the impressive freshman.

Fitzgerald repeated his incredible play over the next few weeks, including an effort against Toledo in which he snagged six balls for 121 yards and his first two collegiate touchdowns. After catching a touchdown pass against Boston College, one that would begin an amazing streak of catching a scoring toss in an NCAA-record eighteen consecutive games, Larry had a spectacular contest the next week against Virginia Tech. The Hokies came into this game as the number-three team in the nation and left Lane Stadium wondering who the hell was Larry Fitzgerald. The Minnesota native caught five catches, three for touchdowns, including his final one in the left edge of the end zone with heavy coverage, to tie the contest at 21. Pitt ended up with 28–21 victory, and while they lost their next two games—the latter against West Virginia 24–17 in which Fitzgerald caught a then career-high eleven catches for 159 yards—they ended the season 9-4 with a victory over Oregon State in the Insight Bowl.

Much was expected from Pitt and Fitzgerald in 2003, and the receiver didn't disappoint, having the greatest campaign for a receiver in school history. The Panthers started the season in the top ten and rose to seventh after convincing victories over Kent State and Ball State, games in which

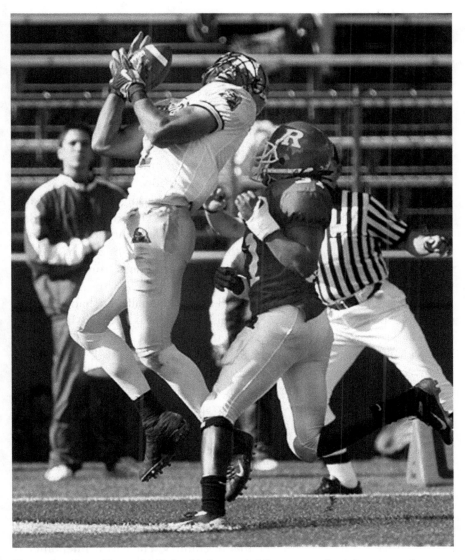

Pitt receiver Larry Fitzgerald (*in the white jersey to the left*) was a star from the moment he stepped on the field for the Panthers. He would catch a touchdown pass in an NCAA-record eighteen straight games while leading the nation with 128.62 yards per game his second season in a Pitt uniform. That year, he finished second in the Heisman Trophy race. *Courtesy of the University of Pittsburgh Athletics.*

Larry scored five touchdowns. Unfortunately, in a third consecutive game against a Mid-American Conference team at Toledo, they were upset 35–31 despite Fitzgerald's career-high twelve catches. The team was devastated going into a contest against a tough Texas A&M team on the road, hoping they could make up for the upset defeat.

Before the contest, *Sports Illustrated* featured what it felt would be one of the premier matchups of the day, Larry Fitzgerald against the Aggies' fine free safety Jaxson Appel, but as it turned out, there was no match. With Pitt down 13–9 at the half and their starting running back and center out for the game, as well as two defensive players who would miss the second half, things looked dire. But the Panthers came out and played hard. Fitzgerald, who caught the game's first score, a 34-yard pass from Rod Rutherford, made a spectacular 5-yard grab while being heavily covered to put the Panthers up, 23–13. His third and final touchdown of the day would clinch the victory as he pulled in a 49-yard bomb from Rutherford to complete the scoring in a 37–26 upset win.

His sophomore year was going well, but personally he had issues to overcome. Before the season began, his mother was ravaged by cancer, which had spread throughout her body to her brain. Larry left school to fly back to Minnesota to see his mother. The prognosis was bad, and she was not given much time to live. Fitzgerald had an argument with his mother earlier in the year and had not spoken to her much since. She was being kept alive by a respirator, and he wasn't able to speak with her when he arrived to apologize. She died soon after, and it devastated him. His father, Larry Sr., said, "He was so overwhelmed with grief because they never patched things up. I told him, 'Don't you carry that with you, Larry. Your mother loved you and you loved her. Don't take any other feelings out of this room today.'"[88] It was great advice that inspired his son.

He trained hard while working through the grief, and it showed in his performance. After the Texas A&M game, he continued to show that he was arguably the best player in the country. He had a phenomenal campaign that included a tremendous eight-catch, 207-yard performance against Rutgers. By the year's end, he had pulled in ninety-two catches for 1,672 yards and an NCAA-high 22 scores. He also led the nation in yards per game with a 128.62 average.

Fitzgerald went on to finish second in the Heisman Trophy vote while being the first sophomore to win the Walter Camp Player of the Year Award, capturing the Fred Biletnikoff Award as the nation's top receiver and being a unanimous first-team All-American, the first sophomore at Pitt to be selected unanimously. One could only imagine what his junior season would bring, but unfortunately, that campaign would be left to the imagination. NFL rules prohibited a player from entering the draft until three years after his high school class graduated. There was controversy over whether he would be allowed to participate. Because he went for a fifth year of high school at Valley Forge, Fitzgerald qualified for the draft and was selected by the Arizona Cardinals in the first round.

His NFL career has been as spectacular as his one at Pitt, as he became the youngest player to catch seven hundred passes and is one of two to reach 10,000 yards in his career before the age of thirty. While his career was short with the Panthers, it was spectacular. His number is one of only ten retired by the school, and it seems certain that he'll be elected to both the College and Pro Football Hall of Fame when he becomes eligible. When it comes to impactful two-year careers, none stacks up better than Larry Fitzgerald's at Pitt.

21. OSCAR CHARLESTON

Homestead Grays, 1930–31
Pittsburgh Crawfords, 1932–38

Widely known as a man with a horrific temper—a reputation that has been widely disputed as more research on the man has been done—Oscar Charleston is nonetheless considered one of the greatest players ever to put on a uniform. In Bill James's *Historical Baseball Abstract*, he lists Charleston as the fourth-best player in league history and the Negro League's top center fielder ahead of such greats as Cristobel Torriente and Cool Papa Bell. He had a frame like Babe Ruth, thin legs with a huge chest, and was an incredible natural hitter. While he came to Pittsburgh in 1930 at thirty-three years old, when he was already an established star, he put his stamp in Steel City baseball lore as a member of two of the greatest Negro League teams ever to play the game, the 1931 Homestead Grays and the 1935 Pittsburgh Crawfords.

Charleston had gotten a reputation for a temper that seemingly bordered on insanity at times. He reportedly was tough on the field, as many were during a period when violence and lack of sportsmanship was somewhat the norm, but those who have researched him recently have come to the conclusion that the reputation may have been distorted. In an article about Charleston in *Sports Illustrated*, John Schulian wrote that "you get the feeling…that here is this rough ballplayer who would fight anybody, crash into anything, take out fielders, but was a real puppy dog."[89]

Whether or not Oscar Charleston deserves his fiery reputation, he was one of the best to ever play the game. When talking to Negro League catcher Quincy Trouppe, St. Louis scout Bernie Borgan stated, "In my opinion, the greatest ball player I've ever seen was Oscar Charleston. When I say this, I'm not overlooking Ruth, Cobb, Gehrig, and all of them."[90] The great Buck O'Neil also concurred, stating that "Charlie was a tremendous left-handed hitter who could also bunt, steal a hundred bases a year, and cover center field as well as anyone before him or since.…He was like Ty Cobb, Babe Ruth, and Tris Speaker rolled into one."[91]

Born in Indianapolis in 1896, Charleston served in the army's 24th Infantry in the Philippines, joining when he was only fifteen years old. He ran track in the service and became the only African American to play baseball in the Manila League. Returning in 1915, "Charlie," as he was known, began his magnificent career in his hometown, playing for the ABCs. At the beginning, he pitched and was a center fielder. On the mound, he was 1-1 with a 4.43 ERA in six games for Indianapolis that season. His reputation as a brawler was also on display his rookie campaign, as he and teammate Bingo DeMoss were reportedly arrested for attacking an umpire, which then started a riot.

He pitched occasionally over the course of his long career, appearing in thirty-two games with a 3-7 mark and a 4.42 ERA, but it eventually became obvious that his success would be in center.

Charleston had a breakout season in 1918, hitting .381 for Indianapolis, a springboard for his Hall of Fame career, which took him to several teams over the course of the next twelve seasons. After the second version of the Eastern League disbanded, he decided to sign with the Homestead Grays in 1930, who were an independent team at the time. He became an important member of the 1931 Grays club, which is on the shortlist of teams considered to be the best in the history of Negro League baseball. According to the database on Seamheads.com, the Indianapolis native hit .319 on a team that included Josh Gibson as well as Hall of Fame pitchers Satchel Paige and Joe Williams.

In 1932, Pittsburgh Crawford owner Gus Greenlee was in the midst of trying to build one of the great Negro League dynasties of all time, and that meant raiding his cross-city rivals the Grays. Greenlee talked the now thirty-five-year-old veteran to joining his team as the Crawford manager.

He, in turn, convinced Gibson into coming along also. Charleston was getting heavier as he got older, and his speed wasn't what it was, which necessitated a move to first base full time. As more Hall of Fame talent joined him with the Crawfords, it was becoming apparent that Greenlee's dream was becoming a reality.

Judy Johnson, Cool Papa Bell and Paige had joined Charleston and Gibson, as well as such notable players not in the Hall of Fame like Ted "Double Duty" Radcliffe. They formed a nucleus that dominated the game. Charleston was a standout hitter with a .350 average in 1932 and would continue to hit over .300 for the next two seasons. As a manager, he was also superb. He led the 1934 and 1935 Crawfords to a combined 100-51 mark, while the 1935 squad captured the league championship.

Charleston stayed with the Crawfords through 1938 as Greenlee's financial empire began to crumble. Oscar left the club following that season. He played periodically for the next decade, ending up with a team owned by Branch Rickey called the Brooklyn Brown Dodgers in 1945. Rickey also had him help scout Negro League players to see who would eventually break the color barrier in Major League Baseball. In 1954, he returned to his hometown of Indianapolis, where became the manager of the Clowns, with whom he won the league title. Unfortunately, in October 1954, he died of a heart attack.

Oscar Charleston's career was magnificent and deserving of the honor he received posthumously in 1976 with his election into baseball's Hall of Fame. While his career spanned fourteen teams over almost forty years, it was his time in Pittsburgh with two of the greatest teams ever produced in professional baseball that helped solidify his legend.

Chapter 4

THE ELITE ONES

ATHLETES 20-11

20. BILLY CONN

Boxing, 1934–48

Western Pennsylvania has a rich history in the sport of boxing. From Harry Greb to Fritzie Zivic to Paul Spadafora, this list of champions is impressive indeed. One man, a light-heavyweight champion of the world born in the East Liberty section of Pittsburgh by the name of William David Conn, was among the greatest of them. Conn is regarded as one best boxers of the twentieth century, and his place in history is secure with his election to the International Boxing Hall of Fame. The only problem with Conn's career is that it's not remembered for his title or his sixty-four victories against some of the best of his era. It is remembered for a devastating loss at the Polo Grounds in New York when for twelve rounds it looked like he was about to pull off one of the great upsets in boxing history. He comfortably led heavyweight champion Joe Louis going into the fateful thirteenth round, only to be knocked out after failing to heed his corner's advice and going for a knockout himself.

When Conn was a young teenager, he met a man named Johnny Ray, who had been a boxer in the Pittsburgh area. After he retired from fighting, Ray bought a gym in East Liberty, where Conn and his friends liked to hang around. Billy made a sarcastic comment toward one of the boxers who was training. The comment didn't sit well with Ray, who challenged the young

He may be known for losing the heavyweight championship of the world to Joe Louis in 1941, but make no mistake, Billy Conn was one of the greatest fighters the sport has known. The former light-heavyweight champion finished his career with a 64-11-1 mark and was named by the Associated Press as the ninth-best fighter of the twentieth century. *Courtesy of Tim Conn.*

Conn to come into the ring and put on the gloves with him. He impressed the gym owner with his natural skill, and when asked what his name was, he retorted, "Billy Conn…I can lick any kid in the neighborhood."[92]

Later on, Conn's father asked Ray to train his son so he could defend himself following some issues he was having in the neighborhood with other kids. They immediately developed a good relationship, with Ray referring to Conn as "Junior" (it was because Conn's father was also named Billy, although Conn would dispute being called Junior since he and his dad had different middle names) and Billy calling Ray "Moonie" because of his affection for moonshine.

While Conn was only sixteen years old, Ray felt that the young boxer was good enough to begin his professional career, and with the permission of his father, the trainer teamed up with Johnny McGarvey, a local manager, to co-manage Billy, with the young boxer to receive half of his earnings. Ray was the trainer and decided that he would bring Conn along to difficult fights so he could actually learn the game quicker rather than worrying about his record and only scheduling easy tune-up bouts for the young boxer.

He began his career at Valley Bell Park in Charleston on July 20, 1934, by knocking out Johnny Lewis in the third round, and then, true to his word, Ray matched him up with tough fighters. The East Liberty native, who eventually would be known as the "Pittsburgh Kid," fought older and sometimes bigger boxers; his record stood at only 8-6 when he met George Liggins on September 9, 1935, at Duquesne Gardens in Pittsburgh. After winning a four-round decision, Conn felt confident and began a twenty-eight-bout unbeaten streak, going 27-0-1.

Billy Conn was now a contender, and his level of opponent was increasing with each fight. Still a very young boxer, Conn stood in with the former middleweight champion of the world, Teddy Yarosz, from nearby Monaca, Pennsylvania, at the Duquesne Gardens. Before the fight, writer Chas Kramer of the *Sports Journal* called the young East Liberty native "Pittsburgh's greatest ring natural." He went on to say, "Billy Conn is the greatest figure to come upon the boxing scene in Pittsburgh since the halcyon days of Harry Greb."[93]

The young fighter came into the bout as an underdog, but in a thrilling battle, he upset the former champion with a split decision. While he defeated Yarosz in a rematch, he also lost to contenders Young Corbett III, the former world welterweight champion; Solly Krieger; and Yarosz in a third match, with Conn getting retribution against Corbett and Krieger in rematches. As Conn was getting older, it was increasingly difficult for him to maintain his weight, so he eventually put himself in position as a light-heavyweight contender. In 1939, he fought for the light-heavyweight crown against the defending champion, Melio Bettina, who had won the vacant New York State Athletic Commission (NYSAC) world title only a few months earlier. The fight was at Madison Square Garden in New York and was not only for the NYSAC belt but also the vacant National Boxing Association (NBA) world championship. Conn emerged victorious with a unanimous decision. The Pittsburgh Kid had now become a world champion at only twenty-one years old.

He retained both championships in a rematch against Bettina at Forbes Field before defeating future light-heavyweight champion Gus Lesnevich twice in defense of his title. Billy was now one of the best fighters in the business and was named *Ring Magazine*'s Fighter of the Year in 1940. He was young and confident and looked toward greater things in his career, namely becoming the first light-heavyweight champion to win the heavyweight title. He gave up his light-heavyweight championship to focus on that goal. Conn put himself in position for a shot at Joe Louis's belt in 1941 by defeating such impressive heavyweight contenders as Bob Pastor and Lee Savold. On June 18, 1941, he finally got that opportunity as he faced the legendary champion at the Polo Grounds in New York. As the fight went on, it was shaping up to be a night for the ages for Billy Conn as well as the history of boxing. Then, stunningly, it tuned into a disastrous evening for the challenger.

Conn was twenty-five pounds lighter than the champion and an 11-5 underdog in the bout. Billy was a masterful boxer, though, and his skills came to the forefront in the fight. For twelve rounds, it looked like the crown would soon be his. The East Liberty native staggered Louis in the twelfth, which unfortunately ended up being Conn's undoing. He was ahead on two scorecards going into the thirteenth and tied on another. If he won only one of the remaining three rounds, he would become the first light-heavyweight champion to win the heavyweight championship.

Conventional wisdom dictated that the smaller fighter should stay away from the heavier champion and just box and move. But Conn was confident and cocky. He said to Ray before the round, "I've got him!" Ray screamed back, "Box! Stay away!"[94] Unfortunately, the young fighter's ego took over, as did the desperation of Louis. About one minute into the round, the champion hurt the smaller challenger. There was no better finisher at the time than Joe Louis, and before the thirteenth round came to an end, so did Conn's hopes. What had looked like a great historical moment ended by Conn being knocked out with two seconds left in the round.

He would be given a rematch, one that ended up being called off after Conn broke his hand in a fight with his father-in-law, Jimmy Smith, a former Major League Baseball player. Both boxers ended up serving in the army during World War II, and the much-heralded rematch wouldn't take place for four years, after both were discharged. It was a one-sided fight at Yankee Stadium on July 19, 1946, with Louis winning via an eighth-round knockout.

Two years later, Conn fought twice more before ending his career with a knockout over Jackie Lyons and finishing with a 64-11-1 record. His place in history is confirmed—he's a member of the International Hall of Fame and was ranked as the ninth-best fighter of the twentieth century by the Associated Press in 1999. Despite all the accolades, it's his first fight against Louis for which he will be remembered forever. While it's a night that should have ended differently had Billy's ego not taken over, the loss does not take away from the fact that he is a legend in the city of Pittsburgh.

19. WILLIE STARGELL

Pittsburgh Pirates, 1962–82

Every kid who grew up in Western Pennsylvania as a baseball fan during the 1960s and 1970s had one thing in common. Whether it was softball, baseball or wiffle ball, when they came to the plate they all stepped into the batter's box and started to whip the bat around in a windmill fashion as they waited for the pitch. It was something they did in honor of one of their heroes, one of the greatest power hitters in the history of the Pittsburgh Pirates. His name was Wilver Dornell Stargell.

Stargell is known for his legendary windmill prep as he faced the pitcher; his prodigious tape measure home runs; his famed restaurant in Pittsburgh, which gave out free chicken every time he'd hit a home run (a tradition started when Hall of Fame announcer Bob Prince began to scream, "Chicken on the Hill with Will" after he smacked a homer); the stars he put on his teammates' pillbox hats in the late 1970s when they'd do something special on the field; and, finally, his nickname "Pops," as the beloved leader of the last world championship team this franchise has produced to date in 1979.

Born in Earlsboro, Oklahoma, before moving to the Bay Area in California as a child, Pops grew up in an atmosphere filled with major-league talent.

Willie Stargell certainly had a magnificent career, but it was toward the end of his career in 1979 that he truly showed how spectacular he was. At thirty-nine years old, he hit thirty-two home runs, capturing the National League Most Valuable Player as well as the MVP Awards in both the National League Championship Series and the World Series. *Courtesy of the Pittsburgh Pirates.*

He attended Encinal High School in Alameda, which produced such players over the years as Jimmy Rollins, Bernie Williams, Dontrelle Willis, Tommy Harper and Curt Motten. While the Hall of Famer attended the school, his team was incredibly talented, as it included Harper and Motten.

Growing up in the projects of Alameda, Pops did have his moments where he got into trouble, but he credited his mother for helping him through those difficult times and getting him to develop his toughness and leadership abilities that were prevalent in his twenty-year career. "Mom taught me it's important how you treat people. When you grow up in the project, there is no reason to be thin-skinned. If you were they stayed on you. I've learned you've got to be able to take what you dish out."[95]

After their playing days at Encinal, Harper received a $20,000 signing bonus from the Cincinnati Reds, while Stargell was only offered $1,500 from the Pirates. With such a low offer, Willie considered taking a job at a local Chevrolet plant, where he'd make almost that amount on a monthly basis and have a chance to pursue a career in management. To Stargell, he felt that opportunities in a plant would come up on other occasions, but playing major-league baseball could be a once-in-a-lifetime chance. He signed a contract with Pittsburgh in 1958.

Early on in his minor-league career, Stargell played for Pittsburgh affiliates in the South, where he faced racial insults on almost a nightly basis. He tried to ignore the taunts and keep focused on the task at hand, hitting 22 home runs at Asheville before moving to their AAA team in Columbus, Ohio, where he finished the season with 27 homers and 82 RBIs in 1962. Stargell was so impressive that he was brought up to the Bucs as a late-season call-up and never went back to the minors.

Pops played the first part of his career in a stadium that was a nightmare for power hitters, Forbes Field. While Forbes was 300 feet down the right field line, there was a screen that rose from the brick fence. The fence quickly shot out to 408 feet and then a center field distance of 457 feet. The left field line stood at 365 feet. Home runs were not an easy task. Stargell did his best to overcome such challenges, averaging almost twenty-four homers per year while clearing the right field roof at the legendary facility an incredible seven times.

His power numbers weren't magnificent at Forbes Field, figures that Stargell would estimate later on cost him a shot at 600 home runs in his career because of the expansive ballpark. Despite the challenges at Forbes, he still was one of the best players in the game, being named to the *Sporting News*' all-star team in 1965 and 1966. While one could only imagine what he would have done in a more hitter-friendly park, it would have been difficult to hit another 17.8 per year in one to bring him to the 600–home run plateau. One thing is for sure: it did cost him hitting 500 home runs in his career. That would all change midway in 1970, when the Pirates moved to a stadium with more hitter-friendly dimensions, Three Rivers Stadium.

Stargell's statistics rose immediately. He smacked 31 homers in 1970, playing the second half of the season at Three Rivers before having his greatest campaign in 1971. It was a special season for the Bucs, as they won the franchise's fourth world championship, and Pops was a big reason for it, hitting a league-high 48 home runs while knocking in 125. There were many who felt that he should have been the National League MVP, but he finished second to the Cardinals' Joe Torre in the voting. As wonderful as the season was, Willie had a very disappointing postseason, going hitless in fourteen at bats in the NLCS before hitting only .208 in the World Series, although he scored the series-winning run in the eighth inning of game seven. He would enjoy two more incredible campaigns in 1972 and 1973, but it would take eight more years until he had his postseason retribution.

In 1972, the Pirates enjoyed their best regular season since 1925 before losing to the Reds in the NLCS. Stargell continued his wonderful power numbers with 33 long balls before enjoying another all-star year in 1973. The team was playing without their team leader that season, as Roberto Clemente had tragically died in a plane accident on New Year's Eve. The team was in mourning all season and struggled on the field. Stargell, though, had an incredible year, leading the National League in both home runs and RBIs, with 44 and 119, respectively, and setting a National League record with 90 extra base hits.

Willie was thirty-three in 1974, and he would begin to accrue injuries that caused his numbers to decline. In 1975, he was permanently moved to first base from left field, as he suffered from cracked ribs. The injury also hampered him at the plate, as his home runs dropped to twenty-two, his lowest total since 1967. A brain aneurysm suffered by his wife, Doris, who thankfully survived, and an injured elbow that occurred during a fight against the Phillies would cause Stargell's statistics to suffer more, as his homers dropped to thirteen in 1977. For all intents and purposes, his career was over at thirty-six.

Great champions seem to find a way to overcome adversity, and Willie Stargell was no different. He rebounded in 1978 with twenty-eight homers, winning the *Sporting News* Comeback Player of the Year Award. That season set up a year for the ages for the aging slugger.

At thirty-eight years old, Stargell was now the spiritual leader of the team in 1979. He celebrated his teammates' achievements by putting stars on their hats, but most of the memorable moments were due to his efforts. He clouted 32 home runs, while finally winning the National League Most Valuable Player Award, finishing in a tie with Keith Hernandez of St. Louis. He made up for his poor performance in 1971 by hitting .455 in the NLCS and .400 in a World Series, during which Pops hit three home runs, including the series-winning shot in game seven. For his efforts, he made a clean sweep of MVP awards, being named the Most Valuable Player in both series. It was a wonderful campaign, but injuries would severely hamper the rest of his career, which ended three years later. With the help of his 1979 performance, Stargell went from a great player to a Hall of Fame inductee in 1988, his first time on the ballot.

He went into coaching after that and was credited by Chipper Jones as helping him become a Hall of Famer with the advice given to him as a rookie. Sadly, on the day PNC Park was to open and a statue was to be dedicated in his honor, an ailing Willie Stargell died, the result of a stroke he experienced while he was in the hospital to have his gallbladder removed.

It was a devastating moment for fans who had come to celebrate his excellence that day. His numbers—475 home runs in a Pirate uniform and the only man to hit a ball out of Dodger Stadium, while finding the upper deck at Three Rivers four times—made him an icon, as did the fact that he led the team to two world titles. But he loved the city of Pittsburgh as much as the town loved him. "Pittsburgh isn't fancy, but it's real. It's a working town, and money doesn't come easy. I feel as much a part of this city as the cobblestone streets and the steel mills. People in this town expect an honest day's work, and I've given it to them for a long, long time."[96] The fans certainly appreciated his efforts, as they cherish him today.

18. BUCK LEONARD

Homestead Grays, 1934–50

Buck Leonard combined with the great Josh Gibson to form one of the most powerful duos in professional baseball history as they helped the Homestead Grays become arguably the most successful franchise in the Negro Leagues. Josh Gibson was called the "Black Babe Ruth," while Leonard was referred to as the "Black Lou Gehrig." For Gibson, it was a comparison on the basis of power, while for Buck it was that of position too—a comparison as to who was arguably the best first baseman of all-time.

Born Walter Fenner Leonard in Rocky Mount, North Carolina, on September 7, 1907, Leonard was given the nickname Buddy by his family. His younger brother, Charlie, couldn't pronounce his nickname, as he would call him Buck instead of Buddy. His brother's interpretation of the nickname stuck.

Buck's baseball career came as a result of the Depression. He was only able to attend school through eighth grade, quitting after his father passed away in 1919 during the flu pandemic. He eventually found work in a railroad shop and played semipro baseball on the side. In the midst of the Depression in 1933, the railroad shop to cut back its workforce. Leonard was becoming a very talented baseball player and ended up leaving home to pursue a full-time career on the diamond because of the cutbacks. He signed with the Portsmouth Firefighters before heading over to the

Buck Leonard (*second from the left*) was one of the longest-tenured Homestead Grays, playing seventeen seasons with the team. He was often compared to Lou Gehrig and is considered one of the greatest first basemen ever to play the game. *Courtesy of the Rivers of Steel and the Josh Gibson family.*

Baltimore Stars midseason for potentially more money. He was given an opportunity with the Stars to be paid a percentage of the gate rather than a set amount. It was with Baltimore that he was taught how to play first base by player-manager Ben Taylor, who was getting older and wanted to give up his spot at the position.

Buck became very effective at first under Taylor, but the promise of more money never came to fruition, as the Stars went bankrupt before the 1933 campaign ended. With no team to play for, he hooked on with the Brooklyn Royal Giants to end the season. In the off season, Hall of Famer "Smoky" Joe Williams was a bartender in New York and told Grays owner Cum Posey about the young Rocky Mount native. Posey signed Leonard for the 1934 campaign, which allowed Leonard more stability as he became a star for the Grays over the next seventeen seasons.

With the Grays, Leonard became more of a leader and was able to learn quite a bit about the game from Posey. He thought that the Grays owner was "kind of a quiet guy but he knew baseball. Taught me two or three things I've never forgotten. Taught me how to hit left-handed pitchers, taught me to use an open stance with left-handers. Taught me how to throw the ball when the pitcher's covering first base. And he told me not to try to steal any bases; told me to quit running. I wasn't fast enough to steal bases."[97]

In 1934, there was a Pittsburgh baseball war in the Negro Leagues, as Gus Greenlee had stolen most of the top talent from the Grays for his Pittsburgh Crawfords. Homestead struggled, while the Crawfords were producing some of the greatest teams the league had ever seen. While times were tough for Homestead, Leonard remained a star, never hitting less than .333 those first three seasons in a Gray uniform, with a magnificent .386 average in 1935.

After three years of playing with a struggling club, Buck Leonard would get the opportunity to play with a winning one. The Crawfords were falling apart financially, and the team was collapsing. Gibson returned to Homestead in 1937 as the era of Leonard and Gibson duo began. Josh Gibson's home runs were legendary, while Leonard had incredible gap power. Buck hit a career-high thirteen home runs with a .376 average that year as the Grays dominated league play with a 54-18-1 mark, winning the second league championship in franchise history. It would be the first of nine consecutive league titles the Grays would secure.

As he gained stature as a ball player, Buck Leonard was becoming a tradition in the marquee game of the Negro League calendar, the East-West Game. The East-West Game was an all-star game for the Negro Leagues. Between 1935 and 1948, Leonard would be selected a record thirteen times.

He was at his best in the all-star contest, hitting .313, with home runs in the 1937, 1941 and 1943 classics; 14 RBIs; and a .563 slugging percentage.

Going into the 1938 campaign, Buck decided to marry Sandra Wroten, a widow. Her late husband had owned a funeral home that Leonard wanted no part of, so they sold the business; she became a teacher, and the future Hall of Famer continued to play year-round to help support her as well as his mother and siblings. He began to play on the winter league circuit in Puerto Rico, Cuba and Venezuela between 1935 and 1955, as well as barnstorming games (postseason exhibition games that would generate extra income for the players) in the United States, some against major-league players. In series of barnstorming games in California during the 1943 off season, Major League Baseball commissioner Kenesaw Mountain Landis put an end to the series following the eighth game. At that point, Leonard was showing the major-leaguers just how talented he was, hitting .500 to that point.

In the regular season for the Grays, Leonard and Gibson continued to dominate league play. Leonard hit a career-high .417 in 1938 before following it up with a .395, twelve-home-run season one year later. Buck went on to have a wonderful career with Homestead, hitting .348 for the period, with a 1.037 OPS, hitting below .300 once between 1933 and 1947. Against the major-leaguers during the barnstorming contests he played in, Buck Leonard showed that he could handle the pitchers in the majors with a .382 average.

While he would never get the chance to prove that he was better than Lou Gehrig, as some suggested, including Hall of Famer Monte Irvin, Buck did have his moments when he thought his opportunity was imminent. He was offered to the Pittsburgh Pirates during the 1938 campaign by the sports editor of the *Pittsburgh Courier*, Chester Washington, along with several other Negro League stars. Unfortunately, the offer was more intended to put pressure on the majors to sign African American players and was never taken seriously by the team. A year later, Pirates president Bill Benswanger offered them tryouts, but they never came to fruition. In 1943, Washington Senators owner Clark Griffith asked Gibson and Leonard, who were playing half of their season in Washington as part of the Homestead-Washington Grays, if they were interested in playing in the majors. When both said they were, Griffith promised to get back to them, but never did. Whether it was the owners who were afraid to sign African Americans or the Negro League owners who feared that the league would fall apart if their players began to sign with the majors, the opportunities never came about until Branch Rickey signed Jackie Robinson in 1945.

The Negro League owners were correct. Once Robinson and the others began to integrate the majors, the Negro Leagues quickly declined and all but came to an end in 1948. The Grays would play two more seasons against less than stellar competition before folding in 1950. In 1952, Buck Leonard was offered a contract by St. Louis Browns owner Bill Veeck to play in the majors, but he was now forty-four years old and knew that his time in professional baseball was over. "I was not bitter by not being allowed to play in the major leagues. I just said, 'The time has not come.' I only wish I could have played in the big leagues when I was young enough to show what I could do. When an offer was given to me to join up, I was too old and I knew it."[98]

While he never got the opportunity to play in Major League Baseball, he did play for a very short time in the minors at forty-six years old. He was successful in his abbreviated time, hitting .333 in ten games for Portsmouth of the Piedmont League. Leonard retired after that and became a truant officer in the Rocky Mount School System before opening a real estate agency in his hometown and becoming an officer with the local team in the Carolina Leagues. Finally, in 1972, he received baseball's ultimate honor with his election into the Hall of Fame.

Whether or not Leonard was better than Gehrig remains in question, but Buck is arguably the best first baseman the Negro Leagues ever produced. He is also one of the greatest baseball players ever to play in the city of Pittsburgh.

17. JAROMÍR JÁGR

Pittsburgh Penguins, 1990–2001

At forty-seven years old, Jaromír Jágr is a freak of nature. Jágr played with the Calgary Flames until he was cut in January 2018 in his twenty-fourth NHL season. Not thinking that he was ready to give up the game, he came back to his native country, the Czech Republic, to play with the team he co-owns, Rytiri Kladno. Remarkably, in February 2019, the ageless wonder laced up his skates for his thirtieth professional season of hockey. Looking at his graying beard as he skates down the ice now, one is reminded of twenty-nine years before when he was a young eighteen-year-old rookie with the Pittsburgh Penguins. He burst onto the NHL in an impressive manner, not only soon becoming the best in the game while he wore the Penguin uniform but also etching his name among the top three in franchise history along with Mario Lemieux and Sidney Crosby.

A young star in his home country, Jágr was eligible for the 1990 NHL draft. He desperately wanted to play alongside one of the greatest talents in the league, Mario Lemieux, and did some maneuvering in his attempts to do just that. The Penguins were set to draft 5th in the first round that year after a disappointing 1989–90 campaign, and unbeknownst to Pittsburgh Hall of Fame general manager Craig Patrick, Jágr had told the four teams in front of them that he didn't want to play in the NHL. It scared off the four teams from drafting the exceptionally talented right wing. In his discussion with Patrick, Jágr had a different story. According to the GM, "When we asked him that question, he said, 'I'll be there tomorrow if you draft me.' I think other teams backed off because of that. We were happy he was there. We were surprised he was there, definitely."[99] While the front offices in Quebec (now Colorado), Vancouver, Detroit and Philadelphia must have been upset they were lied to, the Penguins were ecstatic. The next maneuver was to try and get him out of Czechoslovakia.

Relations between the Eastern Bloc communist countries and the West were beginning to thaw at that time, but getting Jágr to Pittsburgh wasn't going to easy. No Czechoslovakian player at this time had been able to make it to the United States without defecting. Jaromír Jágr would be the first, although it must have felt like he was doing exactly that. The Czech team was going to Seattle for the Goodwill Games and were boarding the plane in Prague. At that point, it became apparent they were missing their best player. He had taken a flight two days earlier with his mother, Anna, from Frankfurt to the Pittsburgh International Airport and was met with open arms by Patrick and Pens coach Bob Johnson. The Czech hockey establishment was not happy he left.

There were fears of repercussions at home for his father and sister, but those were downplayed a bit since his dad had an important job in the construction business at home and it was felt that he was irreplaceable in the job so he would be safe. There was also the fact that Jágr had a year remaining in his contract at home with Poli Kladno, but his agent, Don Meehan, was certain that if they took the Pens to court, Kladno would lose due to the fact that they signed Jágr as a minor.

While there were still some issues that had to be settled, they had their star. When he arrived, he knew no English, but the team set him up in intensive courses to help him learn. He became a media darling and a huge fan favorite. It didn't hurt that he scored twenty-seven goals his rookie season and finished sixth in the voting for the Calder Trophy, an award given to the Rookie of the Year in the league. With another budding superstar on the roster, the Penguins finally won a Stanley Cup that most fans never thought they would see. Up to that point, the franchise had a disastrous history that saw them mostly finish near the bottom of the standings.

With an array of superior talent on the team, including Jágr, the Pens were now an elite team. Despite the death of their coach, Bob Johnson, in the midst of their Stanley Cup defense, the team ended up in the Stanley Cup finals once again, where they faced the Chicago Blackhawks. In his second season, Jaromír continued his progress with thirty-two goals. In game one of the finals at the Civic Arena, he showed his incredible talent with one of the most remarkable goals in NHL history. Chicago had broken out to an early 4–1 lead, but the Penguins fought back, cutting the deficit to one. At that point, the young winger zig-zagged through the Blackhawk defense before putting the puck past goalie Ed Belfour to tie the game at four. Thanks to Jágr's heroics, Pittsburgh eventually won the game and swept Chicago for their second consecutive cup victory. Jaromír was spectacular in the playoffs, netting eleven goals and twenty-four points in twenty-one games.

He continued his incredible play as the years went on, and when Lemieux decided to take a year off after back surgery and the fatigue caused by his radiation treatments for Hodgkin's lymphoma in 1994–95, Jágr took over as arguably the best player in the game. The 1994–95 campaign was shortened due to a labor dispute, but when the teams came back to play in January, the young Czech was incredible. He captured his first Art Ross Trophy, given to the league scoring leader, accumulating 70 points in only forty-eight games. A year later, he amassed a career-high 149 points and sixty-two goals, finishing behind Lemieux in both categories. His point total broke the record for a European player in the NHL, surpassing Peter Stasny's former mark of 139.

When Lemieux decided to retire in 1997, Jaromír Jágr was prepared to take his place at the top of the scoring race. In his final four seasons in a Penguins uniform, he won the Art Ross Trophy each year while capturing the Hart Trophy in 1998–99 as the league's Most Valuable Player. That season, Jágr scored perhaps the most important goal in franchise history, one that may have kept the team in Pittsburgh.

By that point, the Penguins were struggling financially, and the team needed to advance to the second round of the playoffs to generate enough finances to stay afloat. If not, team owner Howard Baldwin would possibly have to sell the team, which may have caused them to move to another city. It wasn't looking good for Pittsburgh, as they were down three games to two to New Jersey and Jágr had missed the previous four games with a groin pull. Knowing the importance of the task at hand, the NHL leading scorer struggled to play this game, but Jaromír scored the game-tying goal with just under three minutes left to play. With 11:01 left in the first overtime, he scored the game-winner, sending the series to a seventh game, which the Pens won two nights later. After the contest, Jágr said, "That was probably my best game ever. My most important for sure. I'll probably never score a goal that important. Probably if I hadn't scored, the team wouldn't be in Pittsburgh right now."[100]

Unfortunately, Baldwin did declare bankruptcy after the season, but since Lemieux was the one he owed the most money to, he worked out an agreement with the Pens legend, who headed up a group to buy the team. Still struggling financially, the team had no choice but to trade Jágr, their highest-paid player, after the 2001 campaign. In one of the worst trades in team history, they sent the five-time scoring champ to the Washington Capitals for a group that included Kris Beech, Michal Sivek and Ross Lupaschuk. Patrick said he was thrilled with what he got and compared Beech to Ron Francis, claiming that he had the potential to be a difference maker; he was not. None of the players acquired came close to matching Jágr's production.

In 2011, Jágr stated that he wanted to come back to the Penguins, and Pittsburgh offered a one-year contract at $2 million. It was hoped that he would finish his legendary career where it began. In a move that didn't sit well with Pens fans, he chose to sign at the last minute with their cross-state rivals, the Philadelphia Flyers, for a reported $3.3 million.

While the anger in Pittsburgh has subsided, Jaromír Jágr has gone on to enjoy a spectacular career. He won the Masterson Trophy at forty-three years old in 2016 as the NHL Comeback Player of the Year, scoring 27 goals for the Florida Panthers, and stayed in the league until he was let go by Calgary in early 2018. While it's not a certainty that his NHL career is over, it most likely is. He has scored 766 career goals, third in league history, while amassing 1,921 points, second behind only Wayne Gretzky. His career was colorful and will certainly land him in the Hall of Fame as hopefully his number, 68, will also hang above the PPG Paints Arena rafters with Lemieux and no. 21 Michel Briere, never to be worn again by any Pittsburgh Penguin.

16. ROD WOODSON

Pittsburgh Steelers, 1987–96

Rod Woodson was the 10th pick in the 1987 NFL draft for the Pittsburgh Steelers. It was thought that the cornerback out of Purdue University would make a significant difference in a Pittsburgh defense that had struggled over the previous few seasons. While it appeared to be the perfect choice, the Woodson-Steeler marriage did not get off to a great start. Disappointed with the contract he was offered, the young defensive back decided to hold out. He was also a world-class hurdler and threatened to focus his efforts on training for the 1988 Olympic Games rather than become the All-Pro many experts were projecting him to be. Finally, after a prolonged ninety-four-day holdout, he signed his deal in late October and on November 8, 1987, began a career with Pittsburgh that would end with his induction in the Pro Football Hall of Fame.

A consensus All-American his senior season at Purdue, Woodson was not happy with the offer that Pittsburgh gave him following the draft. In college, he was a four-time Big Ten 55-meter hurdles indoor champion and was an All-American in the event in 1985. He was one of the first players to admit signing with an agent before his college eligibility had expired, which made him ineligible for the NCAA track season his senior year. Even though Woodson could no longer run for Purdue, he decided while he was holding out that he'd pursue a spot on the 1988 Olympic track team.

Chuck DeBus of the Los Angeles Track Club was helping him, and in Woodson's first race ran, he had the third-best time in the world that year at 13.29. He qualified for the USA Track and Field Championships but fell over a hurdle and failed to qualify for the finals. Despite the mishap, Woodson did qualify for the Olympic Trials in the event. At that point, Steelers director of communications Joe Gordon knew that a track career wasn't just an idle threat. "Cornerback is our weakest position. Prior to the draft, we knew he had some potential as a track man. At that time, he did not appear as hot a prospect as he is now. Realistically, we have to feel now, track is a possibility."[101]

With the contract negotiations stalled and his status as a potential member of the Steelers secondary in jeopardy, Dan Rooney decided to enter the contract talks and eventually worked out a contract that was satisfactory to both sides. Woodson signed a four-year deal that would give him a bonus between $750,000 and $800,000 and be worth more that

$2 million over the course of the contract, including incentives. Rooney was thrilled and said simply, "We expect him to come in and become a productive member of our team."[102]

The cornerback got a two-week roster exemption, and finally, on November 8, they cut defensive tackle Jackie Cline to make room for Woodson on the roster. He played sparingly against the Kansas City Chiefs in that first game but almost secured his first National Football League interception in the 17–16 victory. Rookies Delton Hall and Thomas Everett did intercept passes that day, as Coach Chuck Noll now had three impressive rookies in his defensive backfield.

Two games later, Woodson did pick off his first NFL pass against the Bengals, returning it 45 yards for his first professional touchdown. He finished the year also showing what an effective returner he was, averaging 8.4 per punt return and 22.3 per kickoff return. As his second season began in 1988, he took over the starting spot at cornerback and became a star. After a solid sophomore campaign, Woodson became one of the best in the game in 1989. He led a young Steeler defense that helped propel the team into their first playoff spot in five seasons and was named first-team All-Pro, a feat he repeated a year later in 1990.

Following a disappointing 1991 campaign for both him and the Steelers, the Chuck Noll era ended in Pittsburgh as Bill Cowher was hired to coach the team. It was a resurrection of sorts for the franchise, with a stellar 11-5 mark and their first division title in eight years. Woodson once again became a first-team All-Pro selection, intercepting four passes and returning the second punt return for a touchdown in his career.

The team was getting closer to being a Super Bowl contender in 1993, and Woodson had arguably the most successful season of his career. He picked off a career-high eight passes, running one back for a score, and was named the Associated Press NFL Defensive Player of the Year. A year later, he ran two back for touchdowns and snagged six more interceptions while garnering first-team All-Pro status for the fifth time in eight seasons. Following a disappointing upset loss to the Chargers in the AFC championship game, 1995 looked like the year the Steelers finally would get back to their first Super Bowl in fifteen years. They would eventually make it, just without their superstar cornerback.

In an opening-day victory against the Detroit Lions at Three Rivers Stadium, Woodson would tear his anterior cruciate ligament in his right knee while stopping to tackle Barry Sanders and was lost for the season—or so they thought. At that time, no one had ever suffered such a severe knee injury in the NFL and came back to play that same season. Woodson was determined to make history and worked hard to get to that point.

Through his intense workouts, Woodson defied the odds and was able to return for the team's Super Bowl XXX matchup against the Dallas Cowboys. He played in only the dime packages, replacing Randy Fuller, and had no tackles, but he allowed no completions to Cowboy receivers. His accomplishment of returning so quickly was an inspiration to the team, despite the 27–17 defeat at the hands of the Cowboys.

Woodson did return in 1996 but turned down a $3 million-per-year extension by the team before the season began. While he played well, with six interceptions, one returned for a touchdown, there were questions whether or not his knee would heal properly to the point that he could return to the status he had before the injury. Pittsburgh still offered a five-year deal at the end of the season with a $2 million bonus, but less money overall throughout the contract. The contract was also backloaded, giving the team some insurance in case his knee didn't heal properly. It was a deal that he didn't feel exemplified his worth to the team and he turned it down.

Pittsburgh went on to draft Chad Scott in the first round and spent most of their salary cap and there was little left to sign Woodson so the player and the team parted ways. There were other clubs that questioned whether he knee would allow him to play at his pre-1995 level, so offers weren't coming in at first.

Usually, when the Steelers let a veteran go, they are good at projecting that his better days are behind him, except in this case. While he eventually would switch from cornerback to free safety, Woodson went on to play until 2003 with the 49ers, Ravens and Raiders and twice led the league in interceptions, including in 2002 with Oakland at thirty-seven years old, a season in which he was selected as a first-team All-Pro for the first time in eight years. He retired with an NFL-record twelve interception returns for touchdowns, and his seventy-one interceptions overall is third in league history as of 2018.

As it turned out, Rooney was correct in 1987 for pushing so hard to sign Woodson. He ended up being selected to the NFL's seventy-fifth-anniversary All-Time Team in 1994 and the Hall of Fame's all-1990s team and was elected to the Pro Football Hall of Fame in 2009. Not a bad résumé for a world-class hurdles man from Purdue University.

15. MEL BLOUNT

Pittsburgh Steelers, 1970–83

When Southern University's Mel Blount was drafted in the third round of the 1970 NFL draft by the Pittsburgh Steelers, he was a talented kid from a small school going to a very bad team coming off a 1-13 campaign. Few understood that Chuck Noll and the Steelers' front office were in the middle of constructing one of greatest, if not the greatest, dynasties in NFL history—one in which Blount would play a pivotal part. While he received recognition in the form of Pro Bowl and All-Pro selections to signify his excellence, there was a far greater honor that he received that is rare in professional sports: the league changed the rules of the game because of him, a rule change that more than forty years later has significantly changed the game of football.

At six-foot-three and 203 pounds, Blount came into camp with experience at both safety and cornerback, as the Vidalia, Georgia native was a physical player whom Chuck Noll thought would make a difference in the Steeler secondary. Blount showed that Noll's evaluation was correct, as he started nine games his rookie season for the injured John Rowser and set a franchise mark for kickoff return average with a 29.7 yards per kick mark. He started nine more contests in his second season, and by 1972, Mel Blount had become firmly entrenched as a starter on a defense that was about to become the league's best.

He swiped nine passes between 1972 and 1974, and his physical play was one of the main reasons teams had trouble passing against the Steel Curtain defense. He scored his first NFL touchdown in 1974, scoring on a 52-yard return against the Eagles, and his interception at the goal line against Minnesota in Super Bowl IX helped Pittsburgh secure their first world championship in the forty-one-year existence of the franchise. His stellar play was a prelude to arguably the greatest season a defensive back ever had for the Steelers.

Now one of the best defensive players in the game, Blount became the first Steeler in twenty-nine years to lead the NFL in interceptions. At that point in franchise history, three men shared the team record with ten pickoffs in 1975; Blount surpassed the trio. He intercepted passes in a team-record six games in a row and grabbed eleven for the season. For his efforts, he not only was elected as a first-team All-Pro and was selected to play in his first Pro Bowl but also captured the NFLs Associated Press Defensive Player of the Year Award. It was a perfect season that ended with the Steelers winning their second consecutive Super Bowl.

After another solid season in 1976, Blount's career took a strange twist. Following a savage hit on Steeler receiver Lynn Swann by George Atkinson of the Raiders, Noll stated to the press that Atkinson was part of a criminal element in the league—that he was the kind of player whose main purpose was to injure another rather than just playing the game and should be kicked out. An angry Atkinson sued Noll for $1 million for the comment. In the trial during the off season, the Steelers coach mentioned while testifying that his own cornerback Mel Blount was part of the so-called criminal element, in his opinion. Blount was incensed and threated to sue his coach for $5 million as he demanded a trade. He also asked the players association to look into voiding his contract and was a holdout at training camp.

Eventually, he came back to Pittsburgh in time for the start of the regular season and regained his normal form with six interceptions, but the league was looking for a way to increase the offense in the game. It decided to control the physical play of defensive backs to achieve this. Before the 1978 campaign, a defensive back like Blount could be as physical with a receiver as he wanted. There were few quarterbacks who threw for big yardage; a 300-yard game was considered a magnificent achievement, and completion percentages just above 50 percent was considered the norm. The head of the rules committee, Hall of Famer Don Shula, wanted to make the passing game more efficient, so he campaigned for a new rule that defensive backs couldn't hit a receiver past 5 yards from the line of scrimmage. Blount was the most physical defensive back in the league, so the rule was called by the media the "Mel Blount Rule." It was thought be many as a way for the NFL to neutralize Blount's effectiveness and bring Pittsburgh back to the pack.

The Mel Blount Rule had much bigger consequences than the committee had anticipated. Passing statistics increased dramatically, and forty years later, the results of the rule change are still staggering. It completely changed the way the game is played. In 1978, if part of the intention was to stifle the Pittsburgh Steelers, the rule ended up a failure, as Steeler quarterback Terry Bradshaw had career years because of it and Pittsburgh eventually won two more Super Bowls in 1978 and 1979.

If they thought this rule would also take Blount out of the game more, they were sorely mistaken. He made the Pro Bowl both Super Bowl seasons for the team, and in 1981, he was selected as a first-team All-Pro for the second time in his career. Two years later, he set the franchise all-time interception mark with fifty-seven, a record he still holds as of 2018.

Mel Blount eventually retired after fourteen seasons in a Pittsburgh Steelers uniform to help kids in need with youth homes in Georgia. He was named by the NFL to its all-time 1970s team and also was placed on its all-time seventy-fifth-anniversary team, as well as being elected to the Pro Football Hall of Fame. He currently runs a youth home in Washington County, Pennsylvania, as he continues to devote his life to kids, trying to help them reach their potential.

14. PAUL WANER

Pittsburgh Pirates, 1926–40

Pittsburgh Pirates aficionados have always supported the players who are the icons in franchise history. There are statues devoted to such luminaries as Roberto Clemente, Willie Stargell, Honus Wagner, Ralph Kiner and Bill Mazeroski, as well as various other things that honor these men throughout the stadium, such as the twenty-one-foot wall in right field to signify Clemente's jersey number. Fans wear clothes with these players adorned on them, and conversations regarding the team's successful past will generally include one or another of these men. There is another player, one who was every bit a legend in Pirates lore, who rarely is included among these Pirates. In fact, it wasn't until his grandson came to PNC Park in 2007 and asked owner Kevin McClatchy why nowhere in the facility there was a place honoring his grandfather that the team even considered doing something for him. His number wasn't even among the ones retired by the franchise. McClatchy agreed that he should be honored, and finally, Paul Waner had his number retired, sixty-seven years after he left the team. Today, he remains still relatively unknown among the Pirate faithful, but make no mistake, he is among the top three ever to wear a Pirates uniform.

Waner's résumé as one of the franchise greats is impeccable—a .340 lifetime average with the Pirates, a franchise high, while garnering 2,868 hits (3,152 in his major-league career). Paul combined with Lloyd Waner to form one of two brother Hall of Fame duos in major-league history. He was the ultimate line drive hitter, as his 605 doubles still ranks as the fourteenth-best figure of all time as of 2018, while his 191 triples are tenth. In 1932, he smashed a then National League record 62 doubles, a figure that only four other men in the game have beaten. Paul Waner won the 1927 Most Valuable Player Award in leading the Pirates to their sixth National League pennant.

While he stands as one of the greatest hitters in Pirates history, his defensive numbers in right field are not to be overlooked either. No one has ever made more putouts in right field as Waner's 4,740, and only three men in baseball history have turned more double plays in right field. He led the league in fielding percentage four times, and if one is looking for sabermetric proof of his excellence in right field, he or she only needs to see that his range factor/game is the fourth best in baseball history. When asked to name the greatest right fielder in Pirates history, Joe Tronzo of the Beaver Valley *News Tribune* said simply, "Paul Waner, when he was sober, was the best right fielder the Pirates ever had. The second-best right fielder the Pirates ever had was Paul Waner when he was drunk."[103] The interesting thing about the comment is that came in 1971, during Clemente's incredible season leading Pittsburgh to the world championship. With so much in his favor, it still took sixty-seven years to retire his number.

Paul Waner was born in Harrah, Oklahoma, in 1903 and was a great prospect, though as a pitcher, when he was signed by the San Francisco Seals of the Pacific Coast League. He hurt his arm in 1923 for the Seals, and his manager, former Pirate Dots Miller, made the fortuitous decision of converting the Oklahoma native to an outfielder. After hitting .369 that season and .325 one year later, Waner cracked .400 in 1925, finishing with a .401 average. It was a decision that must have made Miller wonder why he had him pitching in the first place.

Before the 1926 campaign, the great John McGraw and the New York Giants were considering signing Waner, but a scout persuaded McGraw that the five-foot-eight, 155-pound player was too small for the team, claiming, "That little punk don't even know how to put on a uniform."[104] Pirate owner Barney Dreyfuss didn't agree and gave San Francisco $100,000 for Waner and shortstop Hal Rhyne. In the middle of his rookie season with the Bucs in 1926, when they were playing the Giants, a year in which he hit .336 while leading the league in triples with 22, McGraw reportedly replied to the scout who didn't want to sign him, "That little punk don't even know how to put on a uniform but he's removed three of my pitchers with line drives this week. I'm glad you did not scout Christy Mathewson."[105]

Waner was called "Big Poison," with Lloyd being called "Little Poison," famous nicknames that were thought to come from the fact they were poison to the pitchers they faced. Lloyd disputed that, explaining it was from a fan at the Polo Grounds with a thick New York accent calling them "big person" and "little person." Paul battled alcoholism throughout his career, thinking that it was important to relax in the game—for him, that meant taking a drink before coming to the plate and several before a game.

That little punk went on to be the league MVP in 1927, winning his first batting title with a .380 mark while also capturing the RBI crown (131) and leading the senior circuit in hits (237) and triples (18). He helped the team to capture their second National League pennant in three years, where they faced "Murderers' Row," the great 1927 New York Yankee club, in the World Series. While the Bucs were swept in the series, Waner was phenomenal with a .333 average. It unfortunately would be the only fall classic the Hall of Famer would play in. Two years later, as one of the best players in the game, Waner held out in spring training looking for an $18,000-per-year contract and didn't sign it until mid-April. The Oklahoma native went on to have a very consistent career, winning three batting titles and never hitting below .309 until 1938, when he hit .280.

In 1940, Waner was thirty-seven years old. His best days were behind him, and he had twisted his knee going into second base. He hit only .290 and wasn't considered part of the future for the team, so the Pirates released him in December. He signed on with Brooklyn for the 1940 campaign and would go on to play five more years with the Dodgers, Braves and Yankees during World War II, when most of the game's best players had left for the service. He retired in 1945 and seven years later was given baseball's highest honor as he was elected to the Hall of Fame.

Fast-forward to 2007. His name is finally placed among the team's greats, with his number, 11, emblazoned on the façade of PNC Park, never to be worn again by another Pittsburgh Pirate. It hopefully was to be a renaissance for Waner in the eyes of Bucco fans, yet in 2015, when Major League Baseball was having fans vote for the greatest four players in each franchise's history, Waner didn't make the cut, finishing behind Mazeroski for fourth place. While his is a résumé few can match, Waner continues to be the greatest forgotten legend in Pirates history.

13. JACK HAM

Pittsburgh Steelers, 1971–82

The sign reading "Dobre Shunka" hung over a rail at Three Rivers Stadium for twelve seasons. It was there to celebrate one of the greatest linebackers to ever grace the field for the Pittsburgh Steelers. While the pronunciation of the saying was accurate, the correct spelling was *dobrý šunka*, which is Slovak for "good ham." A strange nickname for most, but in the case of Jack Ham, it couldn't have been more perfect.

The most special thing about having Jack Ham as a Pittsburgh Steeler legend was the fact that he was born and bred in Western Pennsylvania. The Johnstown native played football and was a high jumper at Bishop McCort High School before playing a postgraduate season at Massanutten Military Academy in Woodstock, Virginia. When he finished his final game at Massanutten, he believed that his career was finished. He wasn't being recruited aggressively, with only an offer to cover the cost for books at East Carolina. He decided he'd go to Penn State to continue his education when a twist of fate changed his life. A teammate on Massanutten, Steve Smear, verbally accepted a football scholarship with the Nittany Lions but then changed his mind and went to Iowa. He could see the potential in Ham and suggested to the Penn State coaching staff to take a look at the linebacker. They looked at the game films and liked what they saw, offering Ham a scholarship to continue his career. Ham was thrilled. "I didn't have a lot of confidence in myself. It showed. All you want is an opportunity, and they gave me that opportunity with that scholarship and I ran with it. Of all the people that were instrumental in my life—when you're 18 or 19 years old and you get that opportunity—I took that opportunity and was fortunate that they gave me that scholarship. That's why I'm indebted to them forever."[106] The young freshman would more than pay back that debt. The nickname of the school at the time was "Linebacker U," and Jack would contribute to the legacy quite nicely.

A three-year letterman with the Nittany Lions, Ham had an incredibly productive career, sharing the school record with four blocked punts in a career, three in one season, while accumulating 251 tackles over the course of his time at Penn State. He helped lead the team to two consecutive Orange Bowls in 1969 and 1970 while being named a first-team All-American his senior season. After he finished his career in State College, the linebacker was invited to play in two senior all-star contests, the East-West Shrine game and the Hula Bowl—for the latter, he was named the Outstanding Defensive Player of the Game.

All of a sudden, the kid who thought his football career was over after his final high school game was now the second-round draft pick of the Pittsburgh Steelers. In the course of six drafts between 1969 and 1974, the Steelers were impeccable in their defensive draft choices, and Jack Ham was one of their premier picks. By the final preseason contest in his rookie year, he was making the coaches notice his skill. He picked off three passes that final exhibition contest and was given the starting spot at outside linebacker in his first official game.

He had a solid first two seasons that included a career-high seven interceptions in his second campaign, while helping Pittsburgh turn from a team that usually finished at the bottom of the standings to one that captured the central division crown in 1972. In 1973, he would be recognized as one of the game's best with a selection in his first of eight consecutive Pro Bowls he would play in.

A year later, the Steelers were about to go where they had never been before in forty-two seasons: a spot in their first NFL championship contest in Super Bowl IX. To get there the team had a struggle against the Oakland Raiders at Oakland during the AFC championship game. Ham helped turn their fortunes around that afternoon with the most important interception of his career. With the game tied 10–10 in the fourth quarter, he picked off a pass and returned it to the Oakland nine. Terry Bradshaw quickly hit Lynn Swann from the six to put the Steelers ahead for good 17–10. They went on to defeat Minnesota to win the title in a memorable season in which Ham was elected as a first-team All-Pro for the first time.

The team defended their Super Bowl championship a year later, as Ham continued to excel, being named the NFL Defensive Player of the Year by the *Football News*. Jack was not considered the meanest or most aggressive linebacker in the game, but he was the most cerebral. While he was brilliant on the field, his competitive nature also was very prevalent. A great example was during the 1975 opener at San Diego. Pittsburgh was in front, 37–0, and the starters were pulled out of the contest. A few players were speaking with Ham about his interest in the coal industry as the Chargers picked off a pass inside the five-yard line and were looking to break up the shutout. Ham went immediately back into the contest to preserve the shutout and forced a fumble that he recovered. Teammate Andy Russell remembered the play. "The first play the Chargers ran was a sweep to the right. Bad idea. Ham took their giant tight end, threw him aside, speared the runner behind the line of scrimmage causing him to fumble, which of course Jack recovered. As he slowly walked off the field, he casually flipped the ball to the ref. Returning to our position on the sideline, Jack turned to me smiling and said, 'Where was I?'"[107]

Jack Ham would continue his excellence in leading the team to two more Super Bowl titles in 1978 and 1979 and was named a first-team All-Pro five more consecutive times between 1975 and 1979 before retiring after his eleventh season in 1982. Ham went on to be elected to the Pro Football Hall of Fame in 1988 and became the first and only Penn State player to be selected to both the Pro and College Football Hall of Fame when he was enshrined in the college version in 1990.

Picked to the Pro Football Hall of Fame's All-1970s team; the Hall of Fame's fiftieth-anniversary team, next to Lawrence Taylor; and the league's seventy-fifth-anniversary squad shows the brilliance of Jack Ham's career. In a recent rating by 247sports.com, Ham was selected as the seventh-greatest linebacker in the history of the game. Not bad for a kid from Johnstown who thought his career was done after high school.

12. BILL HARTACK

Horse Racing, 1952–80

The name Bill Hartack is probably the least known of the athletes celebrated in the pages of this book, but there is no question that he belongs here. A jockey during a time when Thoroughbred racing was extremely popular in the 1950s, Hartack quickly became its greatest force. By the time he was twenty-six, he became the youngest jockey ever elected to the sport's Hall of Fame, and no one has won more Kentucky Derby races than his five. A complex man, he also had somewhat of a bitter, cocky attitude toward others, especially reporters. He bristled when someone called him "Willie" and alienated many around him. Whether remembered for all his successes or his dour attitude, there are few if any who were greater on the track than Bill Hartack.

Born in Ebensburg, Pennsylvania, located right outside Johnstown in Cambria County, during the height of the Depression in 1932, Hartack had a tough time growing up in the coal mining town. The diminutive young man often got abused for his size in his youth, but his surly attitude wouldn't allow him to back down from fights. In 1940, his mother was killed in an auto accident. A year later, the house they lived in burned down, and the one that was built to replace it had no heating, phone or bathroom.

His father was a coal miner, and after Bill graduated from Black Lick Township High School, his father didn't want his son to have to work in the mines. Bill tried to join the navy but was turned down due to his size. A friend suggested he go to the Charles Town Races in West Virginia, where he was hired by Norbin Corbin to clean stalls and walk the horses. Eventually, he became an exercise rider at Waterford Park in Cumberland, West Virginia, and took his first mount on October 11, 1952. Three days later, he won his first race, and one of racing's greatest careers had begun in earnest.

In 1953, while still riding on some of the minor tracks in the country, Hartack accumulated 350 victories, second only to Bill Shoemaker in wins for North American jockeys, and began to get a reputation for his skill as a jockey. He started to get rides at some of the bigger tracks in the country, and then in 1955, he began his ascent as one of greatest in the sport. That year, the Ebensburg native began a three-year streak during which he was the leading rider in the country. He entered the winner's circle 1,105 times during that period, capturing victories in 26 percent of the races he ran, an incredible mark for horse racing. While he was winning at a record pace, his bad attitude was also on display, as Hartack was suspended five times in 1955 and 1956.

When taking the suspensions into account, the record streak became even more impressive. What was more spectacular was the fact that in 1956 and 1957, his winnings totaled $2,343,955 and $3,060,501, respectively, smashing any records that were held at the time. Up until 1956, no one had ever won more than $2 million in a year, but Hartack became the first to break both the $2 million and $3 million plateaus. While impressive, it was his mount in the 1957 Kentucky Derby that truly put him above everyone else.

In 1956, the young jockey got his first ride in the Derby, taking a horse named Fabius to a second-place finish. He captured his first Triple Crown race later that year when he rode Fabius to a victory in the Preakness, defeating Needles, the horse he lost to in the Kentucky Derby. A year later, he got aboard Iron Liege at Churchill Downs and made history that afternoon. Hartack had ridden well, but as he was coming down the stretch, Shoemaker was gaining on him aboard Gallant Man and looked to be a certainty to pass his rival on the way to victory. Inexplicably, Shoemaker stood up, thinking he had won— the famed jockey apparently misjudged the finish line. By the time he realized what he had done, he quickly sat down and tried to push Gallant Man to victory, but Iron Liege passed him and won by a nose.

By that point, Bill Hartack was a huge star in horse racing. As his stature grew, so did his reputation for being difficult. When someone compared Bill to Ted Williams, Hartack responded, "I've always admired him. A couple of times when he spat at the fans he was right. And when he was fined, I think he was right, too. If the fans would only put themselves in his shoes and have to take the guff and stuff they'd go crazy. But as I say, I don't want people coming and introducing themselves all the time."[108]

Many owners like Fred Hooper were avoiding Hartack because of his attitude. At times, Bill would get off horses and refuse to ride them if he felt they were not 100 percent. Hooper said after one incident that "this guy has gotten too big and too smart. He'll never ride another horse for me."[109] As difficult as he was to work with, Bill Hartack's talent outweighed his attitude, and he continued to get to ride the best horses.

In 1959, he was voted into the Hall of Fame and then won three more Kentucky Derby races—in 1960 aboard Venetian Way, in 1962 on Decidedly and in 1964 with Northern Dancer. He also took Northern Dancer to a win in the Preakness the same year and captured his lone Belmont Stakes as he rode a horse named Celtic Ash in 1960 to a win in New York.

After taking Northern Dancer to victory in 2 Triple Crown races, Hartack went into a slump, winning only 171 races in 1967 and 1968 while only riding in 3 of a possible 12 Triple Crown races since 1964. Hartack knew that his attitude was part of the reason he was having issues. "I go out there to do everything in my power to win. And then I'm disliked for my attitude. Evidently the way I operate is distasteful to certain people. It insults them, and the funny part about it is that insulting anybody is the last thing on my mind. I don't believe in being insulting to anyone, but I do believe in telling the truth, and if it's taken as an insult, well then I can't help it."[110] He was becoming irrelevant, and it looked like his four Kentucky Derby victories would fall one short of Eddie Arcaro's record five wins—that is, until 1969, when the horse racing was reminded of the excellence of Bill Hartack.

Former jockey Johnny Longden was now the trainer of Majestic Prince, a California-based colt, and originally wanted Shoemaker to ride the horse as they prepared for its first race. Shoemaker had been injured in a fall at Santa Anita. With Shoemaker injured, Longden sought Hartack to ride his horse but couldn't find him. Agent Pete Wilson found the jockey for Longden, and the combo went on to win six races in a row, most by significant margins entering the derby. Richard Nixon was in the crowd as the first sitting president to attend a Kentucky Derby and saw longshot Ocean Roar pull ahead at the clubhouse turn. As they came to the last ¼-mile, Arts and Letters had forged to a half-length lead over Majestic Prince. The horse had won his previous races so easily that no one knew how he would respond to a close battle. Hartack was in control, though, and burst out in front as the race was coming to an end. Arts and Letters was coming on down the stretch hoping to pull back in front, but Hartack and Majestic Prince kept the field at bay and won by a neck over Arts and Letters. It was a magnificent victory, giving Hartack five Derby wins in nine tries, tying Arcaro for most victories in the race, although it took Arcaro twenty-one attempts to win his five. It's a record they both share today.

For Hartack, after leading Majestic Prince to a second Triple Crown victory in the Preakness, it was the end of the glory days. Having problems making weight, he went to Hong Kong, where they allowed the horses to carry more weight, and retired from competition in 1980. The Hall of Famer had a magnificent career, winning 4,272 times in 21,535 races for an astonishing 19.8 winning percentage. He finished in the top three 10,513 times, coming in the money in 48.8 percent of his races. He died of a heart attack in a cabin while hunting in 2007 at seventy-four years old with a sad legacy despite his greatness in the sport he loved.

Hartack died alone, never marrying or having any children while chasing away most of those he called friends. Longden described him perfectly: "His riding and his ethics are beyond reproach. He's as smart as they come. But where he can get along with horses, he can't seem to with people."[111]

11. CHARLEY HYATT

University of Pittsburgh (Basketball), 1927–30

The problem with being a legend before the advent of social media—hell, before the advent of television—is that sometimes your incredible accomplishments are forgotten. In the case of the greatest basketball player ever to step on the court for the University of Pittsburgh, Charley Hyatt, his endeavors sometimes seem to have been all but erased.

While he is enshrined in both the Naismith Hall of Fame and the College Basketball Hall of Fame, the only Panther player to be elected to either (Doc

Carlson is in both as a coach)—and one of only eighteen Division I players nationwide to be selected as an All-American in three separate seasons, all while leading Pitt to its only two basketball national championships—Hyatt was left off the initial class to the school's Hall of Fame. Charles Smith and Billy Knight, both fine players in their own right and deserving of the honor, were included, despite the fact that they don't have Hyatt's credentials. Even though the team didn't wear numbers in his era, many have called for his banner to be hung next to those who have numbers retired; the school has yet to give Hyatt such an honor. It would seem Charley Hyatt hasn't been given the respect at Pitt that his career so richly deserves. Nonetheless, he is not only the greatest player the program has ever produced but also one of the best athletes ever to grace the city of Pittsburgh.

A native of Uniontown, Pennsylvania, an industrial town located forty-six miles outside Pittsburgh, Hyatt was part of an impressive array of athletic talent born in that city. On the town's Wikipedia page, such luminaries of the sports world as Chuck Muncie, Terry Mulholland, Ernie Davis, Stu Lantz, Sandy Stephens, Kaleb Ramsey and Wil Robinson are listed under notable people; the member of two Halls of Fame, Charley Hyatt, is not. Nonetheless, he is also arguably the local high school's greatest alumnus. Uniontown High School has a wonderful tradition in men's basketball that began in 1925, when the young junior led the school team to the state title while losing only two games, one to the freshman team at the University of Pittsburgh and the other to a Wichita club in the semifinals of the national high school tournament. One year later, as a senior, Uniontown once again won the Western Pennsylvania Interscholastic Athletic League (WPIAL) championship before losing while trying to defend their state title.

Hyatt gave credit for Uniontown's success to their coach, Abe Everhart, and told of the differences in the game he played versus the way basketball is played in the modern era. His thoughts may give insight to why his career seemed to be ignored. "We had great coaching by Abe Everhart Sr. The game has changed drastically; I could play in any era. Back in the day a man 6-1 was considered a giant, but now there are a lot of taller players. Also the basketball is made better and is rounder and not lopsided and shoots truer. In my day it was a matter of a team scoring 30 points, but now an individual player scores 30 points and it is not uncommon."[112]

After his impressive high school career, he moved on to the University of Pittsburgh, where he played for the iconic coach Doc Carlson. During Hyatt's sophomore season in 1927–28, the man they nicknamed "Clipper" was the final piece Carlson needed to create the best team in the nation.

Only eighteen men have been named as a first-team All-American in three different seasons, and Pitt's Charley Hyatt was one of them. The Uniontown native led the Panthers to their only two national championships and was elected to both the Naismith Basketball Hall of Fame and the College Basketball Hall of Fame. *Courtesy of the University of Pittsburgh Athletics.*

Pitt stood at 14-0 that year, a record that included a dominant 64–33 victory over the defending eastern champion Dartmouth College, and they faced a tough Notre Dame team at home trying to keep their undefeated record intact.

Proving Hyatt's earlier point, the Panthers were a scoring juggernaut, averaging 38 points per game, one of the highest marks in the history of the game at the time. It was a closely fought game, with the Irish leading 15–8 at the half. Pitt battled back to tie the game at 22, but time was running out and it seemed the game would go into overtime. Then Hyatt took a pass from Paul Zehfuss under the basket and tossed in a layup as time ran out for the 24–22 win. Carlson remembered the emotional scene after Hyatt's winning score: "Hyatt tossed the winning field goal in the last few seconds. It was the only time Pitt was ahead during the game. The finish was something to see. Men cried, women fainted, and I felt a warm spot on the top of my head—somebody was kissing my bald pate!"[113]

Charley's big basket was the key moment in a perfect 21-0 season, as he led the nation in scoring and was named an All-American for the first time along with teammate Sykes Reed. It was Reed who, later in life when talking about his teammate's dominance, made the statement that "Charley Hyatt would score 50 points in a game today and you don't need much more than that to win."[114] In 1936, when the Helms Athletic Association was formed and selected national champions from seasons before the NCAA tournament was held, it picked this Pitt team as the best from that season. A year later, the team slipped back a bit, but in 1929–30, they would have another memorable year.

The Panthers stood at 7-0 while playing a difficult schedule before hosting a tough Montana State team led by future Hall of Famer John "Cat" Thompson. Hyatt was incredible, scoring 27 of his club's 38 points, including the winning bucket with under ten second left in a 38–37 win. They would lose twice that campaign but finished with a 23-2 record and a second Helms national crown, which made them one of ten schools to win two or more National Championships in the pre-tournament era. Once again Charley Hyatt was the nation's leading scorer and was named All-American for the third consecutive time.

After his career was over, he decided not to continue as a professional player with the life at the time for a pro player not being the glamorous one it is today. Charley decided to play AAU ball in California, where he won three national Amateur Athletic Union (AAU) titles as a player, the last as a player/coach, and was named an AAU All-American seven times.

As spectacular as his career was, Hyatt was also an innovator, developing a one-handed shot in a time when players shot with two hands. He also was one of the first to shoot with his left hand.

In 1959, he was enshrined in both the Naismith and Helms Halls of Fame and was part of the initial class to the College Basketball Hall of Fame in 2006. Carlson said of his star, "Naturally, I say Hyatt is the greatest basketball player I ever saw. He had the most deeply ingrained desire to play of anybody I ever met. Basketball was his whole life. Nothing else mattered. He would average 30 points a game today. I've never seen anybody who could compare to him."[115]

With all he accomplished, it's still confusing why he is not given the honors by his school and others that he deserves. One of the greatest athletes we've ever seen in Western Pennsylvania certainly should be given his just due.

Chapter 5

THE ICONIC FIGURES

THE TOP 10 ATHLETES

10. TONY DORSETT

University of Pittsburgh (Football), 1973–76

Football at the University of Pittsburgh hit its lowest point in the program's history as the 1970s were in their infancy. A 3-8 and 1-10 finish in 1971 and 1972 made many wonder if the school should consider dropping the program to a minor collegiate level. Chancellor Wesley Posvar and AD Casimir Myslinski decided to see if they could turn around this once proud program by hiring a successful young coach from Iowa State by the name of Johnny Majors. While hiring a young coach was nice, without recruiting proper talent, a return to national prominence would be difficult. Then came a young running back from Hopewell High School in Aliquippa, Pennsylvania, by the name of Tony Dorsett, and everything changed.

He was just a skinny kid, five-foot-eleven and 175 pounds, but he was one of the most sought-after backs in the country. The young freshman was a Parade All-American, garnering the most votes among all running backs, and was perhaps the finest player in Pennsylvania after rushing for 1,238 yards and twenty-three touchdowns his senior season. When looking at him play in what was the top Pennsylvania High School All-Star contest at the time, the Big-33 game, Majors looked in awe and knew that Dorsett was a player he could build his program around.

To rebuild such a decrepit program, the new coach knew that he needed a huge class of incoming freshman that first year to begin his quest. According to assistant head coach Jackie Sherrill (who soon became the head coach once Majors went back to his alma mater at Tennessee in 1977), Majors brought in at least seventy-six kids that year, including such talents as quarterback Robert Haygood, tight end Jim Corbett, kicker Carson Long, future All-American Al Romano and Gary Burley, just to name a few, but Sherrill's main focus was to secure Dorsett. He went about it by trying to recruit his friend at Hopewell, Ed Wilamsowski. The coach remembered that "Ed was white and Tony was black, and at every school they visited, they were separated [in the college dorms]. I don't know if I was smarter than the others, but I didn't separate them. I knew Tony was very, very close to Ed. We kept them together."[116] It was a unique approach at the time for sure, but Dorsett would concur in an interview forty years later that it was one of the main reasons he came.

Dorsett almost left the team before his Panther career began, as he was miserable at the difficult training camp that Majors ran in nearby Johnstown. "It was pretty damn hard and pretty damn hot, and I was ready to come home." Fortunately, the young back decided to stick it out. He said he decided not to leave camp because of "a conversation with my mom and with Jackie [Sherrill]. It was just really hard. I was pretty introverted—quiet and shy. I hid behind those big, dark sunglasses. I didn't feel like I fit in very well socially. The only time I was really comfortable was on the football field."[117] When the Hopewell back broke 100 yards in his first collegiate game against Georgia, both Majors and Sherrill knew that their efforts were worth it, and the freshman was so thrilled he decided to stay.

As time went on that first year, he quickly became a star, beyond anything anyone could have imagined. In the season's third game against Northwestern, he broke the school record for yards in game with 265 and eventually would eclipse the school record for rushing yards in a season, becoming the Pitt's first 1,000-yard back, with a national freshman-record 1,586 in the regular season (adjusted to 1,686 when the NCAA decided to include bowl game stats into the official records). He was named a first-team All-American by the Associated Press, the first freshman in twenty-nine years to be accorded such an honor, and led the Panthers to a 6-4-1 mark and a spot in the Fiesta Bowl. Perhaps the most amazing thing about his freshman year was the fact that the school career rushing record was only 1,957, by Marshall Goldberg, and he was about to obliterate it in only his second year.

While the Aliquippa native quickly broke that record in his sophomore season, it was his worst campaign in a Pitt uniform, as he ran for 1,004 yards while missing his only game in his college career with an injury. Despite the minor setback, he finished thirteenth in the Heisman Trophy voting after an eleventh-place finish his freshman season. Wanting to get back to the form he showed that first year, Dorsett came out with a vengeance in 1975.

It was a fine season that included a school-record 268-yard performance at Army, the highest rushing total at the time in historic Mitchie Stadium, and against the University of Notre Dame he had a contest for the ages. It had been twelve years since Pitt had defeated the Irish, but on a November day at Pitt Stadium, that streak came to an end—along with his Panther single-game rushing record. Dorsett was amazing that day, with runs of 57 and 71 yards, along with a touchdown catch of 49. He ended the day with 303 yards rushing, a school record that still stands today, and 74 more yards receiving as Pitt upset Notre Dame, 34–20. The team ended up in the Sun Bowl, where they won their first bowl game since the 1937, as the All-American had 142 more yards. He ended the campaign being selected as a first-team All-American, becoming the first back in NCAA history to top 4,000 yards after his junior year, and came in fourth in the Heisman.

Big things were projected for both Dorsett and the Panthers in 1976, and neither disappointed. The season began at Notre Dame with the home team looking for revenge after the 1975 upset. The Irish went ahead early 7–0, but the home fans quickly found out that it was to be a long day for Notre Dame after the Panthers' first offensive play from scrimmage when the Heisman Trophy candidate rambled for 61 yards. Pitt went on to outscore the Fighting Irish 31–3 the rest of the game in a dominant 31–10 victory as Dorsett finished with 181 yards.

He never failed to gain less than 100 yards in any single game in 1976, rushing for more than 200 yards in three out of four games during the middle part of the season. The one game in which he didn't have more than 200 yards was a contest at Navy. That day, he may have finished with only 180, but on a 32-yard touchdown run in the fourth quarter, he broke Archie Griffin's NCAA record for rushing yards in a career.

Dorsett went on to run for 224 yards in his last regular season game in a Panther uniform, a 24–7 win against archrival Penn State that marked the first time they defeated a Joe Paterno–led Nittany Lion team. Also on that evening, the All-American became the first back in NCAA history to rush for more than 6,000 yards, adding to his impressive record.

Pitt was undefeated, number one in the nation and playing in the Sugar Bowl against Georgia. Dorsett had captured the Heisman Trophy by this point in time, and neither he nor the team would be denied their destiny in a 27–3 win. That afternoon, Tony set a Sugar Bowl record with 202 yards, finishing his career with 6,526. On top of the Heisman, Dorsett was a unanimous first-team All-American while also capturing other prestigious awards, such as the Maxwell Award and the Walter Camp Award. Most importantly, he was part of the last national championship squad in school history to date.

While Tony Dorsett went on to a Hall of Fame career with the Dallas Cowboys and was elected to the College Football Hall of Fame, as well as having his number retired by the program and being selected to the initial class of the University of Pittsburgh Hall of Fame, his life has been difficult. He announced in 2013 that he was showing signs of a brain condition that is being suffered by many retired football players, chronic traumatic encephalopathy (CTE). Despite the diagnosis, his career at Pitt was historic. With the fact today that players are allowed to declare for the NFL draft after the third year following their high school graduation, his records at the school will be almost impossible to eclipse, although even if that rule didn't exist, it's doubtful that anyone could ever reach the heights the Aliquippa native did during his majestic run.

9. SIDNEY CROSBY

Pittsburgh Penguins, 2005–19

When the National Hockey League shut down the season in 2004 due to a player lockout, the results were thought to be potentially devastating to a league that had often struggled to remain relevant among the top four professional circuits in North America. It turned out to be just the opposite, as the league has continued to grow fiscally after the salary cap was instituted because of the strike. As good as it was for the league, it was even better for the Pittsburgh Penguins. The team had been struggling both on the ice and financially for the previous few seasons and had been desperately looking for a replacement for Mario Lemieux as the club's resident superstar. The league held a lottery for the first pick of the draft since there were no standings the year before to base a draft order on. It was weighted with several factors, including franchises performance over the previous three seasons. While Pittsburgh had a better chance than some, it was still a crapshoot as to who would get the first pick.

While not to the talent level of Mario Lemieux, Sidney Crosby was nonetheless one of the greatest players in NHL history. With a leadership skill second to none, he led the Pittsburgh Penguins to three Stanley Cup championships in his career and four eastern conference crowns, as well as two Olympic gold medals with Canada. *Courtesy of David Finoli.*

Luck was on their side, as they won the lottery and chose a player who turned out to be that replacement for Lemieux, a young kid from Halifax, Nova Scotia, by the name of Sidney Crosby.

Crosby wasn't the biggest player on the ice by any stretch of the imagination, standing at only five-foot-eleven, but his preparation was intense and his desire exceptional. Most importantly, while he didn't match the skills that Mario may have had, his leadership skills were impeccable. He became the major reason why the team not only solved its issues off the ice but also had a renaissance on it in an era that has seen the team outdistance and accomplishments they had during the prime of Lemieux.

Playing with Rimouski of the Quebec Major Junior Hockey League (QMJHL), Crosby was spectacular. He won two consecutive scoring titles with the team and led them to the league championship in 2004–5. He then continued his phenomenal year by helping Canada capture the gold medal at the World Junior Championships. His career in the QMJHL was almost unparalleled, with the second-best points per game in the circuits history at 2.51 per game. Ironically, only Lemieux's mark of 2.81 per game was better.

Much was expected of the young phenom, and he didn't disappoint. He got the opportunity to play with Mario his rookie season and became the youngest player in NHL history to score 100 points in a season, finishing with 102. As good of a rookie campaign as it was, he finished second to Alexander Ovechkin (who had been drafted first the year before but didn't get a chance to play in the NHL that season due to the strike) in the Calder Trophy voting for the league's Rookie of the Year. While Crosby fell short in this occasion, the two went head to head over the next decade many times, with the Penguin captain usually coming out ahead.

Pittsburgh was building a strong young team with players like Marc-Andre Fleury, Evgeni Malkin, Brooks Orpik and Kris Letang, along with Crosby, forming a championship core. The team almost doubled their 58-point output in Sidney's rookie season with 105 points in 2006–7, while the Nova Scotia native led the NHL in points with 120. While Pittsburgh faltered in the first round of the playoffs to Ottawa, Crosby took home three trophies at the end of the season, the Ted Lindsay Trophy, the league MVP according to the Players Association; the Art Ross Trophy as the leading scorer in the NHL; and the Hart Memorial Trophy as the official league MVP.

At twenty years old, he became the Penguin captain. Before the season, a high ankle sprain curtailed a good portion of Crosby's third year as he hit feet first into the boards in a January game against the Lightning. Despite the injury, he came back to help lead the team into the Stanley Cup Finals for the first time since 1992, unfortunately losing to the Red Wings.

In 2009, they made up for the loss with another spectacular run. Now considered one of the best franchises in hockey, Pittsburgh had another phenomenal campaign, as Crosby once again eclipsed 100 points. This time the team was confident of what it could achieve, and after getting past Ovechkin and the Capitals in the second round before easily beating Carolina to win their second consecutive Eastern Conference crown, they waltzed into the finals once again for a rematch with Detroit. While down three games to two to the Red Wings after an embarrassing 5–0 defeat in game five, they battled back to win the final two games, the last contest an exciting 2–1 win in a game during which Crosby hurt his left knee early in the second period. They held on nonetheless in a majestic playoff run to win their third Stanley Cup, as the captain led the league in postseason goals scored with fifteen.

After another excellent campaign in which he became a sniper, eclipsing fifty goals for the first and only time in his career with a league-leading fifty-one, Crosby would suffer a debilitating concussion that threatened his career. In the Winter Classic at Heinz Field in Pittsburgh on New Year's Day 2011, the Pens were facing the Washington Capitals when he was given a blind side hit to the head by David Steckel. The next game, he took a much more innocent hit by Tampa Bay's Victor Hedman but he left the contest once again. He was diagnosed with a much more serious concussion than people anticipated. He was having his best season to date at that point with 66 points in forty-one games, including a twenty-five-game point streak, but he would miss the remainder of the season as well as the first twenty of the next year before returning to play the Islanders on November 11, 2011. Pittsburgh beat New York, 5–0, and Crosby picked up where he left off with four points. Eight games later, he was out with a concussion again after another hit against Boston.

Luckily, he returned before the end of the season and once again took his place as the best player in hockey in a strike-shortened 2012–13 campaign with 56 points in thirty-three games—this year saw another injury when he broke his jaw taking a shot from former teammate Brooks Orpik. The following season, he had a healthy campaign, winning his second scoring title while capturing another Hart Trophy. The team, though, could never recapture their playoff magic of 2008 and 2009, losing in the playoffs, usually in a very disappointing manner.

In 2016, the captain was in a slump, looking like his best days were behind him, and the team was looking like it might have to rebuild after a decade of excellence. The Penguins were faltering, and Crosby was going down with them. As the season was entering its final few months, Pittsburgh was adding some players from the Wilkes-Barre farm team to replace some injured players. As it turned out, what they were doing was adding much-needed speed to the team. Also, with the mid-season addition of Coach Mike Sullivan, they had the direction they sorely needed. Crosby was invigorated and found his scoring touch again, leading the league with forty-four goals after a frenetic second half. Instead of a rebuilding job, the Penguins won their fourth Stanley Cup, with Crosby taking the Conn Smythe Trophy as the playoff MVP despite suffering another concussion in the second round against Washington off a questionable cross check by former teammate Matt Niskanen. One year later, they became the first NHL team to repeat as Stanley Cup champions since Detroit in 1998, with Crosby also repeating, winning the Conn Smythe Trophy again.

Now at thirty-one years old, the player they used to call "Sid the Kid" is a grizzled veteran with 446 goals and 1,216 points in fourteen seasons. He also has been a star on the international level, his most famous moment the game-winning goal in the gold medal game for Canada at the 2010 Winter Olympics against the United States. It was the first of two gold medals he would win (2014 being the other).

Crosby is a certain Hall of Famer and was included in the list of the best one hundred NHL players of all time that the league put out for its 100th anniversary in 2017. There are some who question his greatness, though, especially compared to Lemieux. It may be true that there is no better hockey talent this city has seen than Mario Lemieux; there are few any have seen in the history of the sport who are greater. While he might not be up to his level in talent, Crosby's leadership skills are undeniable. Three Stanley Cups and four conference titles compared to Mario's two and two, with arguably a more talented team, indicate that Sidney Crosby deserves on the shortlist of greatest athletes ever to play in this city and talked about at least in the same breath as Lemieux as far as the impact he made on this franchise. Not a bad return for a lucky bounce of a ball in the 2005 NHL draft.

8. HARRY GREB

Boxing, 1913–26

There was never a time when the sport of boxing wasn't brutal, but in the modern era many rules have been put in place to help minimize injuries and make the sport safer. In the early 1900s, safety was the last thing on a pugilist's mind. For Harry Greb, such rules would have been his ultimate enemy. In the annals of the sport, there was no more feared fighter and certainly few, if any, who were more ferocious. While fighting twice a year would be considered the maximum for most fighters today, Greb fought thirty-seven times alone in 1917. His life was fast and exciting and his death was quick and tragic, but in the minds of boxing experts, he was one of the legends of the ring.

Born in the Millvale section of Pittsburgh in 1894 to Anna and Pius Greb, Harry got his toughness from his father, but it was an attribute that would see the two at odds over his choice of profession. Pius was tough and disciplined and knew that his son was developing into a great athlete, but he was more interested in him becoming a baseball player than a boxer. His father had no respect for the sport, and there were reports that he kicked Harry out of the house at fourteen because he caught him a fight, although others, such as his sister, Ida, claim that he left on his own.

Eventually, he returned home before leaving for good a few years later to pursue a career as an electrician's apprentice for Westinghouse. Greb would once again became enamored of the sport of boxing after hanging out at a local gym. Greb worked for the brother of famed manager George Engle, who saw that the young fighter had talent so he contacted George to tell him how impressed he was with Harry. Eventually, George would manage Greb after a very short amateur career.

He went on to win a boxing tournament in Lawrenceville, near where he grew up, then one in Cleveland that he qualified for with his Lawrenceville victory. After the victory in Cleveland, he decided to turn pro and teamed up with a man named James "Red" Mason to be his manager. His first fight was against Knockout Frank Kirkwood from Coraopolis, Pennsylvania, on May 29, 1913, when Greb won a close decision.

While Harry Greb's official all-time record was 105-8-3, he fought 299 times. At the time, Pennsylvania was a state that didn't allow official decisions in boxing matches, therefore they weren't allowed to have judges at ringside to decide who won a specific fight. To the state, they were considered only exhibition matches. In those situations, the newspaper reporters covering the fight would give their thoughts as to who won. They were called "no decision fights" or "newspaper decision fights" and were not always listed in a fighter's official record—the Kirkwood fight was such a bout.

In his second bout, a technical knockout (TKO) against a fighter named Battling Murphy, the papers began to take notice of his aggressive style. The *Pittsburgh Press* reporter exclaimed, "Greb had the weight and punch and Murphy was joyous when the [first] round ended. Less than a minute after the second round was under way Murphy looked like a passenger and the referee stopped the carnage."[118]

As Greb continued to pile up fights in a rapid manner, he fought more impressive opponents—such as Billy Miske, Battling Levinsky, Gunboat Smith and Tommy Loughran—defeating anyone who came into his path and building a reputation as one of the best fighters in his era. Unfortunately, in 1921, while fighting a man named Kid Norfolk, he was hit with a thumb to the eye and suffered a retinal tear. It would blind him in that eye the rest of his life, but in a testament to his talent and desire, he won a ten-round decision that evening and pushed on to greater moments in the sport.

One year later, he fought a man who would go on to upset Jack Dempsey for the heavyweight title in 1926, Gene Tunney. Tunney lost one fight in his career, and it was this evening for the U.S. Light Heavyweight championship to Greb. Greb was incredible in the ring, violently ripping apart the future heavyweight champion. Tunney described the carnage later on: "It is impossible to describe the bloodiness of this fight. My seconds were unable to stop either the bleeding from the cut over my left eye, which involved a severed artery, or the bleeding consequent to the nose fractures. Doc Bagley, who was my chief second, made futile attempts to congeal the nose bleeding by pouring adrenaline into his hand and having me snuff it up my nose. This I did round after round. The adrenaline, instead of coming out through the nose again, ran down my throat with the blood and into my stomach."[119] Greb won the title with a fifteen-round decision. He defeated another Hall of Famer in Loughran to retain the title before losing it in a rematch with Tunney in 1923. It would be the same year that Greb would fight for the world middleweight championship and forge his way into history.

From middleweights to heavyweights, Greb fought the best there was and challenged middleweight champ John Wilson at the Polo Grounds for Wilson's title. According to the *New York Times*, Greb clearly won the bout, capturing thirteen of the fifteen rounds. A piece on the website Boxing Over Broadway noted that papers were often paid off by managers and promoters before decisions became legal to angle the fight toward their particular fighter. By the time this fight occurred, official decisions were now legal, but the practice still took place to help promote a fighter. In the *New York Evening World Report*, writer Robert Edgren said, "Harry Greb today is the middleweight champion of the world but when Announcer Joe Humphreys…began his announcement 'Winner and new champion' there was no wild burst of applause. It was a victory with no sensational features, and not at all the overwhelming triumph the crowd had expected him to score over Johnny Wilson. Nobody felt sure which would get the decision when the fifteenth round was over."[120]

No matter which version was correct, Greb was the champion, a title he defended with an incredible decision over Mickey Walker in a fight considered one of the greatest of all time. As his vision worsened, he lost the title to Flowers in a fifteen-round decision in 1926 and then in a rematch six months later before retiring.

Harry Greb had the reputation as a partier and was often seen in the press as one, a reputation he vehemently disputed, especially after his retirement in late 1926. There those who also disputed his reputation, saying that he couldn't have been in such tremendous shape had he done the things the reporters claimed. Regardless of their thoughts, he wanted to return to the ring and traveled to Atlantic City to have his eye operated on by a local doctor he had dealt with before, Dr. McGivern. He was also there to have a broken bone removed from his nose that he received in a recent automobile accident. Harry was given a local anesthesia and left the operating room in good condition after the procedure. By the next morning, his heart started to fail and the thirty-two-year-old champion's condition became grave. At 2:30 p.m., Harry Greb was pronounced dead. His fans and family were devastated.

His death was tragic, but his career is still celebrated. He was given his rightful place in the International Boxing Hall of Fame in 1990. Greb was named the tenth-greatest fighter of the twentieth century by the Associated Press in 1999, and noted boxing historian Bert Sugar called him the best middleweight in the history of the sport. Impressive testaments to the greatness that was Harry Greb's career.

7. ROBERTO CLEMENTE

Pittsburgh Pirates, 1955–72

If you look around the city of Pittsburgh, it's fairly simple to deduce who the town's most revered athlete is. There is a statue of Roberto Clemente that greets fans right after they walk over the Roberto Clemente Bridge to PNC Park. Inside the stadium, his number is included on a façade honoring the great players whom the Pittsburgh Pirates have chosen to retire. Peer down to right field and you will see a tall home run fence, exactly twenty-one feet high, to honor this legend. Drive up through the city's Strip District to Lawrenceville and one will find the Roberto Clemente Museum. It's incredible that five decades after Clemente died a hero's death, those who were around and remember that tragic moment so vividly are still choked up when they speak of it, but it wasn't always that way. In his prime in the 1960s, he was often made fun of by the media and fans alike for his heritage, criticisms that most pioneers who broke color barriers (in Clemente's case the barrier nationality also as a Latin American player) at that period faced on their way to greatness.

Born Roberto Clemente Walker on August 18, 1934, in Carolina, Puerto Rico, Clemente was an exceptional natural athlete. He was as successful throwing the javelin as he was on the diamond. It was his excellence as

Roberto Clemente had it all. An incredible offensive player who won four batting titles and the 1966 National League MVP Award, he was also a defensive player extraordinaire who captured twelve Gold Gloves. As good as he was on the field, it was his exceptional spirit off the field that made him special. He was tragically killed in a plane crash in Puerto Rico on New Year's Eve 1972 while trying to take supplies to earthquake-ravaged Nicaragua. *Courtesy of the Pittsburgh Pirates.*

a javelin thrower that is often given credit for his exceptional throwing arm in right field, arguably the strongest the game has ever seen. With a potential bright future in baseball, he chose to pursue a career in the sport and was involved in a bidding war with the Dodgers, Giants and Braves before finally deciding to sign a contract with Brooklyn for $5,000 plus a $10,000 bonus. Because he was given more than $4,000 in total money, the rules at the time in baseball dictated that he be on a major-league roster. If a team chose not to include the player in the majors, they would be subject to a Rule V Minor League Draft. The Dodgers decided to take the gamble.

They had a strong outfield at the time in Brooklyn and a championship-caliber roster, so they sent their new prospect to the farm club at Montreal. There have been differing reports on whether the Dodgers tried to hide him there by warming him up with the pitchers or batting him in unique situations, but regardless, Pittsburgh discovered him while scout Clyde Sukeforth was in Montreal looking at pitcher Joe Black. He was enamored of the young player, and the club decided to take him in the 1954 draft. For former Dodger general manager Branch Rickey, who was now with Pittsburgh, it gave him great pleasure to steal the prospect.

The Pirates were not a very good team in 1955, and Clemente found a spot in their outfield his rookie season. One year later, Brooklyn must have been seething when he broke .300 for the first time with a .311 average. While most players who enjoyed such fast success would have been excited, it was a difficult time for Clemente. He had to deal not only with the issue of race that African Americans had to deal with since Jackie Robinson broke the color barrier in 1947 but also with prejudice of nationality, as Latin American players were not commonplace in the majors yet either. It made it especially difficult on him that many of his teammates didn't respect him because of the fact that Roberto did not want to play unless he was healthy and at his best, sitting when he thought he wasn't. Former Pirate announcer and Pitcher Nellie King stated that "it became kind of a sign that he was a malingerer or didn't have enough [guts] so to speak. He didn't want to play today because so and so was pitching. Gibson or Antonelli. It got whispered around he didn't want to play, he was jaking it."[121]

It also infuriated him that some in the media made fun of him by quoting him phonetically, emphasizing the poor English he spoke. They also called him "Bob" to try to Americanize him. He hated both, especially the quotes, which he felt made him sound unintelligent. He thought the lack of respect by the media was very apparent after the Bucs won the World Series in 1960.

He had a breakout season, hitting .314 with 16 homers and a team-high 94 RBIs. Despite that, he finished only eighth in the MVP voting behind three teammates: the winner, Dick Groat, who missed the last month of the season with an injury; Don Hoak, who finished second; and Vern Law, who was seventh. The slight angered him to the point that he refused to wear his 1960 world championship ring, instead wearing the one he was given for playing in the 1961 All-Star Game. While this may have angered him off the field, it inspired him on it.

In the 1960s, few were the equal of Roberto Clemente. He came out with a vengeance after the slight in 1960, winning his first batting title in 1961 with a .351 average. He went on to capture three more batting titles in 1964, 1965 and 1967, and in 1966, after a 29-home run, 119-RBI campaign in which he hit .317, Roberto was given the respect he deserved when he was named the National League's MVP.

As the 1960s came to an end and the 1970s were beginning, General Manager Joe L. Brown was surrounding his star with many African American players, as well as also aggressively signing Latin American players. Roberto Clemente was going from misunderstood star to a clubhouse leader. He was among the game's best and, quite frankly, arguably the greatest right fielder the game had seen defensively, capturing twelve gold gloves over the course of his career, but he was still somewhat of an unknown figure to many fans across the nation who rarely had the chance to see him play. That all changed in 1971.

Roberto seemed on a mission to lead the team back to the World Series, hitting .341 while needing only 118 hits in 1972 to reach the magical 3,000-hit plateau. As wonderful as he was in the regular season, leading the team to a second consecutive eastern division crown, he was even better in the postseason. Hitting .333 against the Giants in an NLCS series victory for their first pennant in eleven years, he was even more spectacular in a memorable World Series performance. After hitting in all seven games of the 1960 fall classic, he extended his World Series hitting streak to fourteen in 1971. He finished the series with a .414 average, including a clutch home run off Mike Cuellar in game seven, and won the series MVP as Pittsburgh upset Baltimore to win the world championship.

Clemente was on top of the baseball world at thirty-seven years old and enjoyed another fine season in 1972. On September 30, he came into the game against the New York Mets and pitcher Jon Matlack needing one more hit to reach 3,000. He had failed the evening before after what he thought was a hit but instead was ruled an error by official scorer Luke

Quay. This day, he did not leave it to chance, hitting a double in the third to join the elusive 3,000 club. Unfortunately, it turned out to be his last official regular season at bat.

On New Year's Eve, Roberto chartered a plane to take much-needed supplies to earthquake-ravaged Nicaragua. There were reports that the supplies that had been sent were taken by the government headed by Anastasio Somoza Debayle. Clemente felt that since he was so respected in the region, if he personally accompanied the supplies they would get where they needed to go. The DC-7 he chartered was overloaded and not fit for flying. When the plane did take off, it plunged in the ocean not long afterward, killing all on board.

The city as well as all of Latin America was devastated at the loss of their hero. Months later, he became only the second person, with Lou Gehrig being the first, to be inducted into the Baseball Hall of Fame without having to wait the mandatory five years after retirement. Five decades later, the city still mourns and celebrates the man who went from a mocked player to the most revered citizen in Pittsburgh history.

6. JOE GREENE

Pittsburgh Steelers, 1969–81

January 28, 1969, was a seminal day in the history of the Pittsburgh Steelers—and even that might be an understatement. It was the day that the team's new coach, the former defensive coordinator of the Baltimore Colts, Chuck Noll, sat his first draft as a head coach. In fact, it was his first full day as a head coach, being hired the day before by Art and Dan Rooney. To be blunt, this organization was a hot mess and had been for the majority of the thirty-six years it had been in existence. There was no reason to believe this would be such a momentous day, and it was a few years before anyone would realize it. Picking fourth in the first round and in need of a huge influx of talent, Noll had plenty of quarterbacks to choose from, including Notre Dame's Terry Hanratty (whom they got in the next round), Cincinnati's Greg Cook and Marty Domres from Columbia. It made sense to start this massive rebuilding job at quarterback, but Noll was a defensive man and wanted to build his team on defense. He decided to take a defensive tackle out of North Texas State by the name of Joe Greene, prompting many fans in the city to ask, "Who is Joe Greene?" They very quickly found out the answer. The Steeler dynasty was on its way.

Greene was a cocky sort. A talented consensus All-American while playing at a relatively minor program such as North Texas State, he may have been a surprise pick to the city of Pittsburgh, but most experts considered him the best defensive talent in the draft. When asked what he deserved to be paid, he shot out with an immense figure at the time. "I can't say what I'll ask for but it's going to take a $600,000 man to stop OJ [Simpson, the first player taken in the draft]."[122]

He was a bigger-than-life figure at the school, as the name of the North Texas team intertwined with his nickname. There are several different stories as to who had the nickname first, one story being that the school nickname was to honor its defensive unit in 1966, which had the nation's second-ranked rush defense; after the Steelers drafted Greene, some fans mistook the team name of Mean Green for his nickname. Whether the story was true or not, the nickname fit both; their defense was incredible, and Greene was an intimidating, mean defensive force.

The Steelers eventually did sign their impressive defensive tackle, and fans soon found out what a wise pick it was. At six-foot-four and 270 pounds, he improved greatly from week to week to the point that he quickly became one of the best defensive linemen in the game. He was selected to play in the Pro Bowl his rookie season while being chosen as the NFL's Rookie of the Year. Even with his phenomenal performance, the team was 1-13 and not looking close to being a title contender. Three years later, with more pieces in place, their now emotional defensive leader would help take the team to where they had never been before. He was the main cog in an impenetrable defense that took the Steelers to the central division crown in 1972 and their first trip to the playoffs since 1947. Greene was named the Associated Press Defensive Player of the Year for his efforts.

As he was getting along in his professional career, Joe was becoming more mature in the way he played the game but was seemingly enjoying it less. In 1973, he stated, "I used to get a great deal more pleasure out of the game than I do now. I've gotten smarter, I don't play as loose and reckless as I used to. The game gets more conservative, a little dull. When you've been winning for a while, the pressure to keep on winning builds. You don't want to make mistakes."[123]

The game wasn't fun for him, and after a particularly bad stretch in 1974, he decided to quit the team, thinking they weren't at a Super Bowl contending level that he thought they should be. Receivers coach Lionel

The first draft pick in the career of Hall of Fame coach Chuck Noll was perhaps his best. Noll chose Joe Greene from North Texas State in the 1969 draft, and Greene rewarded him with one of the greatest defensive careers in NFL history. He not only was elected to the Pro Football Hall of Fame, but he also became the second Pittsburgh Steeler to have his number retired. *Courtesy of the North Texas State University Athletics.*

Taylor eventually talked him into coming back. Afterward, Greene and his teammates finally did take that big step as contenders. He went on to once again to win another AP Defensive Player of the Year that season as the team captured their first Super Bowl title in a game where Greene became the first player to have an interception, a forced fumble and a fumble recovery in a single Super Bowl contest.

He was perceived as the defensive team leader by most, but not all of the players felt that way. Tom Keating was irritated at him for pulling himself out of a game against the Oilers in 1973. Mike Wagner stated that Greene was treated differently than the rest of the players but seemingly understood: "Chuck generally treated all the players the same—except for Joe. With Joe's personality and Joe's role and Joe's contribution to the team, he just handled him a little differently. Probably rightfully so."[124] Glen Edwards was a little more demonstrative: "When you talk about those Steelers defenses, everybody talks about Joe Greene, Joe Greene, Joe Greene. But that ain't all it was. You know who the man was in the [defensive] huddle? I was. [Edwards was voted team MVP in '74 even though Greene won NFL Defensive Player of the Year.] I was constantly getting on guys, pumping them up. They made Joe out to be the team leader, but as players we said, 'Hell, who made Joe our spokesman?'"[125] Whether he was truly a team leader or not, he was one of the best and most intimidating players on the field.

In 1975, Greene had a tough season, sidelined for almost half of it because of groin injury and a nerve problem in his shoulder, but it was also a year that he showed how feisty he was on the field. He was kicked out of a game against the Cleveland Browns for kicking offensive lineman Bob McKay in the groin and was charged by Denver offensive lineman Paul Howard of also kicking him in the groin so hard that he ripped his scrotum. Two years later, against the Denver Broncos, he punched Howard after the Steelers tackle claimed that the Bronco lineman was holding him. Joe also hit center Mike Montler after Montler's fingers snuck inside Greene's facemask on a previous play.

By 1979, he had tried to show his gentler side, starring in a Coca-Cola commercial where he threw a kid his jersey after the kid gave him a Coke following a game. The commercial is still thought of as one of the most famous of all time.

In 1981, chronic back pain limited his play, as he started only seven games. By the end of the year, he had enough and retired. His spectacular career included ten Pro Bowl appearances, two Defensive Player of the Year awards and an election to the Pro Football Hall of Fame; he was the second player in Steeler history to have his number retired and a spot on the league's seventy-fifth-anniversary team. In 2008, the *Bleacher Report* named him the fourth-toughest player in the history of the NFL. The honors were many for Greene, and they were deserved. He was the first pick in Noll's massive rebuilding process, and the legendary coach couldn't have made a more perfect choice.

5. HUGH GREEN

University of Pittsburgh (Football), 1977–80

Sometimes you have to give credit where it is due. Probably the most important recruit for the University of Pittsburgh in the late 1970s was a little running back out of Pascagoula, Mississippi, by the name of Ray "Rooster" Jones. He was considered one of the top three high school senior backs in the country, but he never blossomed into the superstar many at Pitt hoped he would. He wasn't important because of his efforts on the field but rather because of the defensive player Pitt coaches noticed in the game films while scouting Jones. This player, a six-foot-two, 210-pound defensive end from Natchez by the name of Hugh Green, became one of the greatest players in the program's history.

Green recalled this many years later, saying that the team was looking for someone who could replace their Heisman Trophy winner Tony Dorsett and thought that Jones could be that player. In the films, Green's team played Jones's team twice in 1976, and the coaches were highly impressed. It wasn't that Hugh was an underrated prospect—he was the top defensive lineman in Mississippi—but he was not on the Panthers' recruiting list at the time. The Natchez native averaged thirteen solo tackles per game his senior season while being named All-State his final two years. After watching the films, Sherill and his coaches intensified their recruiting efforts to secure both players and were successful. Jones went on to rush for 1,248 yards in four seasons, a decent career but certainly not one befitting the man who was supposed to replace Dorsett, while Hugh Green became a college football legend and one of the most decorated defensive linemen the collegiate game has ever seen.

Jackie Sherrill had an incredible collection of assistant coaches on his staff in 1978, including future head coaches Jimmy Johnson, Foge Fazio, Pat Jones, Dave Wannstedt and Joe Pendry, who would go on to coach the Pittsburgh Maulers, but it was Hugh Green who got all the attention. While Sherrill may have been looking for Dorsett's replacement in Jones, he found him in Green. The talented defensive end was as impressive his freshman campaign as Dorsett was in 1973. Sherrill put him in the starting lineup his first game in a Pitt uniform, and Green showed his worth with an eleven-tackle performance against Notre Dame that day that included two sacks and a blocked kick. It was the way icons are supposed to start their careers.

Pitt coach Jackie Sherrill recruited Hugh Green after he saw him in a game film going after running back Ray "Rooster" Jones. It was a fortuitous find by Sherrill, as Green became one of the greatest college football players in the history of the game and finished second in the 1980 Heisman Trophy vote at a time when it was thought to be impossible for a defensive player to win the award. *Courtesy of the University of Pittsburgh Athletics.*

There wasn't anything that Hugh Green couldn't do. His speed allowed him to be one of the most devastating pass rushers in the country. Offensive linemen were unable to stop him as he accumulated thirteen sacks that first season. If pass rushing was all he could do, that would have been impressive enough, but his unusual speed for a lineman allowed him to be effective in pass coverage if the coaches needed him to drop back. He was named as a second-team All-American and on the first-team All-East and All-Freshman squads. Johnson claimed, "For a freshman to come in and do the things he did in his first year is incredible. I didn't see a better defensive end all season."[126]

He was now the team's top attraction. Every time he'd make a big stop at Pitt Stadium, PA announcer Roger Huston would scream, "HUUUUUUGH" and then, in a more silent manner, complete his call with "Green." The fans at Pitt Stadium would enthusiastically repeat his call. If the Pitt faithful thought that his freshman campaign was something special, they were in for an even more impressive one in 1978.

Green was now considered one of the best ends in the game as only a sophomore. He didn't disappoint, adding another nine sacks to his career total with sixty-six solo tackles and twenty-nine assists. He could run the 40-yard dash in a time that would make running backs proud, 4.5 seconds, and spent more time in the offensive backfield making game-changing plays than any defensive player in the country. He was named a consensus All-American in 1978 and, before his junior season began, was placed on the Pitt All-Time team. Green was so talented as an athlete that the coaches felt there wasn't a position on the field he couldn't play.

As Hugh began his junior season in 1979, the program was also about to become an elite one. This year was the beginning of a three-year run where the team finished 11-1 each season while winning three consecutive bowl games, and Green would be a vital reason Pitt won twenty-two times in his final two years. He set career highs in tackles (seventy-six) and assists (fifty-nine), with eleven more sacks. After watching Green, ABC broadcaster and former Arkansas head coach Frank Broyles said, "Hugh Green is unbelievable. He's All-World. He's the best lineman I've seen anywhere this year. That's the fastest I've ever seen a defensive end move."[127]

The college football world was now fully aware of his greatness. He was named a Lombardi finalist and was a consensus All-American for the second consecutive season. Before his senior season in 1980, *Street and Smith Magazine* put Green on its All-1970s team. He was the poster boy for just about every college football preseason magazine in 1980 and was being touted as a Heisman Trophy candidate, something unheard of not only for defensive players but also defensive linemen in particular. If anyone thought that the lofty predictions were going to affect Green on the field, they were sorely mistaken.

He had arguably the best campaign of his four-year career with 17 sacks while combining with future Pro-Football Hall of Famer Ricky Jackson for 250 total tackles as one of the great defensive combinations in college football history. The Panthers had one of the great all-time defenses in 1980, allowing only 130 points in twelve games, 36 of them coming in their lone loss to Florida State, 36–22. It was a defeat that cost Green and his team their moment of glory with a recognized national championship, settling for the title in the *New York Times* computer poll only.

Despite the disappointment, Green added to his legendary recognition as one of the game's greats. He had his number retired by the university before his career was over, a rare recognition, while doing Dorsett one better with his third consecutive consensus All-American selection. He won the *Sporting News* Player of the Year; the United Press International Player of the Year; the Maxwell and Walter Camp Awards (the first defensive player to win the Camp Award), given to the nation's outstanding player; and the Lombardi Award as the best lineman in college football. Unfortunately, his historic run to become the first exclusive defensive player to win the Heisman fell short, finishing second to South Carolina's George Rogers. Green took it well, stating, "The Heisman Trophy always went to quarterbacks, running backs and on occasion to a wide receiver. I guess I had the résumé to be in a position to win [the Heisman]. But you don't win an award individually. You win as a team."[128]

Green was drafted seventh overall by the Tampa Bay Buccaneers and had a fine if not spectacular career in the NFL that included two All-Pro selections, but it was a career marred by injuries. In college, though, he was superb, a College Football Hall of Famer. ESPN named him as the fourteenth greatest overall college football player in a poll of the twenty-five greatest, while *Sports Illustrated* named him to its All–Twentieth Century team in 1999 and *College Football News* had him as the fifth-best player in its poll of the top one hundred players of all time, the top defensive player in the ranking. All in all, it was an outstanding career. Thank you, Rooster Jones.

4. ARNOLD PALMER

Golf, 1954–2006

When one thinks of athletes who are bigger than life, they not only look at the final stats but also the magnificent skill that led to their remarkable achievements. Ted Williams swung a bat the way it's taught in the books— or better. It was the epitome of the perfect swing. Pele's remarkable passes, moves and shots, especially his bicycle kick with his back to the goaltender that often sent a ball into the net, left fans breathless, and Mario Lemieux glided effortlessly through an NHL defense to score a goal that fans were certain no human would be able to. These are the remembrances of most of our iconic heroes—not so much a golfer with a cigarette hanging out of his mouth and putting a swing on a golf ball that you'd swear your uncle who never broke 100 would use. This certainly couldn't be the vision of the man who brought golf to a popularity level that it enjoys today, as well as one who was a pioneer in athletes marketing themselves. While his style was not one of the perfect golfer, Arnold Palmer nonetheless brought golf to the masses with his approach.

He was born in Latrobe, Pennsylvania, the home of Mr. Rogers and the banana split, yet looking through the city currently, it's obvious who the favored son is. The airport is named in his honor, as is a bridge, a statue and conservation area at St. Vincent College that's named for his wife, Winnie. This is the same college where dignitaries from all over the world descended to say their goodbyes to Palmer after his death in 2016 at eighty-seven years old, a funeral befitting a king. It was this same city where he was born to be a golfer, to Deacon Palmer, his father, who was the head pro and groundskeeper at Latrobe Country Club, a place that Palmer revered throughout his life.

It was apparent early on that this man was no ordinary golfer. In 1947, Palmer became the first Western Pennsylvania Interscholastic Athletic League (WPIAL) golfer to capture back-to-back high school championships, and then he went one to win the state tournament both years. He took his talents to Wake Forest University to play with his best friend, Buddy Worsham, the brother of the 1947 U.S. Open champion Lou Worsham. Tragically, Buddy was killed in an automobile accident in 1950, and the incident so affected the Hall of Fame golfer that he left school and joined the Coast Guard. When he returned, he was ready to move on and dedicate himself to the sport he was meant to play, winning the 1954 U.S. Amateur

Professional golf has Latrobe, Pennsylvania native Arnold Palmer to thank for its incredible popularity, as he brought the everyday sports fan onto the links to root for a man they considered one of them. His magnificent career ended with sixty-two PGA tour wins and seven major victories. *Courtesy of the World Golf Hall of Fame.*

and then deciding to turn pro. No one knew it at the time, but his career was to be arguably the most important one golf would ever know.

His unique swing looked like that of a weekend duffer, swinging from the bottom of your feet as hard as you could, and while it wasn't what the pros would try to teach a student learning the sport, it was consistent and powerful; most importantly, it was an attitude, the attitude of a gambler who wanted a birdie on every hole and did what he had to get them. It didn't always work out the way he wanted it to, but it certainly did more often than not.

A year after winning the amateur, he captured his first pro event, the 1955 Canadian Open. Despite the fact that he wasn't always popular around the so-called elite golf establishment at the time, his gambling philosophy, his unique swing, an everyman appearance and the fact that he'd talk with the crowd and made them believe he was one of them had the country enthralled with Arnold Palmer.

By the time he arrived at Augusta, Georgia, in 1958, he had won eight PGA tour events and was bringing a hoard of new golf fans to the tournaments, a more blue-collar fan who had previously ignored the sport. The group, called "Arnie's Army," rabidly followed Palmer around the course.

His career had been successful to this point, but he had failed in every attempt to win a major. That would end this weekend, when not only Palmer's future greatness but also his competitive fire were on display. Following a poor practice round, the great Ben Hogan muttered within earshot of Palmer that he was confused what the young Latrobe native was doing in the field. It inspired the man from Latrobe to victory. In an ESPN article, Arnold recalled that the remark "pissed me off. P-i-s-s-e-d....Hogan was another one of the goddamn guys on tour as far as I was concerned. He was no big guy. He was no big deal, and I didn't care what he said. All I wanted to do was beat him, and I did."[129] Palmer certainly did, soundly defeating the great Hogan be seven strokes.

Two years later, in 1960, Palmer won a second Masters, becoming the second player to lead the tournament after each round, but he looked hopelessly out of contention of the U.S. Open in Cherry Hills Country Club near Denver, when he mounted the greatest comeback in the tournament's history. He trailed by seven strokes going into the final round and was told by sportswriters Bob Drum and Dan Jenkins that he had no chance of winning the major during a lunch break between the third and fourth round after Palmer asked them if they thought a 65 could win the major; it was all the inspiration the King needed. He was angry and, ironically, shot a 65. He found out the answer to his question—yes, a 65 can win the tourney—as he bolted in front of a young Jack Nicklaus and the man who had questioned his talent two years earlier, Ben Hogan.

In 1960, Palmer was also credited with two other innovations. The first was when he decided to play in the British Open at a time few Americans played in the tournament. The Open was a failing major that not many took seriously. Arnie took it seriously and made it popular for the greatest players in the game to play there. He eventually won it in 1961, becoming the first American in eight years (Hogan being the last in 1953) to capture the Claret

Jug. The British Open owes its popularity today to the Hall of Famer. His other innovation in 1960 was one that resonates with most professional athletes today. He entered a handshake contract with Mark McCormick of the International Management Group (IMG) to market him to advertisers. While IMG is a giant in the industry today, back then it was a small company in an industry that really didn't exist. Because of his agreement with the company after he won the Masters that year, the marketing opportunities were incredible. It made him an even bigger star, and it made him rich beyond his wildest dreams. It also provided a blueprint to athletes in all sports on how to do the same.

Arnold went on to a fabulous career. While there was the disappointment of losing to Nicklaus at Oakmont in the 1962 U.S. Open, he would win sixty-two times on the PGA tour that included seven majors and more than ninety tournaments worldwide. He was elected to the International Golf Hall of Fame, has a drink named after him, spent more than his fair share both in money and time to charity, built many golf courses, had a tournament named after him, has thirteen streets across this country named in his honor and was awarded both the Presidential Medal of Freedom and the Congressional Gold Medal.

The career of Arnold Palmer was arguably the most important in the history of the sport. For it was Palmer—and not Hogan, Nicklaus, Snead, Hagen, Jones, Woods or any of the others whom experts may claim were better than him—who made the game as wildly popular as it is today, allowing golfers to earn the incredible purses and substantial money that they do outside the sport today.

3. HONUS WAGNER

Pittsburgh Pirates, 1900–1917

As Pirate fans enter PNC Park in Pittsburgh, they are greeted by a towering statue of the man who is widely considered to be the greatest shortstop to ever play the game and arguably one of the top ten talents in the history of Major League Baseball, Honus Wagner. The greatest player in the history of the franchise, Wagner's dominance is far above any other Pittsburgh Pirate, yet given the fact that he retired more than one hundred years ago and his exploits were not recorded on film, sometimes his magnificence is lost on today's baseball fans. To make his story even better, he is also a hometown hero, born right outside Pittsburgh in Mansfield, Pennsylvania, which later on merged with another town, Chartiers, to form what is today known as Carnegie. It's a story that may be forgotten at times but is always worth telling.

Wagner wasn't a bombastic personality by any stretch, as he was considered a fine sportsman as well as a tremendous baseball talent. His kind demeanor off the field is even found in the reason his 1909 American Tobacco Company card, more well known on the collectors' circuit as T-206, is the most expensive card of all time, selling for $3.12 million in 2016. Legend has it that only sixty remained because he had the company pull the card so children wouldn't be influenced to smoke because the sponsor. Of course, there is also the story that it was pulled because he felt he wasn't being properly compensated by the tobacco company, but regardless of the true tale, by all accounts he was an intense competitor on the field but a fine person off who didn't always look for the limelight.

The October 1916 edition of *Baseball Magazine* noted, "No one was ever very close to Wagner. His thoughts and feelings, save for a brief, occasional glimpse, are his own. The recollections of twenty years of brilliant deeds on the diamond must be a source of genuine satisfaction to the greathearted but secretive Pirate."[130] The 1905 *Reach Guide* claimed, "Aside from Wagner's great artistic achievements he has additional merits that entitle him to special distinction. He has a quiet unassuming disposition and remarkable native modesty; is absolutely correct in his living habits; and is a model of deportment on and off the field. Therefore in all ways Wagner represents the greatest development of the model ball player. May his shadow never grow less."[131] It never did.

From most accounts, he always made sure that he was in shape and ready to play, and he didn't drink much alcohol, as many who played the game at that time did. While widely considered the greatest shortstop of all time, he reportedly was a defensive marvel at whatever position he played. Coming up with the National League's Louisville Colonels in 1897, Wagner began his career playing in the outfield, first, second and third. When he came over to the Bucs in 1900 as part of the most lopsided trade in major-league history (only because the Colonels were about to disband and Barney Dreyfuss, the Louisville owner, purchased a piece of the Pirates after disbanding the Colonels), he still played several positions, including shortstop, and didn't begin to play exclusively there until 1903.

There is no greater player in Pittsburgh Pirates history than Honus Wagner. Considered by many historians as the best shortstop the game has ever known, Wagner led the Bucs to four National League pennants and the team's first World Series championship in 1909. He finished his career with 3,420 hits and eight batting titles. *Courtesy of the Pittsburgh Pirates.*

Wagner quickly rose as a star in his hometown, winning his first batting title in a Pirate uniform his first season there while capturing his second in 1903, the year the Bucs won their third consecutive National League pennant and a spot in the first World Series ever. Wagner would be in the national spotlight for the first time in the historic event, and Pittsburgh went in as the heavy favorites. He recorded history in the first game with the first RBI in the history of the fall classic when he knocked in Tommy Leach with the series' first run, but it went downhill from there. The Pirate starting pitchers were hurting, leaving Deacon Phillippe as their only viable option, and Wagner was not 100 percent himself. He hit only .222 in the World Series as the Pirates went on to lose to Boston in eight games. A Boston correspondent for the *Sporting News* was tough on the man they called "the Flying Dutchman," saying, "While Wagner is a fast, gingery player, he is not a wonder as regards to courage. I am half inclined to think old Honus has some yellow in him."[132]

This accusation of cowardice damaged his reputation on the field, and it took him six long years to remove it from his otherwise wonderful character. He continued to be dominant in the league, capturing four more batting titles between 1904 and 1908 and hitting .351 during the period, with a .418 OBP. He also led the National League in doubles and OPS four times in five seasons while leading the circuit once in hits, runs, triples and stolen bases, as well as OBP, and slugging three times apiece. It was a successful period for Wagner, and although team continued to excel, they were never quite good enough to return to the World Series for Wagner's retribution. That came about in 1909, when Pittsburgh won 110 games and their fourth senior circuit pennant. With the NL title, the Bucs returned to the fall classic to face Ty Cobb and the three-time defending American League champion Detroit Tigers.

The series was true theater, with the quintessential sportsman Wagner versus the rough-and-tumble Cobb, whose off-the-field antics were troubling—good versus evil, if you will. Honus was inspired to restore his name, while Cobb was exhausted having to drive through Canada and down New York and Pennsylvania to avoid Ohio, where he was afraid he may be arrested for beating up and stabbing a hotel detective at the Euclid Hotel in Cleveland (a fight instigated by Cobb because he was told he couldn't take the elevator after midnight). Wagner was magnificent, hitting .333 with 6 RBIs, including 2 in an 8–0 game seven victory that gave the Pirates their first World Series championship. Cobb, on the other end, hit only .231.

It was a momentous occasion for Wagner. His reputation was restored. He went on to play eight more seasons, retiring following the 1917 campaign when he was forty-three years old. All told, his career ranks as one of the greatest in the history of the game. With the tenth-highest wins above replacement (WAR) mark in the history of the game, 130.8, Wagner also captured eight batting crowns, has the eighth-highest hit total (3,420), third-most triples (252) and tenth-best stolen base mark (723), while defensively having the fourth-most putouts at short (4,576) and accumulating the eleventh-highest range factor for a shortstop at 5.63. In a testament to his greatness, when he became a member of the inaugural class to the Baseball Hall of Fame in 1936, he received 95.1 percent of the vote, the same as Babe Ruth, and in a recent ESPN poll, he was ranked as the thirteenth-best player in the history of the game.

Wagner went on to a career as a coach with the Pirates for nineteen years, while the number he wore while coaching, 33, was retired. Only a few months after attending the unveiling of his statue outside Forbes Field, he passed away at eighty-one. The statue moved with the team, being relocated first at Three Rivers Stadium and then to PNC, where the Pirates' greatest player continues to greet fans today.

2. JOSH GIBSON

Homestead Grays, 1930–31, 1937–40, 1942–46
Pittsburgh Crawfords, 1932–36

When rating players in a list such as this, it difficult to put one toward the top based on legendary tales. With Hall of Fame catcher Josh Gibson, the legends are many. Did he hit a ball in Pittsburgh one day and the next day it came down in Philadelphia, where a fielder caught it and the umpire said, "You're out…yesterday in Pittsburgh"? Of course not. Did he hit a home run completely out of Yankee Stadium in 1934? There has never been anything to substantially prove that, which brings the feat into question. These stories of course are tall tales and would have no determination in Gibson's rating in this book. Just taking into consideration the facts of this icon's career, he was one of the greatest power hitters the game has ever known. Even though he sadly never played in the major leagues, there's enough fact to overcome the legend that makes Josh Gibson the greatest player ever to grace the diamonds in the Steel City.

Barry Bonds was not a humble man in most instances, but when he broke both the single-season and career home run marks, he made sure to mention the fact that Gibson hit more than 800 in his career (the actual total has been mentioned at 962, although the majority came in exhibition barnstorming games) and 84 in a single season in 1936 (the majority of games he played in that year were barnstorming contests and not official Negro League games). While many of his long balls may have come in exhibition contests, quite a few of those games were against top talent, including contests against major-league players.

It didn't seem to matter who Josh played against, as he always seemed to end up showing off his incredible power. Nicknamed the "Black Babe Ruth," although many who saw Josh play would claim that Babe was the "White Josh Gibson," Gibson was born in Buena Vista, Georgia, and came to Pittsburgh with his family after his father found work at the Carnegie-Illinois Steel factory. He was a talented baseball player and hooked on with the Pittsburgh Crawfords when that franchise was only a semipro boys' team. He attracted the attention of the Homestead Grays in 1929, reportedly playing in isolated contests here and there, but didn't officially join the Grays until 1930, when he was only eighteen.

Like many legends of the game, he was a superstar from the outset. According to the website SeamHeads, he hit .417 in his rookie season for the Grays and was also an outstanding defensive player. He had a powerful arm that could throw out some of the best base stealers in the game, and he was quick defensively. At the plate, Gibson's swing was compact, and he didn't stride toward the plate to generate power; he did so from a flat-footed stance, using the incredible strength from his arms. That approach produced many home runs even outside the legendary tall tales that are often told.

In 1931, he was credited with seventy-five homers against all competition as he led a Grays team that included seven players who are now enshrined in the Baseball Hall of Fame to one of the greatest seasons in Negro League history. Just when he was becoming a superstar with the Grays, he decided to sign with Gus Greenlee and the Pittsburgh Crawfords in 1932, as did many of his Homestead teammates. The balance of power in both the Negro Leagues as well as African American baseball in Pittsburgh immediately went with him.

The Crawfords went from a semipro team to one of the great franchises in professional baseball history. The 1935 and 1936 squads were full of Hall of Fame talents and were league champions on both occasions. Gibson

One of the greatest power hitters in baseball history, Josh Gibson was often compared to Babe Ruth. While he never got a chance to play Major League Baseball, many consider him near or the equal of the Babe when it comes to ranking the greatest player to ever take the diamond. *Courtesy of the Rivers of Steel and the Josh Gibson family.*

was magnificent in a Crawford uniform, especially in 1936, when he hit .433, according to Lawrence Hogan in his book *Shades of Glory*. After the 1936 campaign, the financial situation for the team, as well as Greenlee, became dire, as the team would lose most of its stars, including Gibson, who re-signed with the Grays in 1937. That season in 1937, Gibson smacked perhaps his most prodigious home run, when the *Sporting News* reported he hit a ball in Yankee Stadium 580 feet, 15 feet longer than Mickey Mantle's record homer for the Yankees at the facility. He was phenomenal, teaming with Buck Leonard as a powerful duo that could rival anyone, including Babe Ruth and Lou Gehrig in their primes.

Gibson would also join another Negro League legend, Satchel Paige, in Santo Domingo that year, playing for the Trujillo All-Stars. He led the circuit with a .453 average on the way to the league championship and then rejoined the Grays, where he also was a pivotal part of bringing a Negro League National League championship to the franchise. It was the first of nine consecutive pennants the team would capture.

After four seasons with the Grays, he moved to the Mexican Leagues, where he made more money and had great success with a .467 average his first year and a pennant in 1941. Grays owner Cumberland Posey wanted him back and filed a suit for $10,000, threatening to take his home. He worked out an agreement with Posey and returned to the Grays in 1942, where he continued to lead the team with his spectacular play, including a .474 average in 1943. That was also the year where, unfortunately, Gibson's immense physical attributes began to diminish, as did his mental health. He suffered a nervous breakdown in 1943 and reportedly suffered from alcohol and substance abuse as well as intense headaches. It was found that he had a brain tumor, which most likely caused a majority of his issues. They found the tumor in 1943 and wanted to operate on him then, but Gibson was afraid to have the procedure done given the possibility of paralysis, so he declined. When some of his contemporaries began to return home from serving their country in World War II, they noticed his declining physical stature and health.

He played his last game in 1946 and on January 20, 1947, suffered a stroke and passed away. The shame of Josh Gibson's career was that he never had a chance to play in the major leagues, and from all who witnessed his prodigious power, he would have had a Hall of Fame career there. While Bob Feller thought different, claiming that Gibson couldn't hit a curveball, the fact is that many players couldn't hit Feller's curveball. Josh Gibson's .412 average in exhibition games against major-league all-star teams showed that he could have been a star there.

Gibson once thought that he might have an opportunity to play in the majors when Washington Senators owner Clark Griffith brought him and Buck Leonard into his office to discuss the duo playing for the Senators, but unfortunately nothing came of it. His death ironically came only three months before Jackie Robinson made his debut with the Dodgers as the first African American player in the majors in the twentieth century.

Despite the fact that Gibson never joined Robinson in the majors, his résumé in the game is impeccable. According to Rogan, he hit .359 in his career, with a .648 slugging percentage. Gibson was an icon on the diamond and was voted into the Baseball Hall of Fame in 1972.

Even today, he is rated among the best, despite the fact that he never played in the majors. Those who saw him gave credence to such ratings. Former Cleveland Buckeye Alonzo Boone said, "Josh was a better power hitter than Babe Ruth, Ted Williams or anybody else I've ever seen. Anything he touched was hit hard. He could power outside pitches to right field. Shortstops would move to left field when Josh came to the plate."[133] The great Satchel Paige said, "You look for his weakness and while you're lookin' for it, he's liable to hit 45 home runs."[134]

While it may be tough to rate players based on legend, there is enough factual proof to make the claim that Josh Gibson is the greatest baseball player ever in the history of the sport in Western Pennsylvania.

1. MARIO LEMIEUX

Pittsburgh Penguins, 1984–97, 2000–2006

It's usually tough to pinpoint the exact moment when a struggling franchise turns itself around. For the Pittsburgh Penguins, though, it's easy. The date was June 9, 1984. It's the day the team had the first selection in the NHL draft and decided not to trade it away despite the plethora of outstanding deals they were offered in return for the pick. The reason everyone was desperate to trade for the choice was the fact that a young eighteen-year-old from Montreal by the name of Mario Lemieux was the prize. He was considered a rare, once-in-a-lifetime talent, and luckily for the franchise, he exceeded those lofty expectations. The Penguins had been a laughingstock for the majority of their seventeen-year existence at that point, but they hoped with their new superstar that things would change. Whether they understood the heights Lemieux would take them to when they picked him was uncertain, but they did understand that they would no longer be a laughingstock.

To get Lemieux, they had to produce an embarrassing season in 1983–84 as they were having a hellacious battle with the New Jersey Devils to see who was the worst club in the National Hockey League—with it came the opportunity for the 1st pick. Eventually, Pittsburgh nudged out the Devils for the worst team with an embarrassing 38 points. To do so, they went 3-17-1 in their final twenty-one games of the season. The team would shuttle back and forth many players from their American Hockey League team in Baltimore, giving the appearance that they were doing anything they could to finish last.

It was a talented first round, as such noted players as Kirk Mueller, Eddie Olczyk, Petr Svoboda and future Pen Kevin Hatcher were taken in the round, along with defenseman Doug Bodger and center Roger Belanger by Pittsburgh. But their first choice, Lemieux, was obviously the prize. He was coming off a season with Laval of the Quebec Major Junior Hockey League, where he churned out statistics that one usually only sees in a video game.

A statue outside the PPG Paints Arena celebrating the team's greatest player, Mario Lemieux. Despite injuries and illnesses that limited him to only 915 games in his seventeen-year NHL career, Lemieux put up incredible numbers, finishing with the second-highest points per game, goals per game and assists per game in NHL history. *Courtesy of David Finoli.*

In seventy games, he had 133 goals and 149 assists for 282 points, crushing former Penguin Pierre Larouche's league record of 251. Three decades later, no one has ever come close to his mark. Even more remarkably, he scored 52 points in only fourteen playoff games, showing an ability of being at his best when the games mattered the most.

If Pittsburgh general manager Eddie Johnston had any doubt regarding the caliber of player he had drafted, those thoughts ended after Lemieux's first game. On October 11, 1984, Pittsburgh visited the Boston Gardens to take on the Bruins in the season opener. When the game was barely three minutes old, the young rookie jumped on the ice for his first shift of the game. He quickly took the puck from Hall of Fame defenseman Ray Bourque and broke in on goalie Pete Peeters. He put a fake on Peeters and shoveled a backhand shot past him into the goal at 2:59 of the first period on his first NHL shot. He went on to garner 100 points in the season, becoming only the third NHL player to do so in his rookie campaign, and captured the Calder Trophy as the Rookie of the Year.

Mario had a very successful first three seasons, including breaking the fifty-goal plateau for the first time in 1986–87 with fifty-four despite only playing sixty-three games, as he missed time with a sprained right knee and bronchitis, but it was his experience in the 1978 Canada Cup tournament that seemed to take him from superstar to iconic figure. Playing on a Canadian team filled with legends such as Mark Messier and Wayne Gretzky, Lemieux learned to be great and also learned the effort it took to reach his incredible potential, scoring a tournament-record eleven goals in nine games. "That whole tournament turned my career around. I saw what it took to win, to be a championship team. Seeing how talented players who had won the Cup before—guys like Wayne Gretzky, Mark Messier and Paul Coffey—work so hard every day was a true learning experience. Playing with such great players for five or six weeks also gave me a lot of confidence, and my career took off."[135]

All of a sudden, Mario was among the game's greatest players, battling Gretzky for the best. He won his first scoring title the season following the Canada Cup, netting 70 goals and taking home his first Hart Trophy as league MVP. A year later, he had a season for the ages with 199 points and 85 goals, becoming only the second player in NHL history to have two seasons with more than 70 goals, while setting the league mark with thirteen short-handed tallies. He also became a member of a rare group in hockey history by scoring 50 goals in the team's first fifty games when he hit the mark in Pittsburgh's forty-sixth game of the season. To date, only five players have ever accomplished this rare feat. Taking his legendary season to another level on New Year's Eve, he had perhaps the most remarkable game in the history of the sport, scoring 5 goals five different ways—even-strength, short-handed, on a power play, on a penalty shot and into an empty net—in an 8–6 win over the Devils, becoming the only player ever to perform the feat. It was so impressive that in 2017 NHL fans voted it to be the greatest moment in league history.

As he was becoming one of the best players in league history, injuries would start to become prevalent in his career. In 1990, he has surgery to repair a herniated disk in his back and missed the final twenty-one games of the 1989–90 campaign, as well as fifty the next year, when he developed a rare bone disease because of an infection he developed due to the surgery. He fought his way back to lead the team to their first Stanley Cup that year and captured the Conn Smythe Trophy as playoff MVP with a magnificent postseason run, scoring several highlight reel goals, including some in the finals against Minnesota.

In 1991–92, Mario won his third scoring title but broke his wrist in game two of the second round against the New York Rangers when Adam Graves hit him with a slash. Lemieux quickly returned and once again took the team to a Stanley Cup championship with 34 points in only fifteen games, winning his second Conn Smythe Trophy.

While the 1992–93 season was proving to be the Penguins' best regular season campaign in franchise history, capturing the Presidents Trophy with the league's best regular season record while also setting a mark that still stands today with seventeen consecutive wins, Mario dealt with tragic news that eventually led to his most inspirational moment. The team captain was off to a tremendous start when it was announced on January 12 that he had Hodgkin's Lymphoma. Luckily, it was diagnosed in its early stages and through radiation they were able to cure him. Even though the outcome was positive, radiation treatments for most would have meant an end to the season. Lemieux remarkably returned and did so with a vengeance on March 2, scoring 56 points in the team's final twenty games of the year to unbelievably win the scoring title with 160 points in only sixty games played. He won the Hart Trophy as league MVP once again in one of the most inspirational performances in sports history.

Surgery once again to repair a herniated disk in his back cost him most of the 1993–94 campaign, and he sat out the next season to recover from everything he had been through over the previous few years. After he returned in 1995–96, Mario won two more scoring titles and his third MVP award. He retired after the 1996–97 campaign and was immediately elected to the Hockey Hall of Fame.

His retirement wasn't permanent, as he announced on December 11, 2000, that he was coming back. On December 27, he returned and played a memorable game at the Civic Arena against Toronto in which he scored a goal and two assists, eventually garnering 76 points in only forty-three games despite being away from the game for three and a half seasons. Incredibly, his comeback came at a time when Mario was now one of the owners of the team as part of a group that took the club over in a bankruptcy proceeding. He became the first athlete to own a team he once played for.

Lemieux played off and on for four more seasons, but a reoccurrence of an irregular heartbeat sidelined him indefinitely in December 2005. One month later, on January 24, he retired for good.

His second career as the club's owner has been just as magnificent as his career as a player. He not only helped bring a much-needed arena to the city but also had a hand in making the club profitable over an extended period for the first time in the franchise's history, as well as adding three additional Stanley Cups under his leadership. As good as that all is, it was his play on the ice for which he will always be most known.

Even though his career was marred by injuries, playing in only 915 games in seventeen seasons, his statistics are remarkable. As of 2018, he's eighth on the all-time points list with 1,723 and has the tenth-most goals scored with 690. Taking into account the relatively small number of games he played, those statistics become even more impressive. As far as points, assists and goals per game, he has the second-highest figures in NHL history with 1.88, 1.13 and .75 per game, respectively.

Most experts consistently place him in the top three to play the game alongside Wayne Gretzky and Bobby Orr, but arguably there was no greater talent than Mario Lemieux. While Eddie Johnston and the Penguin hierarchy knew that they were getting a great player in 1984, certainly they had no idea they were picking the greatest athlete ever to play in the city of Pittsburgh.

Chapter 6

NEXT UP

THE TWENTY-FIVE ATHLETES WHO CAME CLOSE

51. LENORE KIGHT (swimming). Born in Frostburg, Maryland, Kight grew up in Homestead, where she represented the Homestead Library Athletic Club. Kight won a silver and bronze medal in the 1932 and 1936 Olympics, respectively. Overall, she set twenty-one United States records and seven world records in her impressive career, which culminated with her election to the International Swimming Hall of Fame.

52. ROBERT PECK (University of Pittsburgh, football). The University of Pittsburgh's first All-American in football also happened to be its first three-time All-American in football.

53. ALBERT WIGGINS (swimming). Albert Wiggins was the first American swimmer to capture AAU championships in three different disciplines. While he never won an Olympic medal, he set four world records and was on the cover of *Sports Illustrated*.

54. BILL FRALIC (University of Pittsburgh, football). The two-time All-American had his number retired by the school his senior season.

55. JEROME BETTIS (Pittsburgh Steelers). The Bus ran for 13,664 yards in his Hall of Fame career, helping to lead the Steelers to their fifth Super Bowl title in his final game.

56. CONNIE HAWKINS (Pittsburgh Rens and Pittsburgh Pipers). Hawkins was the pivotal force in the Pipers' winning the first American Basketball Association championship in 1968, and he secured the MVP award during the regular season.

57. MAURICE STOKES (St. Francis University, basketball). Stokes surprisingly led the Red Flash to the NIT semifinals in 1955, being named the tournament's Most Valuable Player.

58. JOE WILLIAMS (Homestead Grays). One of the most feared pitchers in the Negro Leagues, Joe Williams finally got his just due when he was elected to the Hall of Fame in 1999.

59. PIE TRAYNOR (Pittsburgh Pirates). One of the game's premier third basemen, Pie Traynor hit .320 while leading the Bucs to two World Series.

Harold "Pie" Traynor was considered one of the best third basemen in his time, hitting .320 for the Pittsburgh Pirates. Nicknamed for his love of pies as a child, Traynor went on to manage the Bucs in 1934, almost leading them to the pennant in 1938 before a late-season collapse. He was elected to the Baseball Hall of Fame in 1948. *Courtesy of the Pittsburgh Pirates.*

60. Babe Adams (Pittsburgh Pirates). Leading the Bucs to their first World Series title in 1909, with three wins in the fall classic his rookie year, Adams was one of the greatest control pitchers in the history of the game.

61. Dermontti Dawson (Pittsburgh Steelers). The six-time first-team All Pro at center was finally elected to the Pro Football Hall of Fame in 2012.

62. Trecia-Kate Smith (University of Pittsburgh, track). Smith won seven NCAA track championships at Pitt in the triple jump. She also won the gold medal for Jamaica in the 2005 world championships.

63. Mark May (University of Pittsburgh, football). The school's first Outland Trophy winner, Mark May was not only elected to the College Football Hall of Fame but also had his number retired at Pitt.

64. Michael Moorer (boxing). While known more for his loss to George Foreman, Monessen's Michael Moorer had a fabulous career, winning the World Light-Heavyweight Championship before capturing the heavyweight title.

65. Max Carey (Pittsburgh Pirates). Carey was one of the game's first great base stealers. His 738 stolen bases are still the ninth best in baseball history as of 2018.

66. Paul Coffey (Pittsburgh Penguins). Considered one of the top three defenseman ever to play in the NHL, Coffey came to Pittsburgh in 1987 from Edmonton. He helped lead the franchise to their first Stanley Cup.

67. Bill Dudley (Pittsburgh Steelers). The Hall of Famer was the NFL MVP in 1946, when he won a unique "triple crown," leading the league in rushing, interceptions and punt returns.

68. Hugh Peery (University of Pittsburgh, wrestling). Part of the great Peery wrestling family, Hugh won three consecutive NCAA titles while finishing his career 56-1, winning his final 48 bouts.

69. Joe Schmidt (University of Pittsburgh, football). In an era when Pitt had little success on the field, Joe Schmidt was one of the country's best defensive players. His number, 73, is retired at the school.

70. DAVE PALONE (harness racing). The winningest harness driver of all time, Palone, who spent most of his career at the Meadows in Washington, Pennsylvania, broke the North American record in 2012 with his 15,181st victory and the world record two years later, capturing race number 16,754.

71. ALDO "BUFF" DONELLI (soccer). More well known as the great football coach at Duquesne University, Donelli was one of the country's premier soccer players, becoming the first U.S. player to score a hat trick in international competition, tallying four goals against Mexico in a 1934 World Cup qualifier.

72. MYRTLE McATEER (tennis). McAteer was a force in tennis at the turn of the twentieth century, winning the U.S. Open singles title in 1900. She also captured two women's doubles and a mixed doubles crown at the tournament.

73. MIKE DITKA (University of Pittsburgh, football). A consensus All-American in 1960, Ditka helped reinvent the tight end position as a receiving threat. His number, 89, was retired by Pitt.

74. HOWARD HARPSTER (Carnegie Tech, football). A member of the 1926 squad that pulled off one of the greatest upsets in college football history, against Notre Dame, Harpster was elected to the College Football Hall of Fame in 1956.

75. KATHY STETLER (University of Pittsburgh, swimming). Stetler was the first woman four-year All-American in the school's history. On top of being the first Pitt woman to capture a national championship, she achieved All-American status eighteen times over the course of her four years at Pitt.

Chapter 7

THE LIST

WESTERN PENNSYLVANIA ATHLETES IN THE HALL OF FAME

BASEBALL HALL OF FAME

Name	Inducted	Team
Honus Wagner	1936	Pirates
Connie Mack	1937	Pirates
Fred Clarke	1945	Pirates
Jack Chesbro	1946	Pirates
Rube Waddell	1946	Pirates
Frankie Frisch	1947	Pirates
Pie Traynor	1948	Pirates
Paul Waner	1952	Pirates
Rabbit Maranville	1954	Pirates
Dazzy Vance	1955	Pirates
Joe Cronin	1956	Pirates
Hank Greenberg	1956	Pirates
Max Carey	1961	Pirates
Bill McKechnie	1962	Pirates
Heinie Manush	1964	Pirates
Burleigh Grimes	1964	Pirates
Pud Galvin	1965	Pirates

There are only two sets of brothers in the Baseball Hall of Fame, and one set played in the same outfield for the Pittsburgh Pirates: Paul Waner (*left*) and Lloyd Waner. Born in Oklahoma, Paul was known as "Big Poison," while Lloyd was called "Little Poison." The two were certainly poison to opposing pitchers and helped the Bucs to the 1927 National League pennant. *Courtesy of the Pittsburgh Pirates.*

Name	Inducted	Team
Casey Stengel	1966	Pirates
Lloyd Waner	1967	Pirates
Branch Rickey	1967	Pirates
Kiki Cuyler	1968	Pirates
Waite Hoyt	1969	Pirates
Jake Beckley	1971	Pirates
Joe Kelley	1971	Pirates
Satchel Paige	1971	Crawfords, Grays
Josh Gibson	1972	Grays, Crawfords
Buck Leonard	1972	Grays
Roberto Clemente	1973	Pirates
George Kelley	1973	Pirates
Cool Papa Bell	1974	Grays, Crawfords
Ralph Kiner	1975	Pirates
Billy Herman	1975	Pirates
Judy Johnson	1975	Grays, Crawfords
Fred Lindstrom	1976	Pirates
Oscar Charleston	1976	Grays, Crawfords
Al Lopez	1977	Pirates
Martin Dihigo	1977	Grays
Chuck Klein	1980	Pirates
Arky Vaughan	1985	Pirates
Ray Dandridge	1987	Grays
Willie Stargell	1988	Pirates
Vic Willis	1995	Pirates
Leon Day	1995	Grays
Jim Bunning	1996	Pirates
Ned Hanlon	1996	Pirates
Bill Foster	1996	Grays

Name	Inducted	Team
Willie Wells	1997	Grays
Smokey Joe Williams	1999	Grays
Bill Mazeroski	2001	Pirates
Ray Brown	2006	Grays
Cumberland Posey	2006	Grays
Jud Wilson	2006	Grays, Crawfords
Rich Gossage	2008	Pirates
Billy Southworth	2008	Pirates
Barney Dreyfuss	2008	Pirates
Bert Blyleven	2011	Pirates
Deacon White	2013	Pirates

PRO FOOTBALL HALL OF FAME

Name	Inducted	Team
Bert Bell	1963	Steelers, Steagles, Car-Pitts
John McNally	1963	Steelers
Cal Hubbard	1963	Steelers
Art Rooney	1964	Steelers, Steagles, Car-Pitts
Bill Dudley	1966	Steelers
Walt Kiesling	1966	Steelers, Steagles, Car-Pitts
Bobby Layne	1967	Steelers
Marion Motley	1968	Steelers
Ernie Stautner	1969	Steelers
Earle Neale	1969	Steagles
Bill Hewitt	1971	Steagles
Joe Greene	1987	Steelers
John Henry Johnson	1987	Steelers
Len Dawson	1987	Steelers

Pittsburgh's Greatest Athletes

Name	Inducted	Team
Jack Ham	1988	Steelers
Mel Blount	1989	Steelers
Terry Bradshaw	1989	Steelers
Franco Harris	1990	Steelers
Jack Lambert	1990	Steelers
Chuck Noll	1993	Steelers
Dan Rooney	2000	Steelers
Lynn Swann	2001	Steelers
John Stallworth	2002	Steelers
Rod Woodson	2009	Steelers
Jack Butler	2012	Steelers
Dermontti Dawson	2012	Steelers
Jerome Bettis	2015	Steelers
Kevin Greene	2016	Steelers

COLLEGE FOOTBALL HALL OF FAME

Name	Inducted	Team
Andrew Kerr	1951	W&J
Jock Sutherland	1951	Pitt
Pop Warner	1951	Pitt
Wilbur Henry	1951	W&J
John Heisman	1954	W&J
Robert Peck	1954	Pitt
Edgar Garbisch	1954	W&J
Howard Harpster	1956	Carnegie Tech
Marshall Goldberg	1958	Pitt
Tuss McLaughry	1962	Westminster
George McLaren	1965	Pitt

THE LIST

Name	Inducted	Team
Earle Neale	1967	W&J
Herb Stein	1967	Pitt
Clark Shaughnessy	1968	Pitt
Tom Davies	1970	Pitt
Joe Schmidt	1971	Pitt
Joseph Thompson	1971	Geneva, Pitt
Herb McCracken	1973	Allegheny
Hube Wagner	1973	Pitt
Averell Daniell	1975	Pitt
Joe Skladany	1975	Pitt
Len Casanova	1977	Pitt
Joseph Donchess	1979	Pitt
Lloyd Yoder	1982	Carnegie Tech
Mike Ditka	1986	Pitt
Tony Dorsett	1994	Pitt
Harold Burry	1996	Westminster
Hugh Green	1996	Pitt
Chuck Klausing	1998	IUP, Carnegie-Mellon
Larry Pugh	1998	Westminster
Bill Fralic	1999	Pitt
Joe Fusco	2001	Westminster
Jim Haslett	2001	IUP
Dan Marino	2002	Pitt
Jimbo Covert	2003	Pitt
Harold Davis	2004	Westminster
Mark May	2006	Pitt
Frank Cignetti Sr.	2013	IUP
Joe Micchia	2013	Westminster
Ruben Brown	2015	Pitt

HOCKEY HALL OF FAME

Name	Inducted	Team
Hod Stuart	1945	Bankers, Professionals
Cyclone Taylor	1947	Professionals
Mickey MacKay	1952	Pirates
Frank Fredrickson	1958	Pirates
Bruce Stuart	1961	Victorias
Alf Smith	1962	PAC, Duquesne, Bankers
Riley Hern	1962	Keystones
Jimmy Gardner	1962	Professionals
Jack Stewart	1964	Hornets
Marty Barry	1965	Hornets
Frank Brimsek	1966	Yellow Jackets
Sid Abel	1969	Hornets
Roy Worters	1969	Yellow Jackets, Pirates
Tommy Smith	1973	Professionals, Lyceum, Bankers
Doug Harvey	1973	Hornets
George Armstrong	1975	Hornets
Gordie Drillon	1975	Yellow Jackets
Tim Horton	1977	Hornets, Penguins
Andy Bathgate	1978	Hornets, Penguins
Gerry Cheevers	1985	Hornets
Leo Boivin	1986	Hornets, Penguins
Fernie Flaman	1990	Hornets
Scotty Bowman	1991	Penguins
Bob Johnson	1992	Penguins
Lionel Conacher	1994	Yellow Jackets, Pirates
Mario Lemieux	1997	Penguins
Bryan Trottier	1997	Penguins
Joe Mullen	2000	Penguins

Name	Inducted	Team
Craig Patrick	2001	Penguins
Paul Coffey	2004	Penguins
Larry Murphy	2004	Penguins
Herb Brooks	2006	Penguins
Ron Francis	2007	Penguins
Luc Robitaille	2009	Penguins
Mark Recchi	2017	Penguins

NAISMITH BASKETBALL HALL OF FAME

Name	Inducted	Team
Chuck Hyatt	1959	Pitt
Doc Carlson	1959	Pitt
George Keogan	1961	Allegheny
Ed Wachter	1961	McKeesport Majestics
Ken Loeffler	1964	Geneva
Neil Johnston	1990	Rens
Connie Hawkins	1992	Rens, Pipers
Buddy Jeannette	1994	W&J
Maurice Stokes	2004	St. Francis
Cumberland Posey	2016	Duquesne, Monticello, Loendi
Chuck Cooper	2019	Duquesne

COLLEGE BASKETBALL HALL OF FAME

Name	Inducted	Team
Maurice Stokes	2006	St. Francis
Buddy Jeannette	2006	W&J
Chuck Hyatt	2006	Pitt
Ken Loeffler	2006	Geneva

George Keogan	2006	Allegheny
Doc Carlson	2006	Pitt

INTERNATIONAL BOXING HALL OF FAME

Name	Inducted
Billy Conn	1990
Harry Greb	1990
Charley Burley	1992
Fritzie Zivic	1993
Sammy Angott	1998
Teddy Yarosz	2006

NATIONAL WRESTLING HALL OF FAME

Name	Inducted	Team
Rex Peery	1976	Pitt
Ed Peery	1980	Pitt
Hugh Peery	1980	Pitt
Wade Schalles	1991	Clarion
Stan Dziedzic	1996	Slippery Rock
Kurt Angle	2001	Clarion
Bruce Baumgartner	2002	Edinboro
Robert Bubb	2005	Pitt, Clarion
Carlton Haselrig	2016	Pitt-Johnstown
Tony Gizoni	2017	Waynesburg

NATIONAL SOCCER HALL OF FAME

Name	Inducted	Team
John Jaap	1953	Castle Shannon, Arden, Vestaburg, Jeannette

Name	Inducted	Team
Buff Donelli	1954	Heidelberg, Castle Shannon, Morgan
Ralph Carrafi	1959	Vestaburg
Nick DiOrio	1974	Morgan Strasser, Pittsburgh Strasser, Harmarville, Beadling
Ray Bernabei	1978	Harmarville
Mike Bookie	1986	Vestaburg
Robert Craddock	1997	Castle Shannon, Harmarville
Paul Danilo	1997	Morgan, Heidelberg, Indians
Paul Child	2003	Spirit

INTERNATIONAL SWIMMING HALL OF FAME

Name	Inducted
Jimmy McLane	1970
Lenore Kight	1981
Albert Wiggins	1994

USA TRACK & FIELD HALL OF FAME

Name	Inducted
John Woodruff	1978
Roger Kingdom	2005

USA TABLE TENNIS HALL OF FAME

Name	Inducted
Danny Seemiller	1995
Ricky Seemiller	1998

HARNESS RACING HALL OF FAME

Name	Inducted
Adios	1965
Del Miller	1969
Dave Pallone	2010

THOROUGHBRED RACING HALL OF FAME

Name	Inducted
Bill Hartack	1959

INDIANAPOLIS SPEEDWAY HALL OF FAME

Name	Inducted
Chip Ganassi	2014

UNITED STATED BOWLING HALL OF FAME

Name	Inducted
Louise Fulton	2001

INTERNATIONAL GOLF HALL OF FAME

Name	Inducted
Arnold Palmer	1974
Carol Semple Thompson	2008

INTERNATIONAL TENNIS HALL OF FAME

Name	Inducted
Chuck Garland	1969

NOTES

Chapter 1

1. Thomas, *They Cleared the Lane*, 51.
2. Ibid., 53.
3. Mark J. Spears, "Pioneer Reflects on History," *Boston Globe*, January 23, 2008, http://archive.boston.com/sports/basketball/celtics/articles/2008/01/21/pioneer_reflects_on_history.
4. Paul Zeise, "Cooper's Plight," *Pittsburgh Post-Gazette*, April 25, 2000, 32.
5. *New York Times*, "Chuck Cooper, NBA Player," obituary, February 7, 1984, https://www.nytimes.com/1984/02/07/obituaries/chuck-cooper-nba-player.html.
6. Jim McCurdie, "ARKY VAUGHAN: The Quiet and Talented Shortstop Was at Long Last Welcomed into Hall of Fame—37 Years After Retirement and 33 Years After His Death," *Los Angeles Times*, January 13, 1986, http://articles.latimes.com/1986-01-13/sports/sp-27753_1_arky-vaughan.
7. Ralph Moses, "Arky Vaughan," SABR Online Biography Project, Society for American Baseball Research, https://sabr.org/bioproj/person/4e00be9b.
8. Andrew Martin, "Arky Vaughan: Baseball's Forgotten Star," Baseball Historian, http://baseballhistorian.blogspot.com/2015/05/arky-vaughan-baseballs-forgotten-star.html.
9. McCurdie, "ARKY VAUGHAN."
10. Bill Dundas, "For Antonio Brown, Fighting for His Place in the Sun Has Been a Lifelong Pursuit," SB Nation: Behind the Steel Curtain, June 18,

2018, https://www.behindthesteelcurtain.com/2018/6/18/17459814/ for-antonio-brown-fighting-for-his-place-in-the-sun-has-been-a-lifelong-pursuit-steelers-nfl-news.

11. Jeremy Fowler, "The Antonio Brown 21: What We Learned from an Epic Draft Fail," ESPN, April 21, 2017, http://www.espn.com/blog/afcnorth/post/_/id/91033/small-and-slow-how-antonio-brown-flipped-nfl-draft-on-its-head-in-2010.

12. Finoli and Healy, *Kings on the Bluff: The Next Chapter*, 174–75.

13. Ibid., 178.

14. Rosenfeld, *Charley Burley*, 81.

15. Ibid., 82.

16. Bob Mee, "On This Day: The Fighter Who Was Too Good for His Own Good, Charley Burley, Was Born in 1917," Boxing News, September 6, 2014, http://www.boxingnewsonline.net/on-this-day-the-fighter-who-was-too-good-for-his-own-good-charley-burley-was-born-in-1917.

17. Tom Donelson, "On This Day: The Mysterious Charley Burley," Eastside Boxing, https://www.boxing247.com/news/donelson0607.php.

18. Mee, "On This Day: The Fighter Who Was Too Good for His Own Good."

19. Roy McHugh, "Stautner Undertakes Job of Polishing Diamonds in Rough," *Pittsburgh Press*, July 23, 1964, 46.

20. Rudy Cernkovic, "Michelosen Things Steelers Are in for Rough Season," *Daily Republican*, September 13, 1950, 2.

21. Ed Bouchette, "Hall of Fame Tackle, His No. 70 the Only One Steelers Officially Retired," *Pittsburgh Post-Gazette*, February 17, 2006, 41.

22. Ibid.

23. Jesse Washington, "Splash and Cash: The Legend of Old-School Baller Cumberland Posey," The Undefeated, September 7, 2016, https://theundefeated.com/features/cumberland-posey-only-person-in-basketball-and-baseball-halls-of-fame.

24. Finoli, *Pittsburgh's Greatest Teams*, 60.

25. Ibid.

26. Washington, "Splash and Cash."

27. Baseball Hall of Fame, "Cumberland Posey," https://baseballhall.org/hall-of-famers/posey-cum.

28. Bryan Deardo, "Report: Troy Polamalu Has Some Resentment Towards Steelers," 247sports, March 22, 2017, https://247sports.com/nfl/pittsburgh-steelers/Bolt/Report-Troy-Polamalu-has-some-resentment-towards-Steelers-51912420.

29. Baseball Hall of Fame, "Cool Papa Bell," https://baseballhall.org/hall-of-famers/bell-cool-papa.

30. Ibid.

31. Marino Parascenzo, "Sports Briefing," *Pittsburgh Post-Gazette*, October 6, 1980, 28.

32. Ibid.

33. Ibid.

34. Phil Axelrod, "50 Years Ago, Sihugo Green and Dick Ricketts Led Duquesne to the Title in Basketball's No. 1 Tournament—the NIT," *Pittsburgh Post-Gazette*, March 16, 2005, http://www.post-gazette.com/sports/duquesne/2005/03/16/50-years-ago-Sihugo-Green-and-Dick-Ricketts-led-Duquesne-to-the-title-in-basketball-s-No-1-tournament-the-NIT/stories/200503160249.

35. *2015–16 Duquesne Basketball Media Supplement*, 168.

36. Peter May, "Celtic Greens in Boston: A Guidebook in One Color," *New York Times*, April 26, 2013, http://www.nytimes.com/2013/04/27/sports/basketball/four-boston-celtics-named-green-a-history.html?_r=0.

Chapter 2

37. Anne Shipley, "Once Williams Starts, There's No Stopping," *Washington Post*, August 9, 2004, http://www.washingtonpost.com/wp-dyn/articles/A50662-2004Aug8.html?noredirect=on.

38. Ibid.

39. Athletes in Action, "Struggles: Lauryn Williams," https://athletesinaction.org/olympics/athletes/lauryn-williams.

40. *CBS Pittsburgh*, "Aaron Donald: A Pittsburgh Success Story," February 1, 2017, https://pittsburgh.cbslocal.com/2017/02/01/aaron-donald-a-pittsburgh-success-story.

41. Dan Dahlke, "NFL Draft: Q&A with Pittsburgh Defensive Lineman Aaron Donald," Lombardi Avenue, February 26, 2014, https://lombardiave.com/2014/02/26/nfl-draft-qa-pitt-defensive-lineman-aaron-donald.

42. *CBS Pittsburgh*, "Aaron Donald."

43. Mark Bedics, "6-Time NCAA Wrestling Champ Jumped to NFL Having Never Played a College Down," *Champion Magazine*, January 25, 2018, http://www.ncaa.org/champion/6-time-ncaa-wrestling-champ-jumped-nfl-having-never-played-college-down.

44. Bruce Keiden, "Wrestling Haselrig Devours Competition," *Pittsburgh Post-Gazette*, March 23, 1988, 41.

45. Frank Litsky, "Mike Webster, 50, Dies; Troubled Football Hall of Famer," *New York Times*, September 25, 2002, https://www.nytimes.com/2002/09/25/sports/mike-webster-50-dies-troubled-football-hall-of-famer.html.

46. Ibid.

47. Jeanne Marie, "Bennet Omalu, Concussions, and the NFL: How One Doctor Changed Football Forever," *GQ*, September 14, 2009, https://www.gq.com/story/nfl-players-brain-dementia-study-memory-concussions.

48. Litsky, "Mike Webster, 50, Dies."

49. ESPN, "It's Official: Penguins Sign Russian Star Malkin," via Associated Press, September 7, 2006, www.espn.com/nhl/news/story?id=2574012.

50. Frank Litsky, "A Victory that's Still Memorable 70 Years Later," *New York Times*, August 1, 2006, https://www.nytimes.com/2006/08/01/sports/othersports/01olympics.html.

51. Ibid.

52. Eliott Denman, "Through Good and Bad, 1936 US Gold Medalist John Woodruff Has Never Lost Faith in His Country," *Asbury Park Press*, March 17, 1998, 36.

53. Ibid.

54. Sullivan, *Scouting Report: 1987*, 559.

55. Bob Hertzel, "Big Bucks on Hold: Bonds and Bonilla Make Pirates' Rivals Pay," *Washington Post*, August 26, 1990, https://www.washingtonpost.com/archive/sports/1990/08/26/big-bucks-on-hold-bonds-and-bonilla-make-pirates-rivals-pay/7307ca36-d6f9-450e-a2ce-987bd22e518e/?noredirect=on&utm_term=.57f86754e7c4.

56. *Los Angeles Times*, "Baseball Daily Report: Around the Majors: Leyland Shouts His Displeasure at Bonds," via Associated Press, March 5, 1991, http://articles.latimes.com/1991-03-05/sports/sp-134_1_barry-bonds.

57. Gordon S. White Jr., "Pitt's Marino Questions N.C.A.A. Rule on Professionals," *New York Times*, October 29, 1979, https://www.nytimes.com/1979/10/29/archives/pitts-marino-questions-ncaa-rule-on-professionals.html.

58. Dave Raffo, "When Dan Marino Was Coming Out of College," UPI, January 18, 1985, https://www.upi.com/Archives/1985/01/18/When-Dan-Marino-was-coming-out-of-college-his/7140474872400.

59. *1979 Pitt Football Media Guide*, 64.

60. Gerald Eskenazi, "So Good So Soon," *New York Times*, November 4, 1984, https://www.nytimes.com/1984/11/04/sports/marino-so-good-so-soon.html.

61. *Observer-Reporter*, "Marino Upset by Noll's Comments," via Associated Press, May 13, 1992, 8.

62. Dave Parker and Dave Jordan, "'Roberto Was Our Brother': Dave Parker Recalls First Pirates Spring Training after Clemente's Death," Sporting News, March 22, 2018, http://www.sportingnews.com/mlb/news/roberto-clemente-hall-of-fame-1973-death-pirates-spring-training-dave-parker-essay/1a5a6ga1gkzyg1ev198m4oxr62.

63. Joe Posnanski, "Parker Worthy of Cooperstown Consideration," Major League Baseball, November 28, 2017, www.mlb.com/news/pirates-great-dave-parker-has-strong-hof-case/c-262481168.

64. Jack Sell, "Scout Noll: Terry Is Mobile in Mobile," *Pittsburgh Post-Gazette*, January 28, 1970, 20.

65. Ibid.

66. MacCambridge, *Chuck Noll*, 250.

Chapter 3

67. *Sports Daily*, "Ralph Kiner Recalls Being a Pilot during World War II," Subway Squawkers, November 10, 2009, http://thesportsdaily.com/2009/11/10/ralph-kiner-recalls-being-a-pilot-during-world-war-ii.

68. Finoli and Ranier, *Pittsburgh Pirates Encyclopedia*, 283.

69. John J. Burbridge Jr. in Tan, *National Pastime*, 69.

70. MacCambridge, *Chuck Noll*, 299.

71. WTAE-TV, "Rooney Tells Why the Steelers Passed on Marino, Cheerleaders, Helmet Logos," October 2, 2007, http://www.wtae.com/article/rooney-tells-why-steelers-passed-on-marino-cheerleaders-helmet-logos/7433870.

72. Marino Parascenzo, "In a Class of Her Own: One of the Greatest Amateurs in Women's Golf History Scores Another (and Uexpected) Triumph," *Pittsburgh Quarterly Magazine* (Summer 2015), https://pittsburghquarterly.com/pq-sports/item/738-in-a-class-of-her-own.html.

73. Ibid.

74. *Pittsburgh Press*, "Carol Wins US Amateur Title," August 19, 1973, 69.

75. Ibid.

76. Mike Bires, "Q&A: Hall of Famer Carol Semple Thompson Still First Lady of Amateur Golf," *Beaver Valley Times*, May 6, 2018, http://www.timesonline.com/sports/20180506/q-amp-a-hall-of-famer-carol-semple-thompson-still-first-lady-of-amateur-golf.

77. Chris Willis, "The Career of Hall of Famer Pete Henry," *Coffin Corner* 27, no. 5 (2005): 3.

78. Ibid., 1.

79. Finoli, *When Pitt Ruled the Gridiron*, 177.

80. Ibid., 178.

81. Ibid., 217.

82. Craig Meyer, "Marshall Goldberg, Pitt's Prototype," *Pittsburgh Post-Gazette Interactive*, October 25, 2017, https://newsinteractive.post-gazette.com/thedigs/2017/10/25/marshall-goldberg-pitt-football-prototype.

83. *Pitt 1983 Football Media Guide*, 34.

84. Tom McMillan, "Kingdom's Athletic, Academic Future at Pitt Unclear," *Pittsburgh Post-Gazette*, July 9, 1984, 12.

85. Gary Mihoces, "Receiver, Linebacker Grabbed by Steelers," *Indiana Gazette*, January 30, 1974, 16.

86. Phil Musick, "Lambert: Rare Praise," *Pittsburgh Press*, August 22, 1974, 38.

87. Ed Bouchette, "It's Over," *Pittsburgh Post-Gazette*, July 12, 1985, 9.

88. Tim Layden, "So Good, Too Soon?: Driven by Tragedy, Sophomore Larry Fitzgerald Has Become the Nation's Top Wideout, Perhaps Its Best Player. The Pros Want Him, but Will the NFL Let Him in a Year Early?," *Sports Illustrated Vault*, December 8, 2003, https://www.si.com/vault/2003/12/08/355712/so-good-too-soon-driven-by-tragedy-sophomore-larry-fitzgerald-has-become-the-nations-top-wideout-perhaps-its-best-player-the-pros-want-him-but-will-the-nfl-let-him-in-a-year-early.

89. Jeremy Beer, "Hothead: How the Oscar Charleston Myth Began," Society for American Baseball Research, https://sabr.org/research/hothead-how-oscar-charleston-myth-began#footnote13_jw51qw4.

90. Ibid.

91. James, *New Bill James Historical Baseball Abstract*, 189.

Chapter 4

92. Kennedy, *Billy Conn*, 17.

93. Ibid., 69.

94. Roy McHugh, "Roy McHugh Remembers: Conn's Loss to Louis Still a Knockout Tale," *Pittsburgh Post-Gazette*, November 29, 1999, http://old.post-gazette.com/sports_headlines/19991129mchugh4.asp.

95. Finoli, *50 Greatest Players in Pittsburgh Pirates History*, 29.

96. Ibid., 31.

97. Ralph Berger, "Buck Leonard," SABR Online Biography Project, Society for American Baseball Research, https://sabr.org/bioproj/person/231446fd.

98. Ibid.

99. Pete Blackburn, "How Jaromír Jágr May Have Manipulated the 1990 NHL Draft in His Favor," *Fox Sports*, October 20, 2016, https://www.foxsports.com/nhl/story/how-jaromir-jagr-may-have-manipulated-the-1990-nhl-draft-in-his-favor-090116.

100. Finoli, *Classic Pens*, 126.

101. Mike Janofsky, "Career Hurdle for Woodson," *New York Times*, June 26, 1987, https://www.nytimes.com/1987/06/26/sports/career-hurdle-for-woodson.html.

102. Ed Bouchette, "Woodson Signs Four-Year Steeler Pact," *Pittsburgh Post-Gazette*, October 29, 1987, 28.

103. Finoli, *50 Greatest Players in Pittsburgh Pirates History*, 21.

104. Joseph Wancho, "Paul Waner," SABR Online Biography Project, Society for American Baseball Research, https://sabr.org/bioproj/person/9d598ab8.

105. Ibid.

106. Kristian Dyer, "How Legendary Penn State LB Jack Ham Nearly Went Unrecruited Out of High School," Sporting News, http://www.sportingnews.com/us/ncaa-football/news/jack-ham-linebacker-penn-state-unrecruited-nfl-pro-football-hall-of-fame-pittsburgh-steelers-nfl/1i95ip6df39by1pehrczii79kv.

107. Pittsburgh Steelers, "Jack Ham," https://www.steelers.com/history/bios/ham_jack.

108. William Leggett, "Just Call Me Bill," *Sports Illustrated Vault*, April 13, 1959, https://www.si.com/vault/1959/04/13/616031/just-call-me-bill.

109. Ibid.

110. Christine, *Bill Hartack*, 8.

111. Ibid., 10.

112. Fayette County Hall of Fame, "Charley Hyatt," http://www.fayettecountysportshalloffame.com/2010/hyatt.html.

113. Ibid.

114. Sciullo, *Tales from the Pitt Panthers*, 5.

115. Fayette County Hall of Fame, "Charley Hyatt."

Chapter 5

116. Joe Starkey, "Class of '73 Keyed Pitt's Magical Season," *Tribune-Review*, August 27, 2006, https://triblive.com/x/pittsburghtrib/news/s_467818.html.

117. Ibid.

118. Paxton, *Fearless Harry Greb*.

119. Mike Casey, "Phenomenon: Why Harry Greb Was So Great," Boxing News, August 30, 2012, http://www.boxing.com/phenomenon_why_harry_greb_was_so_great.html.

120. Bobby Franklin, "Harry Greb Won the Title from Johnny Wilson but It May Not Have Been Easy," Boxing Over Broadway, July 17, 2018, https://www.boxingoverbroadway.com/harry-greb-won-the-title-from-johnny-wilson-but-it-may-not-have-been-easy.

121. Finoli, *50 Greatest Players in Pittsburgh Pirates History*, 15.

122. *Pittsburgh Press*, "Greene's Asking Price a Big Figure to Tackle," January 29, 1969, 62.

123. Blount, *About Three Bricks Shy*, 235.

124. Don Banks, "1974 Steelers," *Sports Illustrated Vault*, December 29, 2014, https://www.si.com/vault/2014/12/29/106697819/1974-steelers.

125. Ibid.

126. *1978 Pitt Media Guide*, "Hugh Green," 48.

127. *1980 Pitt Media Guide*, "Hugh Green," 18.

128. Bob Barrickman, "Pitt's Green Was One of the Best in College Football History," *Beaver Valley Times*, June 7, 2011, http://www.timesonline.com/d4b1b974-f761-53bd-a5d4-38af4704bc0f.html.

129. Ian O'Conner, "The Force that Drove Arnold Palmer," ESPN, September 26, 2016, http://www.espn.com/golf/story/_/id/17640876/the-force-drove-arnold-palmer.

130. James, *New Bill James Historical Baseball Abstract*, 591.

131. Ibid.

132. Finoli, *50 Greatest Players in Pittsburgh Pirates History*, 8.

133. Baseball Hall of Fame, "Josh Gibson," https://baseballhall.org/hall-of-famers/gibson-josh.

134. Ibid.

135. Joe Pelletier, "Mario Lemieux," Greatest Hockey Legends, http://internationalhockeylegends.blogspot.com/2007/11/mario-lemieux.html.

BIBLIOGRAPHY

Books

Blount, Roy, Jr. *About Three Bricks Shy…and the Load Filled Up.* Pittsburgh: University of Pittsburgh Press, 2004.

Christine, Bill. *Bill Hartack: The Bittersweet Life of a Hall of Fame Jockey.* Jefferson, NC: McFarland, 2016.

Finoli, David. *Classic Bucs: The 50 Greatest Games in Pittsburgh Pirates History.* Kent, OH: Kent State Press, 2013.

———. *Classic Pens: The 50 Greatest Games in Pittsburgh Penguins History.* 2nd ed. Kent, OH: Kent State Press, 2015.

———. *Classic Steelers: The 50 Greatest Games in Pittsburgh Steelers History.* Kent, OH: Kent State Press, 2014.

———. *The 50 Greatest Players in Pittsburgh Pirates History.* Lanham, MD: Rowman & Littlefield, 2016.

———. *Kings on the Bluff: The 1955 N.I.T. Champion Duquesne Dukes.* North Charleston, SC: Createspace, 2016.

———. *Pittsburgh's Greatest Teams.* Charleston, SC: The History Press, 2017.

———. *When Pitt Ruled the Gridiron: Football at the University of Pittsburgh, 1924–1938.* Jefferson, NC: McFarland, 2011.

Finoli, David, and Bill Ranier. *The Pittsburgh Pirates Encyclopedia.* 2nd ed. New York: Sports Publishing Inc., 2015.

———. *When Cobb Met Wagner: The Seven Games of the 1909 World Series.* Jefferson, NC: McFarland, 2015.

———. *When the Bucs Won It All: The 1979 World Champion Pittsburgh Pirates.* Jefferson, NC: McFarland, 2003.

Finoli, David, and Chris Fletcher. *Steel City Gridirons.* Pittsburgh, PA: Maguire Towers, 2005.

Finoli, David, and Robert Healy III. *Kings on the Bluff: The Next Chapter.* North Charleston, SC: Createspace, 2017.

Hollander, Zander. *The 1990 Complete Handbook of Baseball.* New York: Signet Books, 1990.

James, Bill. *The New Bill James Historical Baseball Abstract.* New York: Free Press, 2001.

Kennedy, Paul F. *Billy Conn: The Pittsburgh Kid.* Bloomington, IN: AuthorHouse, 2007.

MacCambridge, Michael. *Chuck Noll: His Life's Work.* Pittsburgh, PA: University of Pittsburgh Press, 2016.

Paxton, Bill. *The Fearless Harry Greb: Biography of a Tragic Hero of Boxing.* Jefferson, NC: McFarland, 2009.

Riley, James. *The Biographical Encyclopedia of the Negro Leagues.* New York: Carroll & Graf Publishing, 1994.

Roberts, James, and Alexander G Skutt, eds. *The Boxing Register: International Boxing Hall of Fame Official Record Book.* Ithaca, NY: McBooks Press, 1997.

Rogan, Lawrence. *Shades of Glory: The Negro Leagues and the Story of African-American Baseball.* Washington, D.C.: National Geographic, 2006.

Rosenfeld, Allen S. *Charley Burley: The Life and Hard Times of an Uncrowned Champion.* Bloomington, IN: 1st Books, 2003.

Sciullo, Sam. *Tales from the Pitt Panthers.* New York: Sports Publishing Inc., 2004.

Sullivan, Marybeth, ed. *The Scouting Report: 1987.* New York: Harper & Row Publishers, 2007.

Tan, Celia, ed. *The National Pastime: Steel City Stories.* Phoenix, AZ: Society for American Baseball Research, 2018.

Thomas, Ron. *They Cleared the Lane: The NBA's Black Pioneers.* Lincoln: University of Nebraska Press, 2002.

Media Guides

Duquesne University Basketball Media Guide.
Duquesne University Football Media Guide.
Pittsburgh Penguins Media Guide.

BIBLIOGRAPHY

Pittsburgh Pirates Media Guide.
Pittsburgh Steelers Media Guide.
University of Pittsburgh Basketball Media Guide.
University of Pittsburgh Football Media Guide.

Newspapers

Asbury Park Press.
Baltimore Sun.
Beaver County Times.
Daily Republican (Monongahela, PA).
Gettysburg Times.
Indiana (PA) Gazette.
Inter-Mountain (Elkins, WV).
Los Angeles Times.
New York Daily News.
New York Times.
Observer-Reporter (Washington, PA).
Pittsburgh Magazine.
Pittsburgh Post-Gazette.
Pittsburgh Press.
Pittsburgh Quarterly Magazine.
Tribune Review.
USA Today.
Washington Post.

Magazines

Coffin Corner.
GQ.
Sporting News.
Sport Magazine.
Sports Illustrated.

Website Database

athletesinaction.org.
baseballhall.org.
baseballhistorian.blogspot.com.
baseballinwartime.com.
behindtheboxscore.com.
behindthesteelcurtain.com.
billjamesonline.com.
bleacherreport.com.
bloodhorse.com.
boston.com.
boxing.com.
boxingnewsonline.net.
boxingoverbroadway.com.
boxrec.com.
cardiachill.com.
collegebasketballexperience.com.
espn.com.
fayettecountysportshalloffame.com.
heinzhistorycenter.org.
hoophall.com.
internationalhockeylegends.blogspot.com.
lombardiave.com.
mlb.com.
paulickreport.com.
pittsburgh.cbslocal.com.
pittsburgh.forums.rivals.com.
racingmuseum.org.
sabr.org.
seamheads.com.
seattlepi.com.
sportingnews.com.
steelers.com.
teamusa.org.
thedailybeast.com.
thesportsdaily.com.
theundefeated.com.
thoroughbreddailynews.com.

umsportshalloffame.com.
upi.com.
usatf.org.
usga.org.
ushmm.org.
wikipedia.org.

ABOUT THE AUTHOR

David Finoli is an author and sports historian who has written numerous titles on the history of sports in Western Pennsylvania. He has written seven other books for Arcadia Publishing and The History Press, including *Pittsburgh's Greatest Teams* and *Unlucky 21: The Saddest Stories and Games in Pittsburgh Sports History*. He is also a contributor to various books, magazines and sports websites. He lives in Monroeville with his family.

Visit us at
www.historypress.com